TM 9-1575

WAR DEPARTMENT TECHNICAL MANUAL

ORDNANCE MAINTENANCE

WRIST WATCHES, POCKET WATCHES, STOP WATCHES, AND CLOCKS

WAR DEPARTMENT • *6 APRIL 1945*

DISCLAIMER:

THIS MANUAL IS SOLD FOR HISTORIC RESEARCH PURPOSES ONLY, AS AN ENTERTAINMENT. IT CONTAINS OBSOLETE INFORMATION AND IS NOT INTENDED TO BE USED AS PART OF AN ACTUAL OPERATION OF MAINTENANCE TRAINING PROGRAM. NO BOOK CAN SUBSTITUTE FOR PROPER TRAINING BY AN AUTHORIZED INSTRUCTOR.

ORDNANCE MAINTENANCE

WRIST WATCHES, POCKET WATCHES, STOP WATCHES, AND CLOCKS

WAR DEPARTMENT • *6 APRIL 1945*

WAR DEPARTMENT
Washington 25, D. C., 6 April 1945

TM 9-1575, Ordnance Maintenance: Wrist Watches, Pocket Watches, Stop Watches, and Clocks, is published for the information and guidance of all concerned.

$$\begin{bmatrix} \text{A.G. 300.7 (12 Sep 44)} \\ \text{O.O. 300.7/2803} \end{bmatrix}$$

BY ORDER OF THE SECRETARY OF WAR:

G. C. MARSHALL,
Chief of Staff.

OFFICIAL:
J. A. ULIO,
Major General,
The Adjutant General.

DISTRIBUTION: AAF (10); AGF (10); ASF (2); S Div ASF (1); Dept (10); AAF Comd (2); Arm & Sv Bd (2); Tech Sv (2); SvC (10); PC&S (1); PE, 9 (5); Dist O, 9 (5); Dist Br O, 9 (3); Reg O, 9 (3); Establishment, 9 (5); Decentralized Sub-O, 9 (3); Gen & Sp Sv Sch (10); USMA (20); A (10); CHQ (10); D (2); AF (2); T/O & E: 9-7 (3); 9-8 (3); 9-57 (3); 9-76 (2); 9-318 (3).

(For explanation of symbols, see FM 21-6.)

CONTENTS

RA PD 77447

Figure 1 — Pocket Watch With Ordnance Markings

DIAMETER OF PILLAR PLATE

RA PD 77421

Figure 2 — Diameter of Pillar Plate of a Watch

RESTRICTED

CHAPTER 1

GENERAL

_____

Section I

INTRODUCTION

1. SCOPE.*

a. This manual is published for the information and guidance of ordnance maintenance personnel. It contains detailed instructions for inspection, disassembly, assembly, maintenance, and repair of pocket watches, wrist watches, stop watches, and message center clocks, and is supplementary to those in the Field Manuals and Technical Manuals prepared for the using arms. This manual does not contain information which is intended primarily for the using arms, since such information is available to ordnance maintenance personnel in TM 9-575.

2. CHARACTERISTICS.

a. The materiel covered in the manual consists of military timepieces issued to the using arms and services for timing operations.

b. **Pocket Watches.** Pocket watches are of American manufacture. All pocket watches are of the open-face type. They are all 16 size.

c. **Wrist Watches.** Wrist watches are all of American manufacture. Several types of cases have been issued. Cup type, and screw bezel and back type had been issued, but now all wrist watches are being issued in the waterproof case. Standard sizes in use are 10½ ligne, 6/0, and 8/0. Wrist watches are authorized for issue to all branches of the service.

d. **Stop Watches.** The term "stop-watch" or "time-interval recorder" is used interchangeably, to designate an instrument used primarily to indicate time intervals of minutes, seconds, and fractions of a second. Formerly a distinction was made between these instruments. The stop watch, as formerly distinguished from the time-interval recorder, was an ordinary timepiece with an additional auxiliary sweep hand for indicating time intervals of seconds and fractions of a second. A time-interval recorder, as formerly distinguished from a stop watch, lacked the hour, minute, and seconds hands of an

_____

*To provide maintenance instructions with the materiel, this technical manual has been published in advance of complete technical review. Any errors or omissions will be corrected by changes or, if extensive, by an early revision.

ordinary timepiece. The terms "stop watch" and "time-interval recorder" are now applied without distinction to an instrument. Such instruments do not function as timepieces, but as indicators of time intervals.

e. Message Center Clock. The message center clock is issued to headquarters for use by message center personnel. The message center clock is mounted in a hardwood carrying case, which provides protection while in transit and a support while set up for use. The clock is of the 8-day type and is fitted with an 11-jewel watch escapement. It is mounted inside a screw bezel type case.

f. Tank Clocks. Tank clocks were formerly standard equipment on the instrument panel of tanks. These are no longer standard for issue and are not being maintained (War Department Supply Bulletin 9-39).

3. ORDNANCE DEPARTMENT MARKINGS.

a. The Ordnance Department numbers each watch with letters which signify the grade of the watch and the service to which it is issued, followed by the ordnance serial number marked plainly on the exterior back of the case. This serial number is the only number referred to in identifying an ordnance timepiece. Each watch is identified by the following ordnance code markings:

(1) For new manufacture:

(a) OA—for 7- to 9-jewel pocket watches.

(b) OB—for 15- to 17-jewel pocket watches.

(c) OC—for 7- to 9-jewel wrist watches.

(d) OD—for 15- to 17-jewel wrist watches.

(e) OE—for 21-jewel railroad grade pocket watches.

(f) OF—for 15- to 17-jewel wrist watches (waterproof case).

(g) OFA—for 15- to 16-jewel wrist watch, waterproof case, Air Corps (Navigation, Type A-11, substitute standard).

(h) OG—for 7- to 9-jewel wrist watch (waterproof case).

(i) OS—for stop watch.

(2) For manufacture prior to 12 November 1940. (Identification to be added at time of repair on watches not previously marked.)

(a) OW—for 7- to 9-jewel pocket watches.

(b) OX—for 15- to 17-jewel pocket watches.

(c) OY—for 7-to 9-jewel wrist watches.

(d) OZ—for 15- to 17-jewel wrist watches.

4. WATCH SIZES.

a. The standard measurement used by American watch manufacturers is the Lancashire gage, which is of English origin. With

2

FUNCTIONAL DESCRIPTION

this system, the 0 size movement, which measures $1\frac{5}{30}$ inch diameter, is used as a basic figure. Every $\frac{1}{30}$ of an inch added increases the number size by one; every subtraction of $\frac{1}{30}$ of an inch decreases the number size by one. To determine the size of a watch, measure the diameter of the dial side of the lower (pillar) plate (fig. 2). The following table (subpar. b, below) shows Lancashire gage watch sizes in terms of fractions of an inch, lignes, and millimeters.

b. Comparative values of standards of measurement:

$$1 \text{ inch} = 25.4 \text{ millimeters}$$
$$1 \text{ millimeter} = 0.03937 \text{ inch}$$
$$1 \text{ ligne} = 2.256 \text{ millimeters}$$
(French unit of measurement)

Watch Size	Fraction Inch	Decimal Inch	Ligne Size	Millimeters
18	$1\frac{23}{30}$	1.766	19.87	44.86
16	$1\frac{21}{30}$	1.700	19.12	43.17
12	$1\frac{17}{30}$	1.566	17.62	39.79
10	$1\frac{15}{30}$	1.500	16.87	38.09
0	$1\frac{5}{30}$	1.166	13.12	29.63
00 or 2/0	$1\frac{4}{30}$	1.133	12.75	28.78
3/0	$1\frac{3}{30}$	1.100	12.37	27.93
4/0	$1\frac{2}{30}$	1.066	12.00	27.09
5/0	$1\frac{1}{30}$	1.033	11.62	26.24
6/0	1	1.000	11.25	25.39
7/0	$\frac{29}{30}$	0.966	10.87	24.55
8/0	$\frac{28}{30}$	0.933	10.50	23.70

Section II

FUNCTIONAL DESCRIPTION

5. GENERAL.

a. This section contains a brief description of watch construction applicable to all ordnance timepieces. It also contains explanations of functioning, and factors which affect functioning of timepieces. Specific features of individual timepieces are contained in later chapters.

b. **Power Assembly.** The power assembly in a watch consists of the mainspring, mainspring barrel, arbor, and cap. The mainspring furnishes the power to run the watch. It is coiled around the arbor and is contained in the mainspring barrel, which is cylindrical and has a gear on it which serves as the first wheel of the train. The arbor is a cylindrical shaft with a hook for the mainspring in the center of the body. The cap is a flat disk which snaps into a recess in the barrel. A hook on the inside of the mainspring barrel is for the purpose of attaching the mainspring to the barrel.

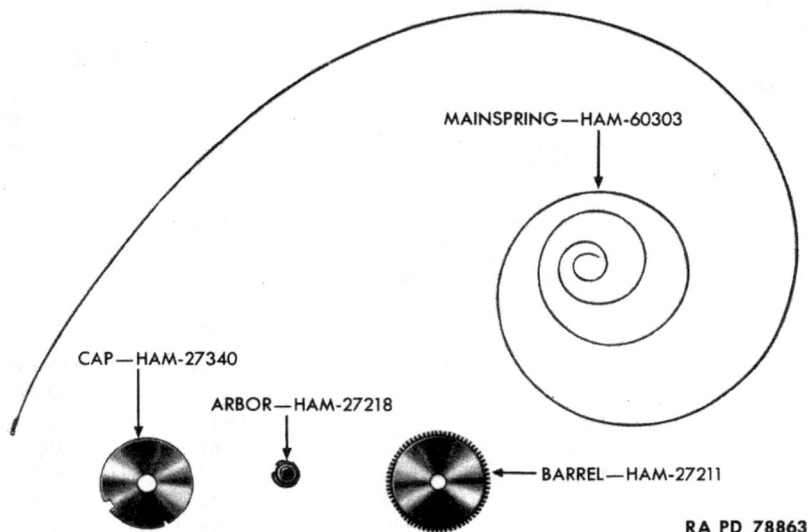

Figure 3 — Watch Movement Barrel Assembly Disassembled

c. **Mainspring.** The mainspring is made of a long thin strip of steel, hardened to give the desired resiliency. Mainsprings vary in size but are similar in design; they have a hook on the outer end to attach to the mainspring barrel, and a hole in the inner end to fasten to the mainspring barrel arbor. Various types of mainsprings used in service timepieces are shown in figures 185 and 218.

d. **Power.** By turning the crown clockwise, the barrel arbor is rotated and the mainspring is wound around it. The mainspring barrel arbor is held stationary after winding by means of the ratchet wheel and click. As the mainspring uncoils, it causes the mainspring barrel to revolve. The barrel is meshed with the pinion on the center wheel, and as it revolves it sets the train wheels in motion. Pocket and wrist watches, in most cases, will run up to 36 hours on one winding. The message center clock is designed to run for a period of 8 days.

6. TRAIN.

a. The train is a set of wheels through which the power of the mainspring is transmitted to the escapement. The first wheel of the train is the mainspring barrel. The second wheel is referred to as the center wheel, because of its position in the movement. The third wheel, fourth wheel, and escape wheel complete the train. The center, third, and fourth wheels are made of brass, mounted on steel

4

FUNCTIONAL DESCRIPTION

Figure 4 — Relative Position of Watch Parts in Typical Movement — Rear View

RA PD 86934

5

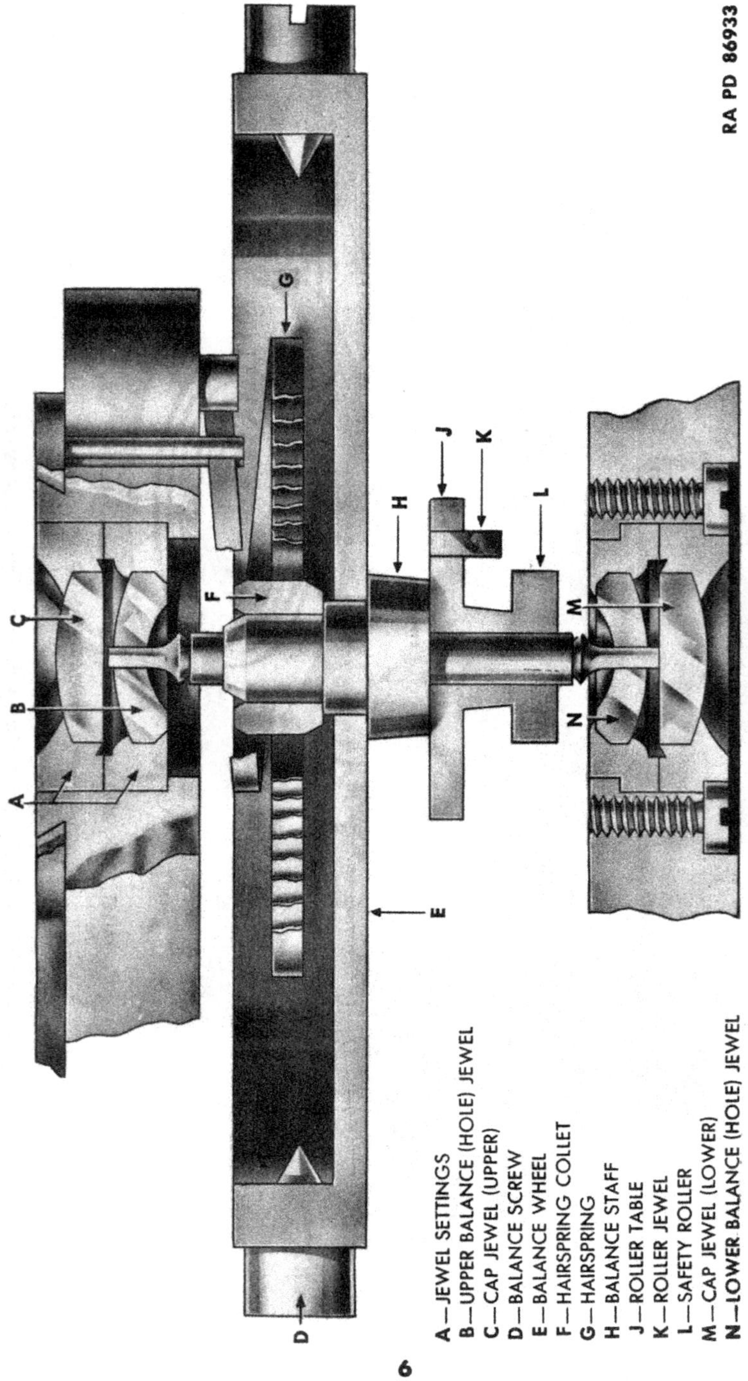

RA PD 86933

A—JEWEL SETTINGS
B—UPPER BALANCE (HOLE) JEWEL
C—CAP JEWEL (UPPER)
D—BALANCE SCREW
E—BALANCE WHEEL
F—HAIRSPRING COLLET
G—HAIRSPRING
H—BALANCE STAFF
J—ROLLER TABLE
K—ROLLER JEWEL
L—SAFETY ROLLER
M—CAP JEWEL (LOWER)
N—LOWER BALANCE (HOLE) JEWEL

Figure 5 — Typical Balance Assembly

FUNCTIONAL DESCRIPTION

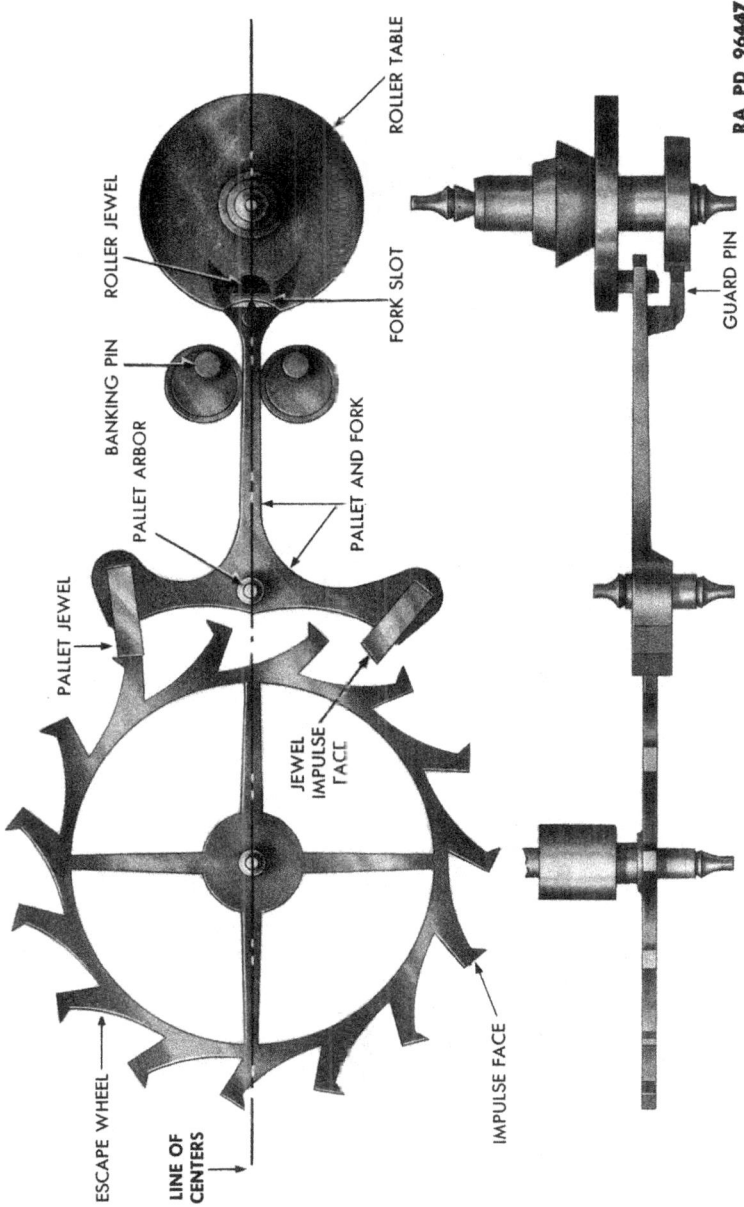

ROLLER TABLE

ROLLER JEWEL

FORK SLOT

BANKING PIN

PALLET ARBOR

PALLET AND FORK

PALLET JEWEL

JEWEL IMPULSE FACE

ESCAPE WHEEL

LINE OF CENTERS

IMPULSE FACE

GUARD PIN

RA PD 96447

Figure 6 — Pallet and Fork at Rest With No Power Being Exerted on Escape Wheel Pinion by Mainspring

7

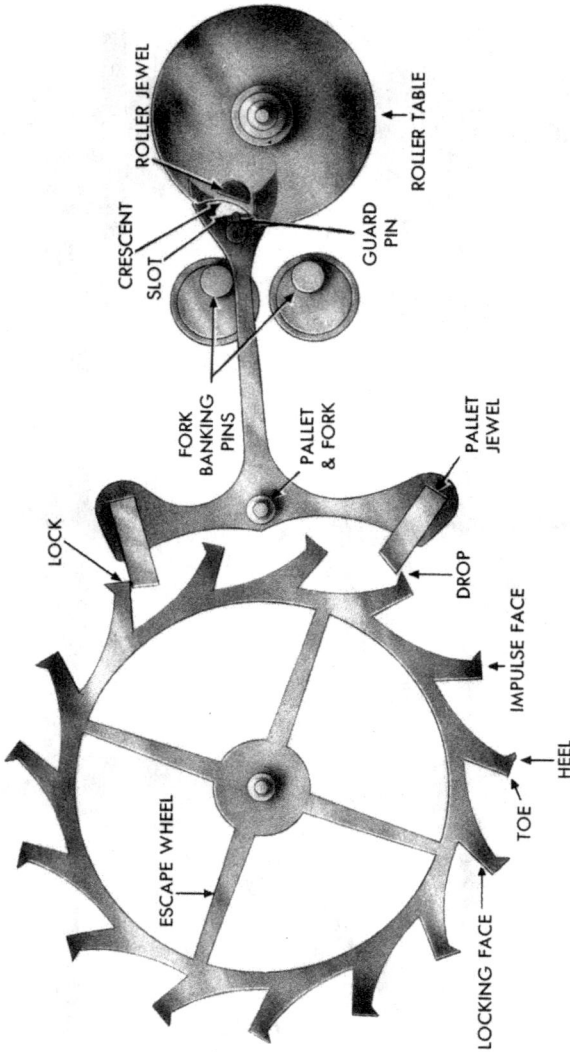

RA PD 96448

Figure 7 — Fork at Rest Against Right Banking Pin and Right Pallet Jewel Engaging Tooth of Escape Wheel

pinions and arbors. The long center wheel arbor projects through the pillar plate and above the dial, to receive the cannon pinion and hour wheel. The cannon pinion receives the minute hand and the hour wheel the hour hand. As the mainspring drives the barrel, the center wheel is rotated once each hour. The center wheel meshes with the third pinion causing it to rotate eight times each hour, or one revolution each 7½ minutes. The third wheel meshes with the fourth wheel pinion causing it to rotate once each minute. The fourth wheel also has a long arbor which projects above the dial to receive the second hand. Watches with a sweep second hand have an auxiliary wheel train that brings an arbor through a hollow center wheel arbor to support the sweep second hand. The fourth wheel in turn drives the escape wheel and pinion 10 revolutions each minute and brings the power of the mainspring down through the train to the escapement.

7. ESCAPEMENT.

a. **Purpose of Escape Wheel** (figs. 7 and 8). If a movement consisted only of the mainspring and a train of wheels, such as that already described, and the mainspring were wound up, the train would run at full speed resulting in the power being spent in a few moments. For this reason, the escapement has been arranged to check it. The duty of the escapement is to allow each tooth of the escape wheel to pass at a regulated interval. The escapement is of no service alone and, therefore, must have some other arrangement to measure and regulate these intervals. This is accomplished by the balance assembly.

b. **Escape Wheel** (fig. 7). The escape wheel is in most cases made of steel and is staked on a pinion and arbor. It is the last wheel of the train and, therefore, connects the train with the escapement. It is constructed so that the pallet jewels move in and out between its teeth, allowing but one tooth to escape at a time. The teeth are "club-shaped" because of the addition of impulse faces to the end of the teeth.

c. **Pallet, Fork, and Arbor.** The pallet jewels are set at an angle to make their inside corners reach over three teeth and two spaces of the escape wheel. The outside corners of the jewels will reach over two teeth and three spaces of the escape wheel with a small amount of clearance. At the opposite end of the pallet, directly under the center of the fork slot, is a steel or brass pin called the guard pin. The fork is the connecting link to the balance assembly.

8. BALANCE AND HAIRSPRING.

a. The rotation of the balance wheel is controlled by the hairspring. The inner end of the hairspring is pinned to the collet, and

ORDNANCE MAINTENANCE — WRIST WATCHES, POCKET WATCHES, STOP WATCHES, AND CLOCKS

RA PD 96449

Figure 8 — Fork at Rest Against Left Banking Pin and Left Pallet Jewel Engaging Tooth of Escape Wheel

FUNCTIONAL DESCRIPTION

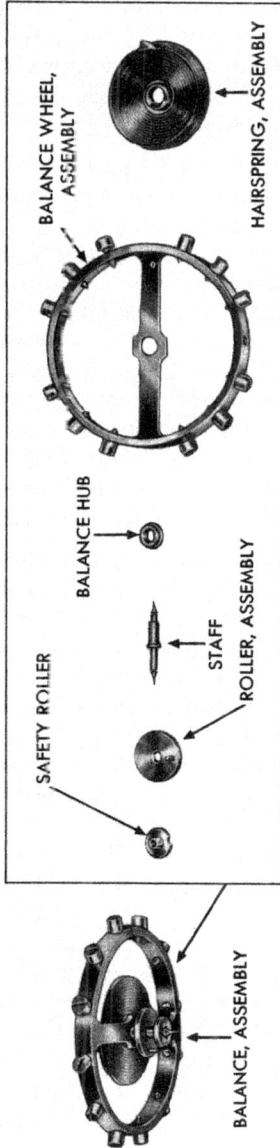

BALANCE WHEEL, ASSEMBLY

HAIRSPRING, ASSEMBLY

BALANCE HUB

STAFF

ROLLER, ASSEMBLY

SAFETY ROLLER

BALANCE, ASSEMBLY

RA PD 78885

Figure 9 — Watch Movement Balance Assembly With Two-piece Roller — Assembled and Disassembled

11

the collet is held friction-tight on the staff above the balance wheel. The outer end of the hairspring is pinned to a stud which is held stationary on the balance cock by the stud screw. The roller jewel is cemented in the large roller assembly, which is mounted on the staff directly under the balance wheel. Under the first roller is a smaller one which acts as a safety roller, necessary because of the crescent cut out in the roller table which allows the guard pin of the escapement assembly to pass through.

b. **Action of Balance Wheel and Fork** (fig. 8). The balance wheel rotates clockwise and counterclockwise on its axis by means of the impulse it receives from the escapement. The motion of the balance wheel is constant due to the coiling and uncoiling of the hairspring. The impulse that has been transmitted to the roller jewel by the swinging of the pallet fork to the left, causes the balance to rotate in a counterclockwise direction. The position of the fork allows the roller jewel to move out of the slot of the fork freely and in the same direction. The fork continues on until it reaches the banking pin. Meanwhile the balance continues in the same direction until the tension of the hairspring overcomes the momentum of the balance wheel. When this occurs the balance returns to its original position, which causes the roller jewel to again enter the slot of the fork.

c. **Pallet and Escape Tooth Action** (fig. 8). The momentum that has been built up during the return of the balance, causes the roller pin to impart an impulse on the inside of the fork slot. This impulse is great enough to push the fork away from its position against the banking pin. As the fork is pushed away, it causes the pallet stone to slide on the toe of the escape wheel tooth. When the pallet stone has slid down to its edge, it frees the escape wheel tooth, thereby unlocking the escape wheel. The escape wheel, being impelled by the force of the mainspring, starts to rotate. As the escape wheel turns, the tooth glides along the impulse face of the pallet jewel, forcing it to move out of the way. The moving pallet carries the fork with it and imparts the impulse to the roller jewel. The right pallet stone intercepts a tooth of the escape wheel to lock it, as the fork moves toward the banking pin. Having a short "run" left to the banking pin, the pressure of the escape wheel tooth against the locking face of the pallet jewel draws the stone deeper into the escape wheel and, therefore, causes the fork to complete its run and holds it against the banking pin. Meanwhile the balance continues in a clockwise direction until the tension of the hairspring overcomes the momentum of the balance and returns it to its original position.

d. **Rate of Escape Tooth Release.** Through the motion of the escapement, the mainspring keeps the balance vibrating, and the balance regulates the train. The escape wheel has 15 teeth and is

FUNCTIONAL DESCRIPTION

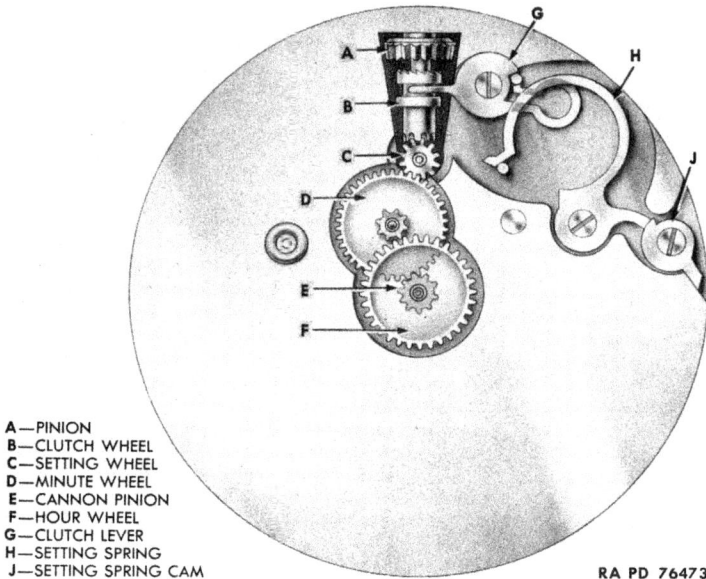

A—PINION
B—CLUTCH WHEEL
C—SETTING WHEEL
D—MINUTE WHEEL
E—CANNON PINION
F—HOUR WHEEL
G—CLUTCH LEVER
H—SETTING SPRING
J—SETTING SPRING CAM

RA PD 76473

Figure 10 — Dial Side of Pillar Plate

allowed to revolve 10 turns per minute. Thus, 150 teeth glide over each pallet stone in 1 minute. The gliding of the escape wheel teeth over the impulse faces of the pallet stones will cause the balance to vibrate 300 vibrations or beats per minute. These vibrations will continue until the force of the mainspring is spent.

9. WINDING AND SETTING.

a. The winding and setting mechanism (fig. 10) consists of the stem, crown, winding pinion, clutch wheel, setting wheel, setting lever, clutch lever, clutch spring, crown wheel, and ratchet wheel. When the stem is pushed in, the clutch lever throws the clutch wheel to winding position. Then, when the stem is turned clockwise, it causes the winding pinion to turn the crown and ratchet wheels. The ratchet wheel is fitted on the square of the mainspring arbor and is held in place with a screw. When the stem and crown are turned, the ratchet wheel turns and revolves the arbor which winds the mainspring, thereby giving motive power to the train. Pulling the stem and crown outward pushes the setting lever against the clutch lever, engaging the clutch wheel with the setting wheel. The setting wheel is in constant mesh with the minute wheel; therefore, turning the stem and crown permits setting the hands to any desired time.

ORDNANCE MAINTENANCE — WRIST WATCHES, POCKET WATCHES, STOP WATCHES, AND CLOCKS

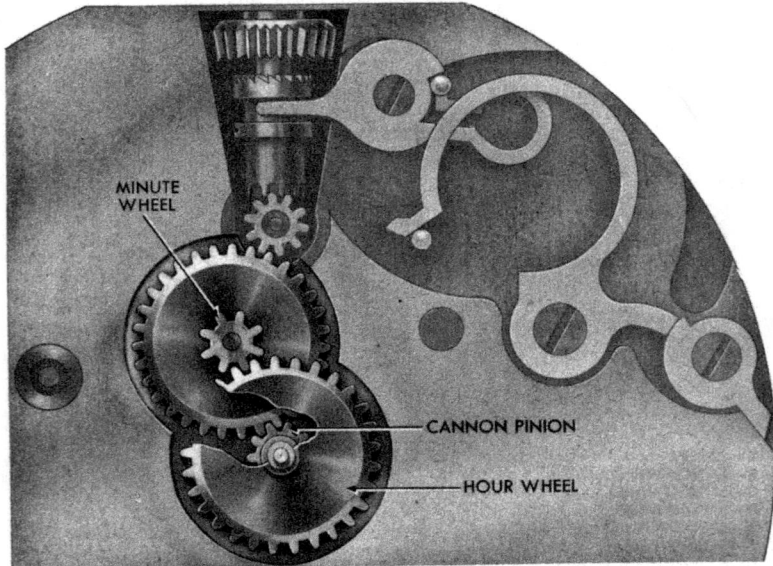

RA PD 78898

Figure 11 — Watch Movement Winding and Setting Mechanism

b. The dial train consists of the cannon pinion, minute, and hour wheels (fig. 11). The cannon pinion is a hollow steel pinion which is mounted on the center wheel arbor. A stud which is secured in the pillar plate holds the minute wheel in mesh with the cannon pinion. To the minute wheel is attached a small pinion which is meshed with the hour wheel.

c. The center arbor revolves once per hour. A hand affixed to the cannon pinion on the center arbor would travel around the dial once per hour. This hand is used to denote minutes. The minute wheel is in mesh with the cannon pinion. The hour wheel has a pipe that allows the hour wheel to set over the cannon pinion. The hour wheel meshes with the minute wheel pinion. This completes the train of the cannon pinion, minute wheel, and hour wheel. The ratio between the cannon pinion and the hour wheel is 12 to 1; therefore, the hand affixed to the hour wheel is used to denote the hours. With this arrangement, time is recorded and read.

10. JEWELS.

a. Materials Used for Jewels. Jewels are used as bearings to reduce metal-to-metal contacts which produce friction and wear. They improve the performance and accuracy of the watch, and materially

FUNCTIONAL DESCRIPTION

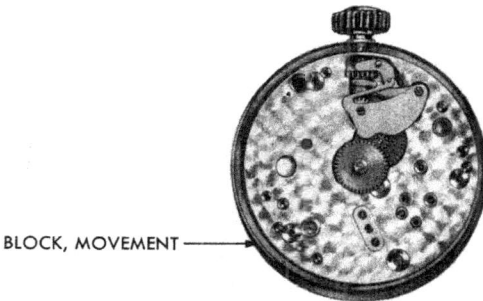

BLOCK, MOVEMENT

RA PD 78871

Figure 12 — Wrist Watch Movement Dial Train

prolong its usefulness. The materials used for making watch jewels
are diamonds, sapphires, rubies, and garnets. The diamond is the
hardest but is seldom used except for cap jewels. The sapphire is the
next in hardness and is the most commonly used because of its fine
texture. Rubies and garnets are softer than sapphires. They add to
the outward appearance of the watch but do not have the fine texture
of the sapphire jewel.

b. **Types of Jewels** (fig. 13). Watch jewels are of four distinct
types, each type having a particular function.

(1) HOLE JEWELS. Hole jewels are used to form the bearing
surface for wheel arbors and balance staff pivots.

(2) CAP JEWELS. Cap jewels are flat jewels. They are positioned at the ends of wheel staffs, outside the hole jewels, and limit
the end thrust of the staff.

(3) ROLLER JEWELS. The roller jewel (pin) is positioned on the
roller table to receive the impulse for the balance from the fork.

(4) PALLET JEWELS. The pallet jewels (stones) are the angular-
shaped jewels positioned in the pallet to engage the teeth of the
escape wheel.

c. **Number and Location of Jewels.** Ordnance watches have
either 7, 9, 15, 17, or 21 jewels. The location of the jewels varies
somewhat in different makes and grades, but the general practice is
as follows (fig. 6):

(1) 7-JEWEL WATCHES. Seven-jewel watches have: one hole
jewel at each end of the balance staff; one cap jewel at each end of
the balance staff; one roller jewel; and two pallet jewels.

(2) 9-JEWEL WATCHES. These have the seven jewels mentioned
in 7-jewel watches, with the addition of a hole jewel at each end of
the escape wheel.

TRAIN

ROLLER JEWEL

CAP JEWEL

OLIVE-HOLE JEWEL

PALLET STONES

RA PD 86955

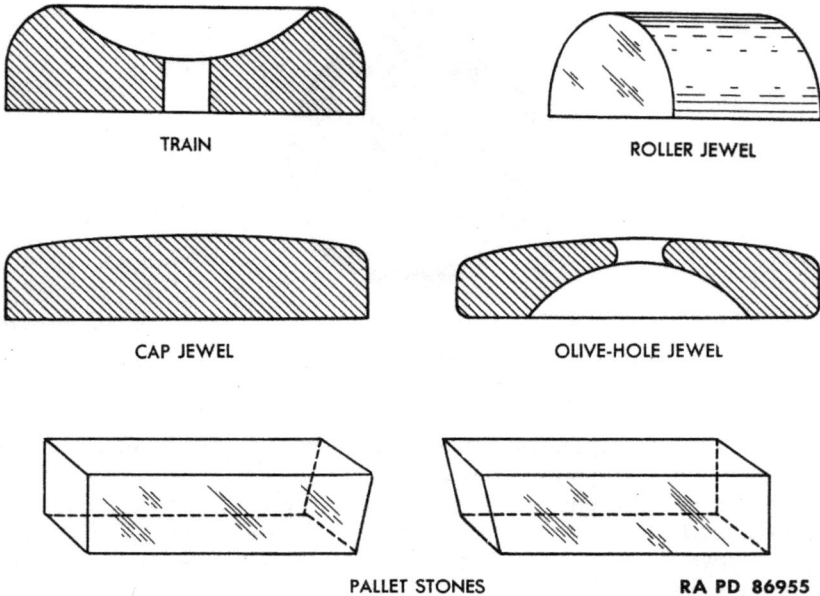

Figure 13 — Jewels

(3)   15-JEWEL WATCHES.   These watches have the nine jewels found in 9-jewel watches, with the addition of the following: one hole jewel at each end of the pallet staff; one hole jewel at each end of the fourth-wheel staff; and one hole jewel at each end of the third-wheel staff.

(4)   17-JEWEL WATCHES.   The 15 jewels in 15-jewel watches are used with the addition of one hole jewel located at each end of the center wheel staff.

(5)   21-JEWEL WATCHES.   These have the 17 jewels found in 17-jewel watches, with the addition of: one cap jewel at each end of the pallet arbor; and one cap jewel at each end of the escape wheel staff.

11.   SUMMARY OF TIMEPIECE TERMS.

a.   The following definitions of timepiece terms are given for the purpose of ready reference.

ARBOR: the mechanical axis of a moving part.

BALANCE WHEEL: the vibrating wheel of a watch or clock.

BALANCE COCK: the bridge holding upper balance jewels.

BALANCE SEAT: the part of a balance staff to which the balance wheel is fastened.

FUNCTIONAL DESCRIPTION

BANKING PINS: the two pins which limit the angular motion of the pallet.

BARREL: the circular box in which the mainspring is housed.

BARREL ARBOR: the axis of the barrel around which the mainspring is wound.

BARREL COVER: the lid that snaps into a recess in the barrel.

BEZEL: the front ring of the case which retains the crystal.

BOW: the ring of a pocket watch case that is attached to the pendant.

OVERCOIL HAIRSPRING: the flat hairspring with its outer coil bent upward and inward, terminating in a circular curve.

CANNON PINION: the pinion with a long pipe fitted frictiontight to center arbor, and on which the minute hand is attached.

CAP JEWEL (END STONE): the flat-faced jewel placed over a hole jewel.

CENTER WHEEL: the wheel that is located in the center of the movement.

CLICK: the detainer or pawl on ratchet wheel.

CLUB TOOTH: the form of tooth used on the escape wheel.

COCK JEWELS: the hole and cap jewels of the balance cock.

COLLET: the small brass collar which fits frictiontight on the balance staff, and to which is pinned the inner end of the hairspring.

COMPENSATING BALANCE: the bimetal balance wheel cut at opposite points, which causes an automatic temperature correction to counteract the variation of the hairspring action caused by heat and cold.

CONICAL PIVOT: the pivot which is cylindrical at the end and gradually widens toward the arbor shoulder. This form of pivot is used on arbors which run on cap jewels.

CYLINDRICAL PIVOT: the pivot, the full length of which is the same diameter up to the shoulder of the arbor, ordinarily used on train wheels.

DOUBLE ROLLER: the roller arranged so the impulse and safety actions are separated instead of being confined to one roller.

DRAW: the inclined position of the locking face of the pallet stone (jewel); this causes the pallet to be drawn toward the escape wheel, and the fork toward the banking pin where it is in position to receive the roller jewel (pin).

DISCHARGING EDGE: the left edge or corner of either pallet stone (jewel).

DISCHARGING PALLET STONE: the left pallet stone (jewel) ("L" stone).

DROP: the distance which an escape wheel tooth has to travel before it reaches the locking face of the pallet after the opposite tooth has escaped.

END SHAKE: the up-and-down play of an arbor between the plate and bridge or between the jewels.

END STONE (CAP JEWEL): the flat-faced jewel placed over a hole jewel.

RECEIVING PALLET STONE: the right pallet stone (jewel) ("R" stone).

ESCAPEMENT: the device in a watch or clock by which the motion of the train is checked, and the energy of the mainspring communicated to the balance.

FORK: the part of the pallet which contains the slot that engages the roller jewel (pin).

FOOT JEWELS: the bottom cap and hole jewels of the balance.

FOURTH WHEEL: the wheel that drives the escape wheel; it has a long arbor projecting above the surface of the dial, to which the second hand is attached.

GUARD PIN: the pin that is located near the end of the fork, serving as a guard against overbanking.

HAIRSPRING: the spring which vibrates the balance.

HAIRSPRING STUD: the outside terminal to which the end of the outer coil of the hairspring is pinned.

HANDS: the revolving pointers used to indicate the time.

HOUR WHEEL: the wheel which fits over the cannon pinion, and to which the hour hand is fastened.

HUB: the part of the balance staff between the balance arms and the roller table.

IMPULSE: the force transmitted by the escape wheel to the pallet by gliding over the angular or "impulse face" of the pallet stone (jewel).

IMPULSE FACE: the angular face of the pallet stone (jewel) over which the escape wheel teeth pass.

IMPULSE ANGLE: the angle of the impulse face of the escape wheel teeth.

LOCKING FACE: the engaging side of either pallet stone (jewel) against which the escape wheel locks.

MEAN TIME SCREWS: balance screws used for timing, usually longer than other balance screws; when turned away from or toward the balance rim, they cause the balance vibrations to become faster or slower.

MINUTE WHEEL: the wheel driven by the cannon pinion.

MINUTE WHEEL STUD: the short stud fixed to the plate on which the minute wheel revolves.

FUNCTIONAL DESCRIPTION

MINUTE WHEEL PINION: the pinion on the minute wheel which drives the hour wheel.

MOVEMENT: the mechanism of a watch or clock without the case or dial.

OVERBANKED: the escapement error causing one side of the fork to rest against the banking pin, and the roller jewel to rest against the other side of the fork, due to movement of the fork and guard pin at a time when the roller jewel is not engaging the fork; this locks the escapement and stops the motion of the balance.

PENDANT: the small neck or knob of a pocket watch to which the bow is attached.

PINION: the small gears that mesh with the wheels of the train.

PIPE: the extension of the hub of a pinion or wheel.

PLATE: the disk of a watch or clock which forms the foundation of the movement.

POISE: a perfect balance condition brought about by the adjustment of the balance screws in the balance wheel, to equalize the weight of the balance in all pendant positions.

RATCHET WHEEL: the wheel with pointed teeth on the outside diameter mounted over the mainspring barrel arbor meshing with the click, to retain power of the mainspring.

REGULATOR: the movable pointer mounted over the center of the balance cock, one end of which indicates the distance it is moved, and the other end having two pins between which the outermost coil or overcoil vibrates.

REGULATOR PINS: the two pins attached to the end of the regulator between which is placed the outermost coil or overcoil of the hairspring; moving the regulator causes the pins to move, thereby shortening or lengthening the active length of the hairspring; this regulating causes the balance to vibrate faster or slower.

ROLLER JEWEL (PIN): the jewel cemented in the roller table, which receives the impulse from the pallet fork.

ROLLER SEAT: the part of the balance staff on which the roller is mounted.

SAFETY ROLLER: the smaller of the two rollers of a double roller escapement.

SECONDS PIVOT: the prolongation of the fourth-wheel arbor projecting above the surface of the dial, to which is attached the second hand.

STAFF: the metallic axis on which a wheel turns.

TRAIN: the wheels of a watch or clock which connect the power assembly with the escapement.

Section III

INSPECTION

12. GENERAL.

a. Fundamentally, inspection is for the purpose of determining whether or not the timepiece is serviceable. It is also important to determine if lack of first- and second-echelon maintenance is the cause of the apparent failure of the timepiece. Serviceability, as interpreted in this section, is the ability of the instrument to perform its intended functions completely.

13. INSPECTION BEFORE DISASSEMBLY.

a. **Completeness.** Inspect the external appearance of the watch for completeness, including accessories.

b. **Ordnance Markings.** Check the ordnance markings, on the exterior back of the case, indicating the grade and serial number of the watch.

c. **Case.**

(1) POCKET WATCH. Inspect the case for dents, discoloration, scratched or loose crystal, tight fit of bezel and back to case band, worn or loose bow, and broken-loose or sprung hinges.

(2) WRIST WATCH. Inspect for conditions listed in step (1), above, plus worn lugs, unserviceable spring bars, strap, and buckle.

d. **Dial.** Inspect the general appearance and legibility of numerals. Check radium luminous markings of dial and hands in the dark.

e. **Winding and Setting Mechanism.** Wind the watch fully and, while winding, check by feel, the operation of the click and click spring, and for any slippage which would indicate that the winding wheels are not in mesh. It should be possible to wind the watch fully; if the stem continues to turn without winding fully, it indicates that the mainspring is broken or slipping. Pull the stem out to setting position. The stem should enter the setting position with a slight click, without excessive force, and remain in that position during the setting operation. While the stem is in that position, turn the hands backward to check fit of cannon pinion. If the cannon pinion is too tight, the watch will stop. Do not confuse this with the hack watch, as it is designed to stop when in the setting process. If the cannon pinion is too loose, the stem will turn too freely.

f. **Hands.** See that the hands do not rub on the dial or crystal, or hook on each other while turning them through a complete revolution. When set at the 12:00-hour position, the minute and hour hands

INSPECTION

should both point at the twelfth-hour graduation. See that the hands are tight on their pipes. If hands rub on dial or crystal, straighten them; if they are loose on their pipes, tighten them.

g. Balance Assembly. Remove the case back and, if the watch is running, observe the action of the balance assembly. The balance should be rotating no less than 225 degrees in any position. Check the condition of the hairspring; it should be true in the flat and concentric with the hairspring collet. It should also clear the balance arm. If the watch is magnetized, it will cause it to run erratically or stop. Check it for magnetism (par. 34). Check the balance wheel for trueness, and the balance pivots for end and side shake; if there is too much end or side shake, it indicates the possibility of a bent or broken pivot or jewel, and it will be necessary to disassemble the balance assembly for further inspection.

h. Train Wheels. Check the exposed portion of the train wheels for burred, bent, or broken teeth, leaves on the pinions, and broken pivots. If any of the wheels exposed have bent or broken teeth, leaves on the pinions, or a broken pivot, a blocked train will result.

i. Watch Record. Check the watch record for the date it was last repaired, what was done to it, and whether or not previous trouble is indicated at this time. Determine whether or not enough time has elapsed to warrant cleaning.

j. Regulation. If the timepiece is running and appears to be in serviceable condition, set it according to a master timepiece, and allow it to run in a horizontal and two vertical positions for 24 hours in each position (dial up, dial down, and pendant down), noting variations in time in each position, to determine whether or not there is a position or poise error. Units having a timing machine available can perform these checks on the machine in just a few minutes. However, the rate obtained on a machine is only on indication of the rate at the time of the check. It is advisable to allow the watch to run for at least 24 hours before it is declared serviceable. Permissible tolerances are as follows:

(1) POCKET WATCH, RAILROAD GRADE. The mean time daily rate in any two extreme positions should not exceed 12 seconds in 24 hours.

(2) WRIST WATCHES. The mean time daily rate in all positions should stay within the range of from minus 15 to plus 45 seconds in 24 hours.

(3) POCKET WATCHES. The mean time daily rate in any two extreme positions should not exceed 30 seconds in 24 hours.

ORDNANCE MAINTENANCE — WRIST WATCHES, POCKET WATCHES, STOP WATCHES, AND CLOCKS

14. INSPECTION OF TIMER MECHANISM, ELGIN STOP WATCH.

a. **Completeness.** Inspect as outlined in paragraph 13 a.

b. **Ordnance Markings.** Inspect as outlined in paragraph 13 b.

c. **Case.** Inspect as outlined in paragraph 13 c.

d. **Dial.** Inspect as outlined in paragraph 13 d.

e. **Hands.** See that sweep second hand does not rub on the dial or crystal, and does not hook on the minute recording hand. See that the sweep hand stops indicating, that the connecting pinion is disengaged from the seconds wheel, and that the sweep second hand and minute hand return to zero when the crown is pushed in, indicating the return of the fly-back lever to the grooves in the heart cams.

f. **Winding Mechanism.** Check the smoothness of operation; check winding wheels for mesh; check operation of click and click spring; check for broken or slipping mainspring; and check the pendant screw to see that it is properly seated, retaining the winding bar in position.

g. **Balance Assembly.** Inspect as outlined in paragraph 13 g.

h. **Train Wheels.** Inspect as outlined in paragraph 13 h.

i. **Stop Watch Mechanism.**

(1) Start the mechanism in motion by pressing the pendant plunger, and observe the action of the sweep second hand. See that it does not catch on the minute recording hand or rub on the dial or crystal.

(2) Press the pendant plunger again to see that the hands stop.

(3) Press plunger again and see if the hands return to zero.

(4) Remove movement, take off hands and dial while repeating steps (1) to (3), above, and observe the action of the seconds register wheel, minute register wheel, minute register, intermittent wheel and spring, actuating lever and spring, actuating cam wheel, actuating cam wheel spring and hook, actuating cam wheel pawl, the upper fourth wheel, connecting lever, and pinion.

(5) Check each of the above for burs, rust, looseness or breaks, and deteriorated or gummy oil which would affect normal operation and make the instrument unserviceable.

j. **Watch Record.** Check as outlined in paragraph 13 i.

Section IV

GENERAL MAINTENANCE

15. TOOLS AND SUPPLIES.

a. Third- and Fourth-echelon Tools (figs. 14 and 15).

Name	Federal Stock No.	Manufacturer's Part No.
BLOCK, wood (maple), watch repair	39-B-418	A-7579260
BLOCKS, movement, 8¾, 10/0 to 18 size, set (1)	W-18-B-1150-30	MCE-40409
BLOWER, air (Feola type) (1)	W-18-B-1153-300	HV-35405
BOX, metal, Mr (or equal) w/o contents	W-41-B-1835-750	
BROACH, cutting, Nos. 15 to 70, set (1)	W-18-B-1376-500	HV-35455
BRUSH, watchmaker's, 4 row, med. stiff, No. 2 (2)	38-B-55-65	HV-35564
BRUSH, watchmaker's, 4 row, med. soft, No. 3 (2)	38-B-55-66	HV-35565
COMPASS, small, for testing magnetism (1)	W-18-C-1598	MCE-36438
DEMAGNETIZER (1)	W-17-D-67B	HV-36449
FILE, flat, hand, sm., No. 4 cut, w/safe edges (1)	W-41-F-2028	MCE-34044
FILE, screw-head, large (1)	W-41-F-2332	HV-34868
GLASS, loupe, watchmaker's dble. lens, for use w/glasses or w/o glasses (1)	W-18-G-1101-60	HV-36778
INSERTER, w/disks (for inserting unbreakable crystal) (1)	W-18-I-495	
OILER, gold tipped, No. 3 (1)	W-41-O-30	MCE-40451
OPENER, case, wood handle (1)	W-18-O-417	HV-36969
PLIERS, bow contracting (1)	W-18-P-24010	HV-41250
PLIERS, side cutting, 4½ in. long (1)	W-41-P-1992-25	MCE-40735
PLIERS, snipe nosed, 4½ in. long (1)	W-41-P-1920	MCE-40732
REMOVER, hand (w/plunger)	W-18-R-341-200	KN-310A HV-38612
SCREWDRIVER, jeweler's (0.025-100) GGG-S-121-A (set of 6) (1)	W-41-S-1325	KN-250
TWEEZERS, jeweler's, straight point, 4½ in.	W-41-T-4205	HV-43110
TWEEZERS, watchmaker's, straight point, long (1)	W-41-T-4207	HV-43131
VISE, pin, dble. end, 4 in. (1)	W-41-V-356	MCE-40623
WINDER, mainspring (KN-123A)	W-18-W-1099-300	
WINDER, mainspring with accessories	W-18-W-1099-500	KN-128
WRENCH, sleeve (10 prong) (1)	W-41-W-2561	KN-145
WRENCH, watch case, waterproof (Waltham)	41-W-3814	
WRENCH, watch case, waterproof, combination box and spanner	41-W-3814-125	

b. Third- and Fourth-echelon Supplies.

Name	Federal Stock No.	Manufacturer's Part No.
CEMENT, watch glass, tube (2)	52-C-1688	HV-18062
OIL, watch, bottle, with dropper	14-O-680	EL-56A
PAPER, watchmaker's, no lint (1,000 sheets) box (2)	53-P-22910	MCE-15618
PEG WOOD (¹⁄₁₆ x 6 in.) pcs. (3)	39-P-340	MCE-40506
PITH, hard, bundle (2)	39-P-328	HV-40507
WASHER, timing, 6 gross 8/0 D 16's size asstd.	18-W-100-25	
WIRE, brass, assorted, 14 to 21 bundle (1)	22-W-671-200	MCE-44529

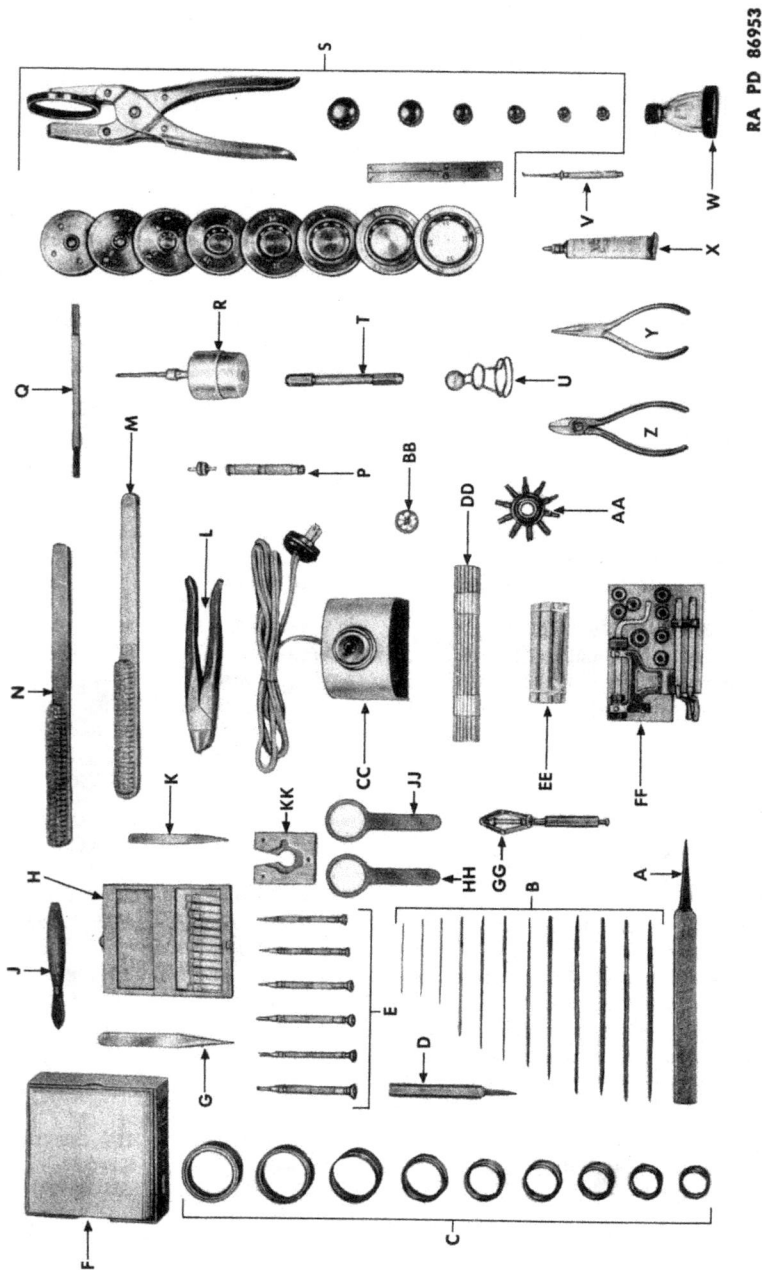

RA PD 86953

Figure 14 — Watch Repair (Junior) Tool Set, Set No. 2

GENERAL MAINTENANCE

RA PD 86953A

A—FILE, FLAT, HAND, SM., NO. 4 CUT, w/SAFE EDGES, (1) MCE-34044—W-41-F-2028

B—BROACH, CUTTING, NOS. 15 TO 70 SET, (1) HV-35455—W-18-B-1376-500

C—BLOCKS, MOVEMENT, 8¾, 10/0 TO 18 SIZE SET, MCE-40409—W-18-B-1150-30

D—FILE, SCREW HEAD, LARGE, HV-34868—W-41-F-2332

E—SCREWDRIVERS, JEWELER'S (0.025-100) GGG-S-121A (SET OF 6) (1) KN-250—W-41-S-1325

F—PAPER, WATCHMAKER'S, NO LINT (1,000 SHEETS) BOX, (2) MCE-15618—53-P-22910

G—TWEEZERS, WATCHMAKER'S, STRAIGHT POINT, LONG (1) HV-43131—W-41-T-4207

H—WASHERS, TIMING, 6 GROSS 8/0 D 16'S SIZE (ASS'TD) MCE-44529—22-W-671-200

J—OPENER, CASE, WOOD HANDLE (1) HV-36969—W-18-O-417

K—TWEEZERS, JEWELER'S STRAIGHT POINT, 4½ IN. (1) HV-43110—W-41-T-4205

L—PLIERS, BOW CONTRACTING (1) HV-41250—W-18-P-24010

M—BRUSH, WATCHMAKER, 4 ROW, MEDIUM STIFF NO. 2, HV-35564-38-B-5565

N—BRUSH, WATCHMAKER, 4 ROW, MEDIUM SOFT NO. 3, HV-35565—38-B-5566

P—WINDER, MAINSPRING, KN-123A—W-18-W-1099-300

Q—WIRE, BRASS, ASSORTED, 14 TO 21 BUNDLES (1) MCE-44529—22-W-671-200

R—BLOWER, AIR (FEOLA TYPE) (1) HV-35405—W-18-B-1153-300

S—INSERTER, w/DISKS (FOR INSERTING UNBREAKABLE CRYSTAL) (1)—W-18-I-495

T—VISE, PIN, DBLE. END, 4 IN., MCE-40623—W-41-V-356

U—LOUPE, WATCHMAKER'S DBLE. LENS, FOR USE w/or w/o GLASSES (1) HV-36678—W-18-G-1101-50

V—OILER, GOLD TIPPED, NO. 3 (1) MCE-40451—W-41-O-30

W—OIL, WATCH, BOTTLE, EL-56A-14-O-680

X—CEMENT, WATCH GLASS, TUBE, HV-18062—52-C-1688

Y—PLIERS, SNIPE NOSE, 4½-IN. LONG (1) MCE-40732—W-41-P-1920

Z—PLIERS, SIDE-CUTTING, 4½-IN. LONG (1) MCE-40735—W-41-P-1992-25

AA—WRENCH, SLEEVE (10 PRONG) (1) KN-145—W-41-W-2561

BB—COMPASS, SMALL, FOR TESTING MAGNETISM (1) MCE-36438—W-18-C-1598

CC—DEMAGNETIZER (1) HV 36449—W-17-D-670

DD—PEGWOOD (⅛ x 6 IN.) PCS. (3) MCE-40506—39-P-340

EE—PITH, HARD, BUNDLE (2) HV-40507—39-P-338

FF—WINDER, MAINSPRING, WITH ACCESSORIES, KN-128—W-18-W-1099-500

GG—REMOVER, HAND (w/PLUNGER), KN-310A, HV-38612—W-18-R-341-200

HH—WRENCH, WATCH CASE, WATERPROOF (WALTHAM)

JJ—WRENCH, WATCH CASE, WATERPROOF, COMBINATION BOX AND SPANNER

KK—BLOCK, WOOD (MAPLE), WATCH REPAIR A-7579260—39-B-418

Legend for Figure 14 — Watch Repair (Junior) Tool Set, Set No. 2

BOX, METAL
M4-RA-DD-C106
W-41-B-1835-750

RA PD 86646

Figure 15 — Metal Box M4 (or Equal) Without Contents

Name	Federal Stock No.	Manufacturer's Part No.
c. Fifth-echelon Tools (figs. 16 and 17).		
ANVIL, 4 milled slots, 16 graduated holes, 1¾ in. diam (1)	W-18-A-459-500	MCE-35049
BLOCKS, movement, set of 8, 10/0 to 18 size	W-18-B-1150-300	MCE-40409
BLOCKS, watch case, set	39-B-418	A-7579260
BLOWER, air (Feola type) (1)	W-18-B-1153-300	HV-35405
BROACH, cutting, Nos. 15 to 70 (set) (1)	W-18-B-1376-500	HV-35455
BROACH, pivot, cutting, American (12)	W-18-B-1376-525	HV-35443
BROACH, pivot, round, American (12)	W-18-B-1376-700	HV-35444
BRUSH, dial (1)	38-B-1263	HV-126
BRUSH, washout, bone handle (2)	38-B-5570	HV-35590
BRUSH, watchmaker's, 4 row, medium soft, No. 3 (2)	38-B-5566	HV-35565
BRUSH, watchmaker's, 4 row, medium stiff, No. 2 (2)	38-B-5565	HV-35564
BRUSH, watchmaker's, 4 row, soft (2)	38-B-5568	HV-35566
BURNISHER, bell-metal (1)	W-18-B-1451-200	HV-35810
CALIPERS, sliding, millimeters, w/vernier, measuring 1⁄10 mm, 1⁄28th-inch	W-41-C-314	HV-37875
CALIPERS, truing, for both wrist and pocket watches (1)	W-18-C-99-300	HV-36062
CALIPERS, vernier, English and metric, 0-5 w/ratchet (1)	W-41-C-372	MCE-37874

GENERAL MAINTENANCE

Name	Federal Stock No.	Manufacturer's Part No.
CHUCK, 3 jaw (W. W. pattern) (1)	W-40-C-965-900	HV-28
CHUCK, balance, large	W-40-C-972	HV-237
CHUCK, balance, small (W. W. No. 2)	W-40-C-972-300	HV-236
CHUCK, wire (for Peerless lathe, W. W. pattern) (Nos. 4, 26, 28, 30, 34, 38, 40, 46, 50) (1)	W-40-C-995-200	MCE-39584
COMPASS, small, for testing for magnetism (1)	W-18-C-1598	MCE-36438
CUP, alcohol w/cover (1)	W-18-C-1984-400	MCE-36308
CUP, oil, set (3) in wood base and w/3 different size oilers (1)	W-18-C-1988-50	MCE-36338
DEMAGNETIZER, complete w/cord and plug	W-17-D-670	HV-36449
DRILL, pivot, mascot, 4 to 26 (12)	W-41-D-1860	MCE-36581
DRILL, twist (set of 36) (1)	W-40-D-1253	MCE-36618
FILE, screw-head, large (1)	W-41-F-2332	HV-34868
FILE, screw-head, small (1)	W-41-F-2330	HV-34872
FILE, Sw-patt., hand, sm., 6 in. (1 cut No. 6) (2)	W-41-F-2038	HV-34046
FILE, Sw-patt., hand, sm. cut. No. 4, 6 in. w/safe	W-41-F-2028	MCE-34044
FILE, Sw-patt., needle cut, No. 0, 4 in. long, 8 files w/rd. knurled hdls. (set 1)	W-41-F-2100	MCE-34908
FRAME, saw, 2 in. deep (1)	W-41-F-3419	HV-41909
GLASS, loupe, watchmaker's dble. lens, for use w/glasses or w/o glasses (1)	W-18-G-1101-50	HV-36778
GRAVER, turning and pivoting (set 6)	M-18-G-1298	MCE-38556
HAMMER, 2½ in. head, complete w/handle (1)	W-41-H-491	HV-38707
HOLDER, chuck, for tailstock (for Peerless lathe)	W-40-H-548-950	HV-39842
INSERTER, crystals, unbreakable, set (1)	W-18-I-495	
LAMP, alcohol, facet shaped, w/wick and burners (1)	W-57-L-348	HV-39368
LAMP, electric, watchmaker's (1)	W-17-L-5354	
LATHE (Peerless, W. W. pattern), w/accessories (1)	W-40-L-29-75	HV-39640
LEVELER, hairspring (1)	W-18-L-1050	HV-20
MALLET, br., 2 in. br. hd., 9 in. hardwood handle, No. 910 (1)	W-41-N-385	MCE-40360
OILER, gold tipped, No. 3 (1)	W-41-O-30	MCE-40451
OPENER, case, wood handle (1)	W-18-O-417	HV-36969
PIPE, bow, plain, 1-6 in. pr. (1)	W-18-P-22379	HV-35261
PLIERS, bow contracting (1)	W-18-P-24010	HV-41250
PLIERS, end cutting, 4 in. (1)	W-41-P-1736	HV-40716
PLIERS, flat nosed (rough jaws) 4 in. (1)	W-41-P-1770	HV-40728
PLIERS, rd. nosed, 4½ in. (1)	W-41-P-1911	MCE-40729
PLIERS, side cutting (1)	W-41-P-1992-25	MCE-40735
PLIERS, snipe nosed, 4½ in. (1)	W-41-P-1920	MCE-40732
REMOVER, hand, w/plunger (1)	W-18-R-341-200	HV-38612
REMOVER, wrench, hairspring collet	W-18-R-341-175	KN-19
REMOVER AND REPLACER, jewel, 6 prongs, covering size of American made watches (1)	W-18-R-341-400	HV-39087

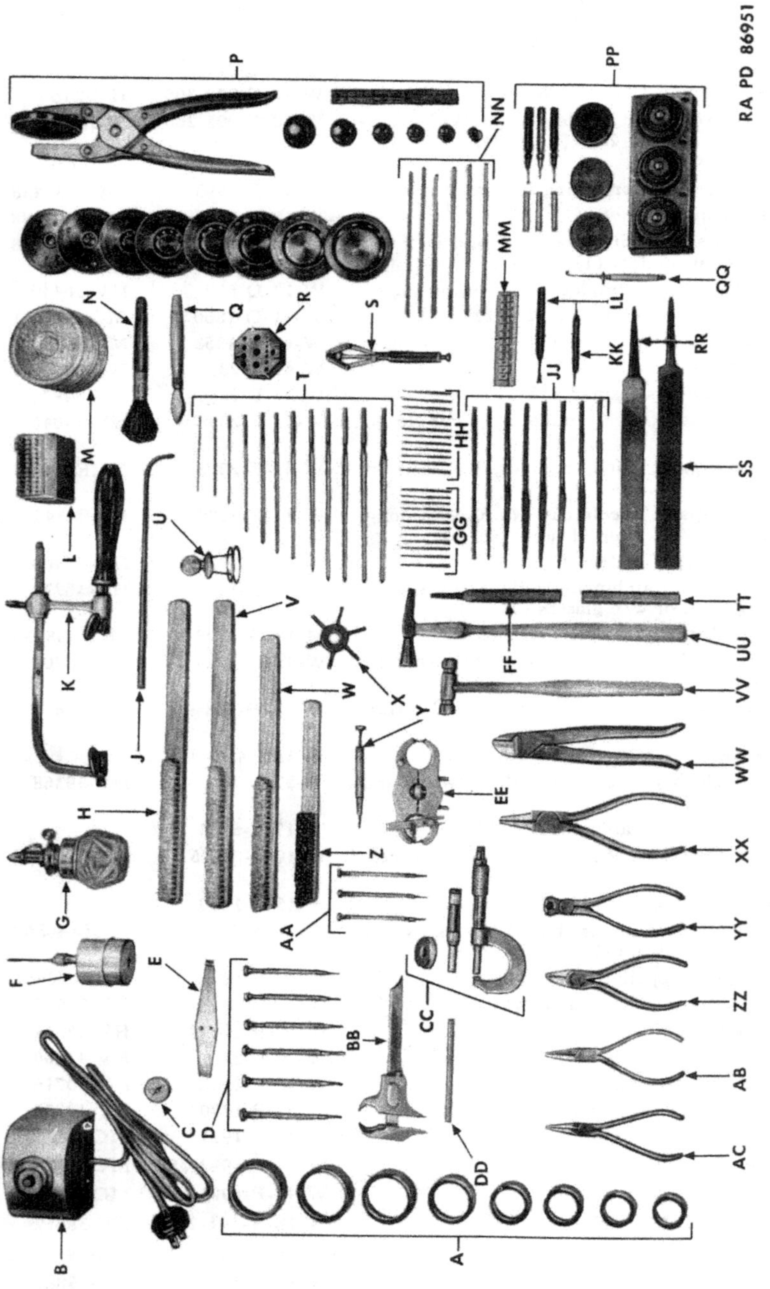

RA PD 86951

Figure 16 — Watch Repair (Senior) Tool Set, Set No. 1

GENERAL MAINTENANCE

RA PD 86951A

A—BLOCKS, MOVEMENT, SET OF 8, MCE-40409—W-18-B-1150-300
B—DEMAGNETIZER, HV-36449—W-17-D-670
C—COMPASS, MCE-36438—W-18-C-1598
D—SCREWDRIVER, JEWELER'S, KN-250—W-41-S-1325
E—SCALE, BALANCE, HV-41978—W-18-S-261-15
F—BLOWER, AIR, HV-35405—W-18-B-1153-300
G—LAMP, ALCOHOL, HV-39368—W-57-L-348
H—BRUSH, SOFT, HV-35566—38-B-5568
J—PIPE, BLOW, HV-35261—W-18-P-22379
K—FRAME, SAW, HV-41909—W-41-F-3419
L—DRILL, TWIST (SET OF 36) MCE-36618—W-40-D-1253
M—CUP, ALCOHOL, MCE-36308—W-18-C-1984-400
N—BRUSH, DIAL, MCE-35586—38-B-1263
P—INSERTER, CRYSTAL, SET—W-18-I-495
Q—OPENER, CASE, HV-36969—W-18-O-417
R—ANVIL, MCE-35049—W-18-A-459-500
S—REMOVER, HAND, w/PLUNGER, KN-310A—W-18-R-341-200
T—BROACH, CUTTING, SET, HV-35455—W-18-B-1376-500
U—GLASS, LOUPE, HV-36778—W-18-G-1101-50
V—BRUSH, MEDIUM STIFF NO. 2, HV-35564—38-B-5565
W—BRUSH, MEDIUM SOFT NO. 3, HV-35565—38-B-5566
X—REMOVER AND REPLACER, JEWEL, HV-39037—W-18-R-341-400
Y—SCREWDRIVER, BALANCE, KN-22A—W-41-S-1313
Z—BRUSH, WASHOUT, HV-35590—38-B-5570
AA—SCREWDRIVER, JEWELER'S (SET OF 3) HV-42100—W-41-S-1326

BB—CALIPERS, SLIDING, MILLIMETER, HV-37875—W-41-C-314
CC—CALIPERS, MICROMETER, MCE-37874—W-41-C-372
DD—BURNISHER, HV-35810—W-18-B-1451-200
EE—CALIPERS, TRUING, HV-36062—W-18-C-99-300
FF—FILE, SCREW HEAD, LARGE, HV-34868—W-41-F-2332
GG—BROACH, PIVOT, CUTTING, HV-35443—W-18-B-1376-525
HH—BROACH, PIVOT, ROUND, HV-35444—W-18-B-1376-700
JJ—FILE (SET OF 8) MCE-34908—W-41-F-2100
KK—LEVELER, HAIRSPRING, HV-20—W-18-L-1050
LL—REMOVER, WRENCH, H/SPRING COLLET, KN-19—W-18-R-341-175
MM—DRILL, PIVOT, MCE-36581—W-41-D 1860
NN—GRAVER (SET OF 6) MCE-38556—W-18-G-1298
PP—CUP, OIL (SET OF 3), w/3 OILERS, MCE-36338—W-18-C-1988-50
QQ—OILER, MCE-40451—W-41-O-30
RR—FILE, MCE-34044—W-41-F-2028
SS—FILE, HV-34046—W-41-F-2038
TT—FILE, SCREW HEAD, SMALL, HV-34872—W-41-F-2330
UU—HAMMER, HV-38707—W-41-H-491
VV—MALLET, BRASS, MCE-40360—W-41-M-385
WW—PLIERS, BOW CONTRACTING, HV-41250—W-18-P-24010
XX—PLIERS, MCE-40729—W-41-P-1911
YY—PLIERS, END CUTTING, HV-40716—W-41-P-1736
ZZ—PLIERS, SIDE CUTTING, MCE-40735—W-41-P-1992-25
AB—PLIERS, SNIPE NOSE, MCE-40732—W-41-P-1920
AC—PLIERS, FLAT NOSE, HV-40728—W-41-P-1770

Legend for Figure 16 — Watch Repair (Senior) Tool Set, Set No. 1

RA PD 86952

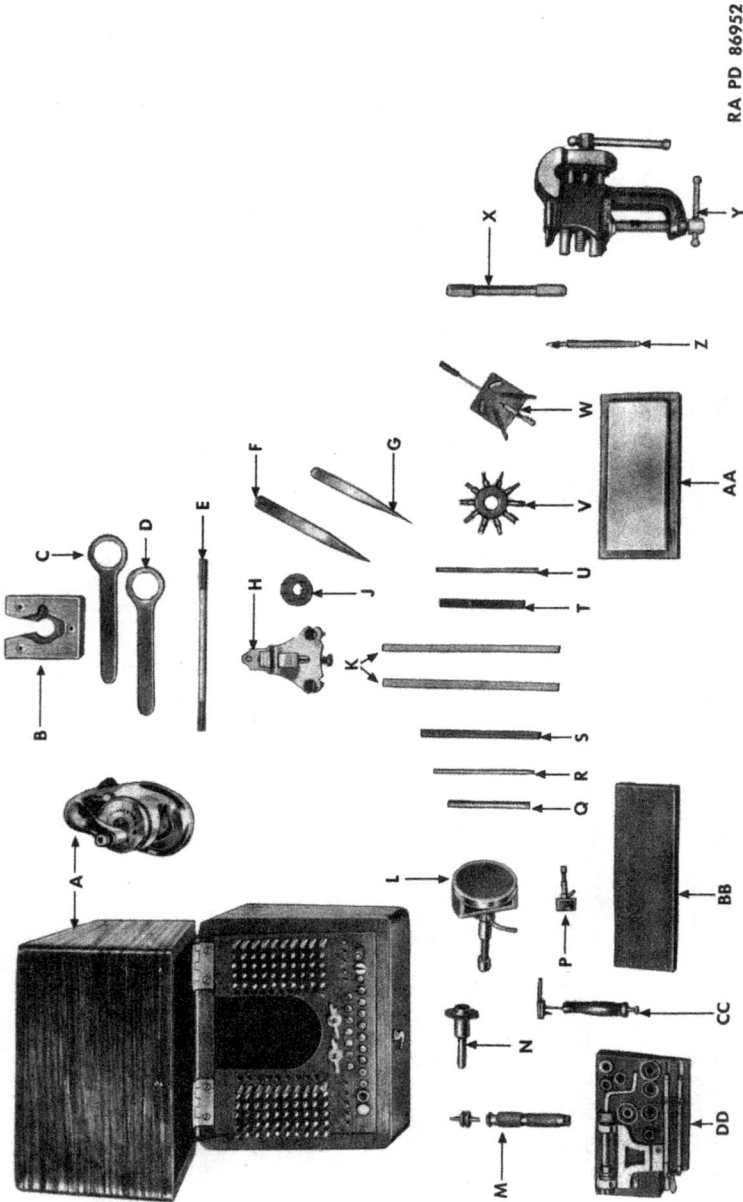

Figure 17 — Watch Repair (Senior) Tool Set, Set No. 1

RA PD 86952A

A—TOOL, STAKING, 100 PUNCHES,
  KN-18-B—W-18-T-3289-200
B—BLOCK, WOOD (MAPLE), WATCH REPAIR
  A-7579260—39-B-418
C—WRENCH, WATCH CASE, 19-E-122-5
  —W-41-W-3814-125
D—WRENCH, WATCH CASE,
  HAM-ST-3433—41-W-3814
E—WIRE, BRASS, NOS. 14-21 BUNDLE,
  MCE-44529—22-W-671-200
F—TWEEZERS, STRAIGHT POINT, LONG,
  HV-43131—W-41-T-4207
G—TWEEZERS, STRAIGHT POINT, 4½-IN.,
  HV-43110—W-41-T-4205
H—TOOL, POISING, w/AGATE JAWS,
  HV-395—W-18-T-3288-925
J—UNDERCUTTERS, BALANCE SCREW
  (NI P/TD, SET OF 7) HV-35099—
  W-18-U-170
K—SLIPS, POLISHING, BOXWOOD,
  HV-35813—W-41-S-5638
L—CHUCK, BALANCE, SMALL (WW NO.
  2), HV-236—W-40-C-972-300
M—WINDER, MAINSPRING, KN-123A—
  W-18-W-1099-300
N—SAW, CIRCULAR, AND ARBOR,—¾ IN.
  HV-76A—40-S-651-140
P—CHUCK, BALANCE, LARGE, HV-237—
  W-40-C-972
Q—STONE, OIL, SLIP, TRIANGULAR,
  HV-42860—W-41-S-5644-50

R—STONE, OIL, SLIP, TRIANGULAR,
  HV-42853—W-41-S-5644
S—STONE, OIL, SLIP, SQUARE, HV-42863
  HV-42863—W-41-S-5577
T—STONE, OIL, SLIP, SQUARE, HV-42876
  —W-41-S-5645
U—STONE, OIL, SLIP, SQUARE, HV-42854
  —W-41-S-5641
V—WRENCH, SLEEVE (10 PRONGS),
  KN-145—W-41-W-2561
W—SETTER, JEWELS AND PALLET STONES,
  HV-29—W-18-S-1501-700
X—VISE, PIN, DOUBLE END CHUCK—
  MCE-40623—W-41-V-356
Y—VISE, BENCH, NO. 707, HV-43358—
  W-41-V-97
Z—VISE, PIN, w/CHUCK, HV-40605—
  W-41-V-340
AA—STONE, HARD, BOXED, MCE-42821—
  W-41-S-5333-25
BB—STONE, OIL, COMBINATION, COARSE
  AND FINE, HV-42812—
  W-41-S-5414
CC—TOOL, COMBINATION, HV-60—
  W-T-3288-625
DD—WINDER, MAINSPRING,
  w/ACCESSORIES, KN-128—
  W-18-W-1009-500

Legend for Figure 17 — Watch Repair (Senior) Tool Set, Set No. 1

ORDNANCE MAINTENANCE — WRIST WATCHES, POCKET WATCHES, STOP WATCHES, AND CLOCKS

Name	Federal Stock No.	Manufacturer's Part No.
REST, slide, 3 in. slide for Peerless lathe, w/6 cutters and shoes (W. W. pattern) (1)	W-40-R-1890-173	HV-40066
SAW, circular and arbor, ¾ in. (1)	W-40-S-651-140	HV-76A
SCALE, balance (for matching balance screws) (1)	W-18-S-261-15	HV-41978
SCREWDRIVER, balance (1)	W-41-S-1313	KN-22A
SCREWDRIVER, jeweler's (0.025-100) (GGG-121-A) (set of 6) (1)	W-41-S-1325	KN-250
SCREWDRIVER, jeweler's asst'd. (12)	W-41-S-1326	HV-42100
SETTER, jewels and pallet stones (1)	W-18-S-1581-700	HV-29
SLIPS, polishing, boxwood (2)	W-41-S-5638	HV-35813
STONE, hard, Arkansas, 2 x 5 in. boxed (1)	W-41-S-5333-25	MCE-42821
STONE, oil, comb., 6 x 2 x 1 in., 1 side coarse and 1 side fine (1)	W-41-S-5414	HV-42812
STONE, oil slip, square, 3⅛ x ⅛, hard, Arkansas (1)	W-41-S-5641	HV-52854
STONE, oil slip, square, 3½ x ³⁄₁₆, India (1)	W-41-S-5577	HV-42863
STONE, oil slip, square, 3½ x ³⁄₁₆, jasper (1)	W-41-S-5645	HV-42876
STONE, oil slip, triangular, 3½ x ⅛ x ⅛, hard, Arkansas (1)	W-41-S-5644	HV-42853
STONE, oil slip, triangular, 3½ x ¼ x ¼, hard, Arkansas (1)	W-41-S-5644-50	HV-42860
SWITCH, foot, for motor	17-S-20387	
TOOL, combination, No. 60 (1)	W-18-T-3288-625	HV-60
TOOL, poising, w/agate jaws	W-18-T-3288-925	HV-395
TOOL, staking, 100 punches (punches reversible, may be used as stumps), set (1), tools, friction jeweling removers, staff and roller	W-18-T-3289-215	KN-18R
TWEEZERS, straight point, 4½ in.	W-41-T-4205	HV-43110
TWEEZERS, watchmaker's, straight point, long	W-41-T-4207	HV-43131
UNDERCUTTER, balance screw-in, ni-plated base (7 in set) (1)	W-18-U-170	HV-35099
VISE, bench, No. 707 (1)	W-41-V-97	HV-43358
VISE, pin, double end chuck, w/reversible chucks, from 9 to 3 mm, 4 in. long, No. 53 (1)	W-41-V-356	MCE-40623
VISE, pin, w/chuck (for holding small broaches No. 11)	W-41-V-340	HV-40605
WHEEL, carborundum, grinding		MCE-39796
WHEEL, crystal, grinding		MCE-42898
WINDER, mainspring	W-18-W-1099-300	KN-123A
WINDER, mainspring, w/accessories	W-18-W-1099-500	KN-128
WRENCH, sleeve (10 prongs)	W-41-W-2561	KN-145
WRENCH, watch case, 0.72 CTC of pins	W-41-W-3814-125	19-E-122-3
WRENCH, watch case, waterproof	W-41-W-3814	HAM-ST-3933

d. Equipment.

Name	Federal Stock No.	Manufacturer's Part No.
BENCH, watchmaker's, flat top, walnut finish (1)	41-B-509	MCE-35218
CLEANER, watch, electric, heavy duty (L and R Mfg. Co.) (1)	W-18-C-844	

GENERAL MAINTENANCE

BENCH — W-41-B-509　　　　　　　　← LAMP — W-17-L-5354

STOOL — W-26-5-35890

Figure 18 — Watchmaker's Bench, Flat Top, Walnut Finish

ORDNANCE MAINTENANCE — WRIST WATCHES, POCKET WATCHES, STOP WATCHES, AND CLOCKS

CLEANER — W-18-C-884

JAR — 18-J-500

BASKET — 18-B-994-750

RA PD 86648

Figure 19 — Electric Watch Cleaner

Name	Federal Stock No.	Manufacturer's Part No.
MOTOR, lathe, $\frac{1}{12}$ hp., 25 to 60 cycle, 110 volts a-c or d-c (1)	W-17-N-4596	HV-39919
STOOL, adj., oak finish, 18 in. (1)	W-26-S-35890	MCE-35250
TIMING MACHINE	18-T-571-775	

e. Fifth-echelon Supplies (fig. 22).

CEMENT, bottle shredded jewel	52-C-940	HV-18005
CEMENT, watch glass, tube	52-C-1688	HV-18062
CLEANING, liquid, watch washing, noninflammable (L and R Mfg. Co., No. 1 or equal) (gal)	51-C-1329-80	
CLEANING, liquid, watch rinsing, nonexplosive (L and R Mfg. Co., No. 3 or equal) (gal)	51-C-1329-65	

GENERAL MAINTENANCE

HOLDER, TOOL

CHUCK—W-40-C-965-900

REST—W-40-R-1890-173

CHUCK, WIRE—W-40-C-995-200

MOTOR—W-17-M-4596

Figure 20 — Peerless Lathe With Accessories

CUTTERS, TOOL

SWITCH, FOOT, FOR MOTOR—17-S-20387

LATHE, W-40-L-29-75

35

MACHINE, TIMING—18-T-571-775

PAPER
18-P-21200

COVER, TIMING MACHINE

RA PD 86650

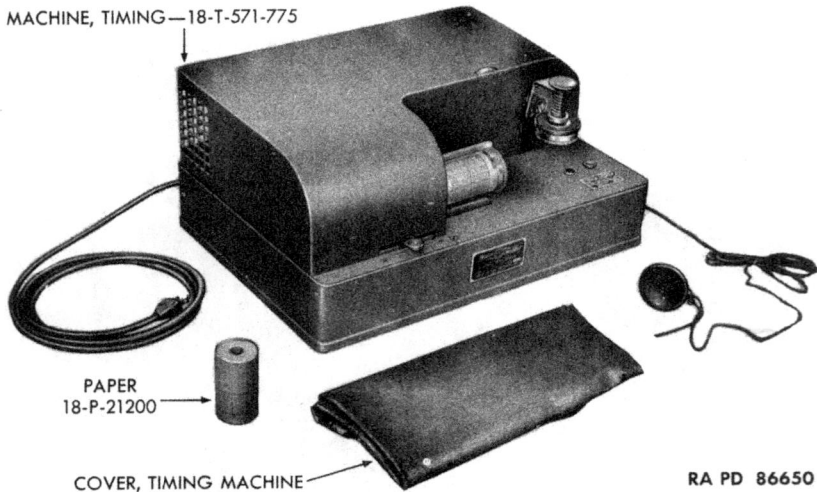

Figure 21 — Timing Machine

Name	Federal Stock No.	Manufacturer's Part No.
OIL, watch, bottle	14-O-680	EL-56A
PAPER, watchmaker's, no lint, box, 100 sheets	53-P-22920	MCE-15617
PEG WOOD, watchmaker's (for wrist and pocket watches)	39-P-325	HV-40510
PITH, soft bundle, 3½ in. long	39-P-330	MCE-40520
ROUGE, stick, hand (for use w/boxwood sticks for polishing pivots, etc.)	51-R-438	HV-18210
SAW, asst'd. 8/0 to 6 size (gross)	41-S-215	HV-41898
WASHER, timing, 6/0 to 18 size, 6 gross asst'd.	18-W-100-25	
WIRE, brass, Nos. 14 to 21, bundle	22-W-671-200	MCE-44529
WIRE, pivot	22-W-2012-75	HV-105
WIRE, spring No. 22	22-W-2011-100	HV-110
WIRE, spring No. 24	22-W-2011-110	HV-110
WIRE, spring No. 26	22-W-2011-120	HV-110
WIRE, spring No. 28	22-W-2011-130	HV-110
WIRE, spring No. 30	22-W-2011-140	HV-110
WIRE, spring No. 32	22-W-2011-150	HV-110
WIRE, steel, tempered, bundle	22-W-2012-50	HV-107
WIRE, steel, tube, soft	22-W-2013	HV-101

16. CARE AND HANDLING.

a. **Care.** Watches and clocks are delicate, precision-built instruments. The length of time a service timepiece renders satisfactory service depends entirely on proper care and handling by both the

GENERAL MAINTENANCE

using arms and the maintenance personnel. Timepieces should not be tossed about carelessly. A shock or jar may bend or break a pivot, crack or chip the jeweled bearings in which the pivots revolve, and render the timepiece unserviceable. Timepieces should be kept away from electrical apparatus which have strong magnetic fields, as induced magnetism may cause the timepiece to run erratically or stop. Opening cases and exposing the mechanism to dust should be avoided. Dust in the movement causes the bearings to clog, oil to gum up, and wheels and pinions to bind, thus causing the movement to stop.

b. **Winding.** Care should be exercised when winding a timepiece. Wind it slowly and cautiously, and wind fully at regular intervals either daily or weekly. Care must be exercised when reaching the end of the winding, for a sudden jerk may cause the end of the mainspring to uncheck or break. A sudden jerk may also shear the teeth off the winding pinion, crown wheel, or ratchet wheel.

c. **Water and Dampness.** If a timepiece has been submerged in water, it should be turned over to the repair section immediately. Water or dampness in a movement will cause all steel parts to become rusted, rendering the timepiece unserviceable. If the watch cannot be returned at once to a maintenance section, rust might be prevented for a few days by dipping the watch in dry-cleaning solvent, drying it under a lamp and flooding the movement with oil. NOTE: *The dial will be discolored by this treatment and it should only be used for a short period.*

d. **Handling of Parts.** After watch parts have been cleaned, do not handle them with the fingers. Place them in a parts tray and keep them covered until ready to assemble. If it is necessary to replace a part after cleaning, all parts that have to be handled during the replacement must be cleaned before final assembly. In cleaning watch or clock parts either by hand or machine, the procedure outlined in paragraph 17 must be followed.

e. **Replacement of Parts.** Replace new parts with extreme care and always use proper tools and methods. Observe extreme precautions in selecting replacement parts. Parts from different manufacturers and from different size watches are not interchangeable. All parts that require replacing must be carefully selected from the Standard Nomenclature List addendum covering the make, model, and size of watch being repaired. NOTE: *All replacement parts are coated with a rust preventive and must be cleaned before installation.*

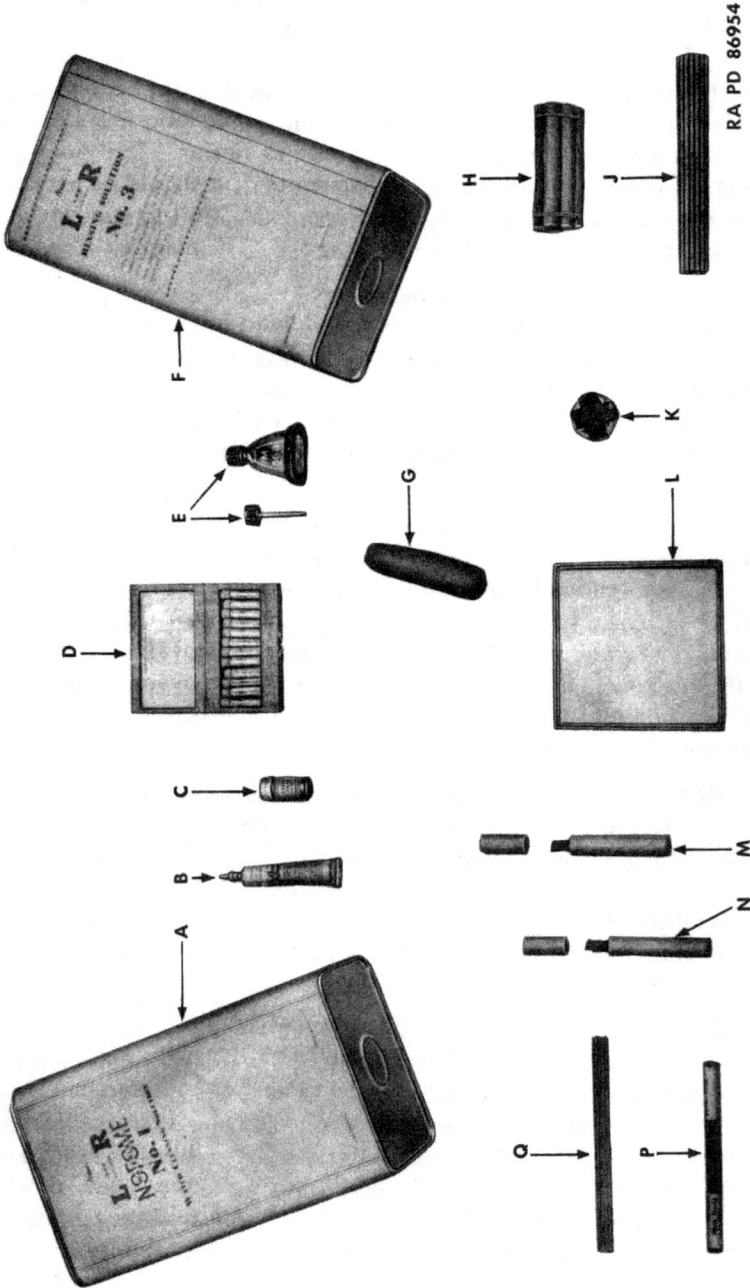

RA PD 86954

Figure 22 — Watch Repair Set (Senior) No. 1 Supplies

RA PD 86954A

A—CLEANING, LIQUID, WATCH, WASHING, NON-INFLAMMABLE (L & R CO. NO. 1 OR EQUAL (GAL.) 51-C-1329-75

B—CEMENT, WATCH GLASS, TUBE, HV-18062—52-C-1688

C—CEMENT, BOTTLE SHREDDED JEWEL, HV-18005—52-C-940

D—WASHER, TIMING 6/0 TO 18 SIZE, 6 GROSS ASSORTED 18-W-100-25

E—OIL, WATCH, BOTTLE, EL-56-A—14-0-680

F—CLEANING, LIQUID, WATCH RINSING, NON-EXPLOSIVE (L & R CO. NO. 3 OR EQUAL) (GAL.) 51-C-1329-50

G—ROUGE, STICK, HAND (FOR USE WITH BOXWOOD STICKS FOR POLISHING PIVOTS, ETC., HV-18210—51-R-438

H—PITH, SOFT, BUNDLE 3½-IN. LONG, MCE-40520—39-P-330

J—PEGWOOD, WATCHMAKERS, FOR WRIST AND POCKET WATCHES, AV-40510—39-P-325

K—WIRE, SPRING NO. 22 TO NO. 32, HV-110 22-W-2011-100 TO 150

L—PAPER, WATCHMAKERS, NO LINT BOX, 1000 SHEETS, MCE-15617—53-P-22920

M—WIRE, PIVOT, HV-105—22-W-2012-75

N—WIRE, STEEL, TEMPERED, BUNDLE, HV-107—22-W-2012-50

P—SAW, ASSORTED, 8/0 TO 6, GROSS, HV-41898—41-S-215

Q—WIRE, STEEL TUBE, SOFT, HV-101—22-W-2013

Legend for Figure 22 — Watch Repair Set (Senior) No. 1 Supplies

Section V

CLEANING AND LUBRICATING

17. CLEANING.

a. Watches and clocks like other mechanical instruments require cleaning to insure the efficiency and accuracy that is expected of them. They require cleaning for two reasons: (1) dust has entered the case, settling on the moving parts, and (2) oil has dried causing pivots to become gummy, which causes wear on parts and lack of power in the train. When a timepiece becomes dirty it will show an erratic rate and become worse each day until the condition is so bad that it will cease functioning entirely.

b. There are two methods used in cleaning ordnance timepieces: the machine method, and the hand method. Cleaning with a watch cleaning machine is preferable to the hand method as it is faster and simpler but, when using it, the proper method must be followed with precautions. There are special manufactured solutions made by the manufacturer especially for use with the cleaning machine, and only these must be used. When cleaning by the hand method, a combination of the following ingredients can be used satisfactorily: mild soap and water, ammonia, and alcohol, followed by at least two separate rinses of benzene or gasoline containing no tetraethyl lead. One possible combination of the cleaner is listed for reference, the materials of which are available in any operational theater.

> 1 gallon boiling water
> 2 ounces soap (mild castile preferred) (by weight)
> 6 ounces ammonia (26 percent solution preferred)
> 12 ounces alcohol

c. When the watch cleaning machine is used, the heavier parts such as the plate and bridges are placed in one compartment of the cleaning basket, and the train wheels, winding and setting parts, dial train, pallet, and all other smaller parts in another compartment, with the balance assembly by itself. The basket is attached firmly to the rotating spindle of the motor and lowered to immerse in the cleaning solution contained in jar No. 1, allowing it to rotate there for 2 minutes only. The basket is then raised slightly above the solution and slowly rotated to expel excessive solution for 20 or 30 seconds. The same process is repeated in the Nos. 2 and 3 jars containing rinsing solution, after which the basket is revolved above the drying coils for 2 minutes. With the drying completed, unfasten the basket and carefully remove the parts. Sharpen a piece of pegwood and run the point in the jewel holes. This will remove any foreign particles that have not been removed by the cleaning machine. Also rub the cap jewels thoroughly to make sure they are clean. Press all pivots into

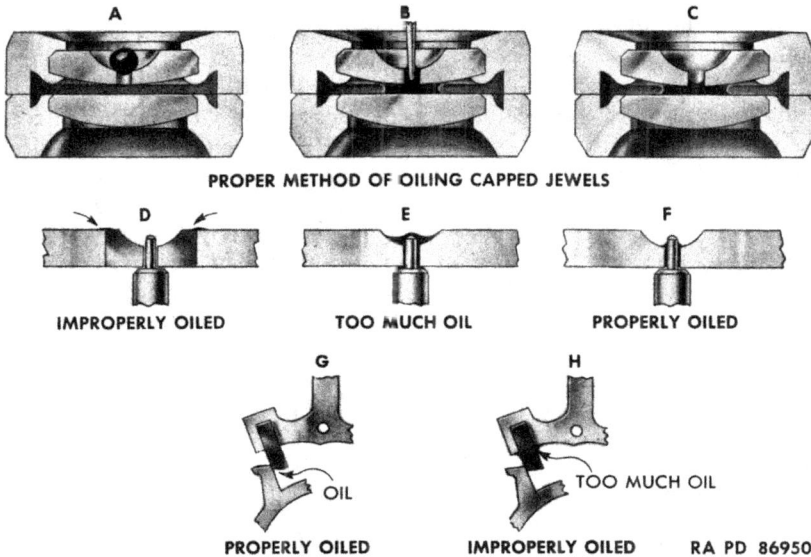

Figure 24 — Proper and Improper Oiling

18. LUBRICATION.

a. **General.** The primary reason for oiling a watch is to reduce friction and wear between moving surfaces. This reduction saves power and makes for smoother operation. The importance of cleaning and thoroughly oiling a watch yearly cannot be emphasized too greatly.

b. **Oiling Capped Jewels.** To place oil in a capped jewel, a small drop should be placed on the oiler and fed into the space between the jewel and the end stone with a fine pointed wire or broach smaller than the jewel hole. The size of the oil bubble should then be examined and increased to its proper proportions by adding a little at a time (fig. 24).

c. **Proper Method of Oiling.** Figure 24 shows a drop of oil after it has been placed in the jewel cup. During this operation care should be taken not to strike the brass setting with the oiler as it may cause the oil to run away from the bearing. B, figure 24, shows the oil being pushed through the jewel hole to the end stone by a fine wire or broach which must be smaller in diameter than the jewel hole. C, figure 24, shows oil in place. Note the quantity of oil. There is sufficient oil to lubricate the bearing, but not so much that the oil will contact the settings. Overoiling a bearing is as harmful as underoiling.

CLEANING AND LUBRICATING

d. Oiling Train Jewels. After the movement has been assembled, oil should be placed in each of the train jewels or bushings. In oiling, the oiler should touch the pivot and the bottom of the oil cup simultaneously, so that the oil flows through the jewel hole to the pivot shoulder immediately. When removing the oiler from the oil cup, lift it straight up so that any possibility of leaving a track of oil across the top surface of the jewel to the setting is eliminated. This condition would tend to draw oil out of the cup onto the setting as shown in D, figure 24. When oiling the center lower jewel, a small quantity of oil should be placed on the center wheel arbor so that the cannon pinion will be properly lubricated during setting. To avoid putting too much oil on the center wheel arbor, apply with an oil-saturated piece of pegwood. E, figure 24, shows how excessive oiling will cause the oil to flow through, and adhere to, arbors and pinions and will travel through the movement. If oil gets on the hairspring, it causes erratic timing. F, figure 24, shows a properly oiled pivot. Oil has run directly through the jewel hole to pivot shoulder, retaining the proper amount of oil on the bearing surfaces.

e. Oiling Pallet Stones. An approved method of oiling the pallet stones is to apply the oil to three teeth of the escape wheel rather than to the pallet stones themselves. As the escape wheel rotates, an even coverage of oil will be distributed upon all the teeth of the wheel and to the face of the pallet stones (fig. 24).

f. Oiling Winding and Setting Mechanism. After cleaning and winding the mainspring, a small amount of oil should be placed in the barrel to lubricate every part of the spring. Apply a small amount of oil to the shoulders of the barrel arbor before inserting it into the barrel. An excessive amount of oil in the barrel will be forced out when the mainspring is wound tightly. All the bearing surfaces in the winding and setting mechanism should be oiled, including the square of the winding arbor, where it runs through the clutch wheel. In the case of a pocket watch, the leaves of the sleeve in the pendant should be oiled in order to lubricate the shoulders of the winding arbor. Never lubricate the setting wheels or the minute and hour wheels or the teeth or pinions of third and fourth wheels.

g. Use Clean Oil. Watch moving parts are subject to a certain amount of wear under normal conditions, but if the watch is improperly oiled, wear will occur more rapidly and the watch will fail to keep time accurately. It is essential that clean oil be used because abrasives in the form of dirt or dust find their way into the oil. The main supply of oil should be kept away from dirt and light, and should be protected from air and contamination as much as possible.

h. Oiling Interval. For best performance, a timepiece must be cleaned, oiled and regulated once each year.

Section VI

TROUBLE SHOOTING, ADJUSTMENT, AND REPAIR

19. WATCH STOPS.

a. **General.** The following is an outline covering the usual causes for the stopping of a watch. These methods apply to pocket and wrist watches unless otherwise noted.

b. **Hands Catching on Dial or Crystal.**

(1) To determine if hands are catching, pull the crown out to setting position. Turn crown and rotate hands a complete revolution clockwise and counterclockwise, and observe the action of the hands. If minute hand is rubbing or catching on the crystal, the hour hand rubbing on the dial or catching on the minute hand, or the second hand rubbing on the dial, it will be obvious.

(2) To correct the condition, remove bezel and realine hands so that they are parallel to each other, with the minute hand tip curved down toward the dial to conform to the curve of the crystal. Raise the second hand enough to clear the dial, yet not enough so it will catch on the hour or minute hand (fig. 25).

c. **Dial Loose or Out of Position.**

(1) A loose dial is usually detected by movement within the case. If the dial is out of position, it will cause the hour wheel pipe or the second hand pipe to bind, which can be readily observed. To determine the cause, remove the movement from the case and check the dial foot screws. Remove the dial and check the feet to see if they are bent, worn, or broken.

(2) To correct these conditions: If a dial has a broken foot, replace it with a new dial. If the feet are bent, straighten them to aline with their respective holes in the pillar plate, and center around the hour and fourth wheel arbors. If the dial foot screws are stripped, replace with new screws.

d. **Broken or Bent Hour Wheel Teeth or Pipe.**

(1) Pull the crown out to setting position and rotate the hands. If the hour wheel teeth are broken or the pipe is bent, they will bind and the hands will stop rotating. To determine the cause, remove the movement from the case and remove hands and dial. Turn the setting mechanism and observe the circular movement of the hour wheel, checking it for trueness, bent teeth, and for proper mesh with the minute wheel pinion. Check the hour wheel pipe. It must fit snugly over the cannon pinion without binding.

(2) If the hour wheel teeth are broken, worn short, or badly bent, the wheel must be replaced. If one or more of the teeth are bent

TROUBLE SHOOTING, ADJUSTMENT, AND REPAIR

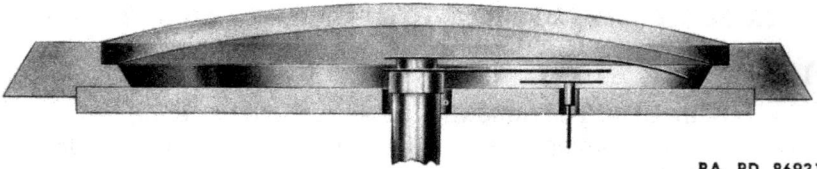

RA PD 86931

Figure 25 — Proper Setting of Hands

slightly, they may be straightened. If the pipe is bent, the wheel must be replaced. If the pipe fits too tightly on the cannon pinion, it can be broached out to fit properly. If the pipe fits too loosely on the cannon pinion, replace the hour wheel.

e. Broken or Bent Minute Wheel and Pinion Leaves.

(1) Pull the crown out to setting position and rotate the hands. If the minute wheel teeth are broken, bent, or the wheel has too much side play on its post, the minute wheel will bind and the hands stop rotating. To determine the cause, remove movement from case and remove hands and dial. Turn the setting mechanism and observe the circular movement of the minute pinion in relation to the hour wheel for trueness, bent leaves, and for proper mesh with the hour wheel teeth. Remove the hour wheel and check the teeth of the minute wheel. Check fit of minute wheel pinion to minute wheel; there should be no movement. Check mesh of minute wheel and cannon pinion as well as the mesh with the intermediate wheel (if provided). Check minute wheel for broken or bent teeth. Check for broken or bent minute wheel post.

(2) If the minute wheel pinion leaves or teeth are broken or bent, the wheel must be replaced. If the minute wheel is loose on its post or the post is broken, a new post must be installed. If the post is bent, the minute wheel will not mesh with the cannon pinion or intermediate wheel (if provided), and the post must be straightened. If the minute wheel teeth are bent or broken, the wheel must be replaced.

f. Broken or Bent Cannon Pinion Leaves or Pipe.

(1) This may be determined by pulling the crown out to the setting position and turning the hands. If the cannon pinion leaves are broken, bent, or do not mesh correctly with the minute wheel, the cannon pinion will bind and the hands will stop rotating. To determine the cause, remove movement from case and remove the hands, dial, and hour wheel. Rotate the cannon pinion and note mesh of cannon pinion with minute wheel.

ORDNANCE MAINTENANCE — WRIST WATCHES, POCKET WATCHES, STOP WATCHES, AND CLOCKS

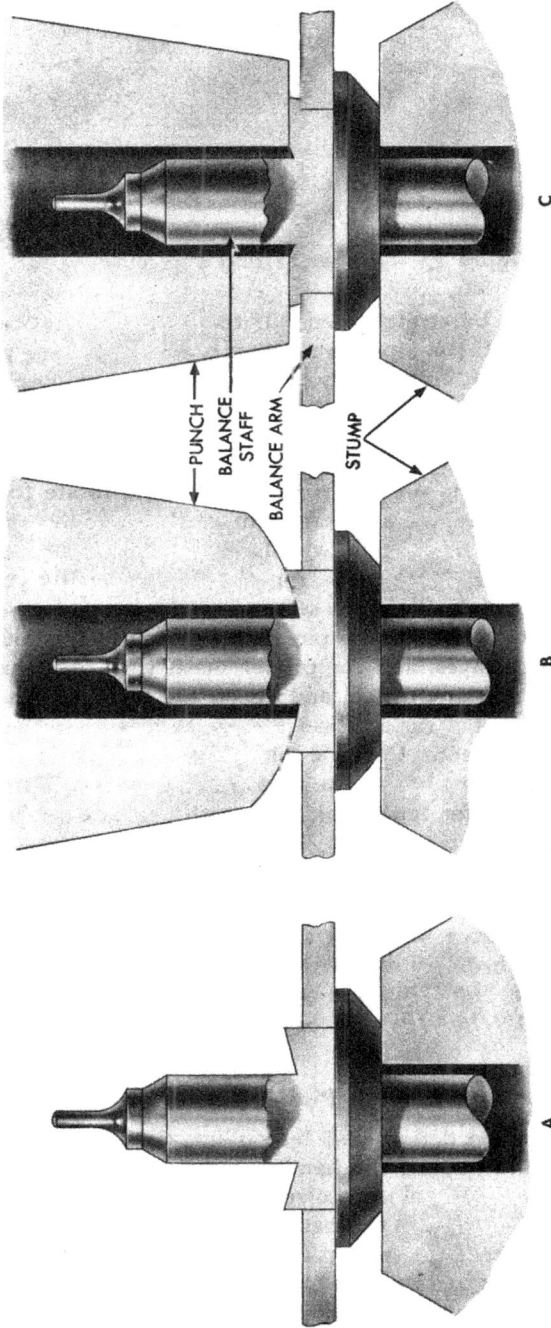

RA PD 96450

Figure 26 — Replacing Balance Staff

46

TROUBLE SHOOTING, ADJUSTMENT, AND REPAIR

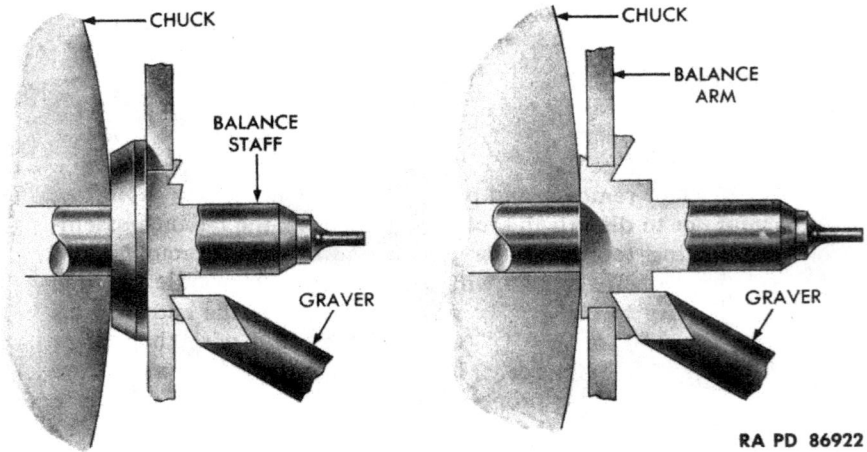

RA PD 86922

Figure 27 — Removing Damaged Balance Staff

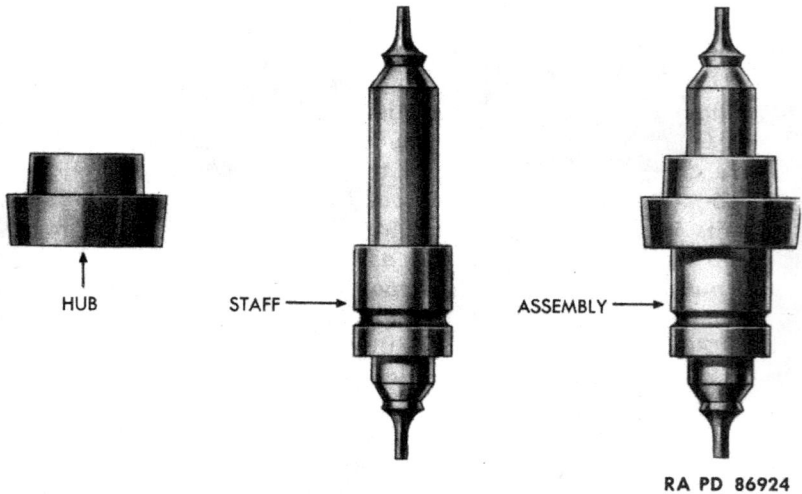

RA PD 86924

Figure 28 — Two-piece Friction Fit Staff

(2) If the leaves of the cannon pinion or the teeth of the minute wheel are broken, bent, or do not mesh properly, the parts affected must be replaced.

g. Bent or Broken Balance Staff.

(1) In order to determine whether or not the staff is bent or broken, remove the movement from the case and, with the tweezers,

TROUBLE SHOOTING, ADJUSTMENT, AND REPAIR

pivot being polished. Excessive heat will reduce the hardness of the steel pivot.

(2) In the case of a badly scored pivot, a jasper stone should be used to reduce the metal of the pivot. Rouge, with a slight amount of oil, should then be applied to the bell-metal burnisher. Apply rouge sparingly. The burnisher must be held parallel to the pivot so as to eliminate the possibility of tapering the pivot. A slight back-and-forth action, together with a sliding movement from side to side of the burnisher toward the end of the pivot, will utilize the application of the rouge and oil and will present a highly polished pivot. CAUTION: *Care must be exercised in the amount of pressure applied to the bell-metal burnisher to prevent the pivot from snapping off.*

i. Friction Jeweling.

(1) It is a simple matter to remove and replace a jewel; however, the preparation for the actual operation cannot be overlocked. The inspection of the size and condition of the new jewel and the depth of the old jewel in regard to "end shake" must be considered.

(2) Using the friction jeweling tool with its proper stump and pump center pusher for the jewel, measure the depth of the old jewel in the plate or bridge. This is accomplished by placing the old jewel on the stump, flat side up, and setting the micrometer to proper depth, being careful not to push the jewel and change its setting in the plate. Note the micrometer reading and push out the old jewel.

(3) The jewel hole in the plate must be inspected for size and condition. It must be slightly larger than the jewel to be replaced to allow for friction fit without cracking the new jewel. If the hole in the plate is oversize, it must be closed to proper size. With the staking tool, use a round-nosed punch of proper diameter to close the hole. Carefully ream the hole to the proper diameter. Reaming will remove any burs and maintain the concentricity of the jewel hole.

(4) Position the new jewel on the plate, flat side up. Press the jewel into place to the proper depth as shown by the micrometer setting. The pump center pusher avoids the danger of marring the jewel hole in the plate. Assemble the movement and check for proper end shake.

j. Bent or Broken Hairspring.

(1) If the hairspring is bent, it may drag on the balance arm or the balance cock and cause the movement to stop just as readily as a broken hairspring. A bent hairspring may also cause the watch to run erratically.

(2) To determine the cause of these conditions, remove the movement from the case and visually examine hairspring from various directions. If the hairspring is broken, it must be replaced. If it is

bent, true the spring in flat so that it will clear the balance arm and center it around the collet. For instruction on detailed adjustment, see paragraph 37.

k. Cracked, Chipped, or Broken Balance Jewels (Hole or Cap).

(1) If a balanced jewel is cracked, chipped, or broken, the watch may stop completely, run erratically, or stop and go. To determine the cause, remove movement from case and remove balance cock and balance assembly. Inspect the jewels.

(2) Cracked, chipped, or broken jewels must be replaced.

l. Broken, Chipped, or Loose Pallet Jewels.

(1) If a pallet jewel is cracked, chipped, or broken, it will stop the watch completely or will cause it to run erratically, or stop and go. This may be determined by removing the movement from the case, removing hands and dial, and observing the action of the pallet jewels through the hole in the pillar plate opposite the pallet jewels.

(2) Cracked, chipped, or broken pallet jewels must be replaced with a new pallet assembly. Loose pallet jewels must be recemented and adjusted for angle and depth (par. 39).

m. Broken, Chipped, or Loose Roller Jewel.

(1) A broken roller jewel will cause the watch to stop. A chipped roller jewel may cause the watch to run erratically or stop and go. A loose roller jewel may cause the watch to be overbanked. To determine the condition of the roller jewel, remove movement from case and observe the action of the roller assembly and roller jewel. Note whether the roller jewel is broken or chipped. Remove the balance assembly and notice if the roller jewel moves when touched with the point of a piece of pegwood.

(2) A broken or chipped roller jewel must be replaced with a new roller assembly. Roller jewels alone are not issued. A loose roller jewel can be cemented into position (par. 39).

n. Broken or Bent Pallet Arbor Pivots.

(1) A broken or bent pallet arbor pivot will cause the watch to stop. This may be determined by removing the movement from the case and removing the balance cock and balance assembly. Release the unused power of the mainspring. Using a feeler, shift the pallet fork from side to side and determine whether or not the arbor is upright and if the pivots are in their respective jewels. Remove the pallet bridge and pallet assembly and see that the arbor is tight in the pivot. If the arbor is a screw type, check to see that it is screwed in tight and that the threads are not stripped.

(2) If a pivot is broken, replace the pallet assembly. If the arbor is loose, tighten it.

TROUBLE SHOOTING, ADJUSTMENT, AND REPAIR

o. Broken or Bent Guard Pin.

(1) A broken guard pin will cause the watch to stop completely. A bent guard pin will cause it to stop and go intermittently. A guard pin that is too long will contact the safety roller and the friction will cause the watch to stop. A short guard pin will allow the watch to become overbanked and stop. To determine the condition, remove movement from case and observe the action of the guard pin to see that it is in the same plane as the safety roller and does not strike the jewel pin. Check guard pin shake with a feeler to see if the pin is too long or too short. If the guard pin is too short, too much guard pin shake will exist; if too long, there will be insufficient guard pin shake. If the guard pin is bent in the horizontal, unequal guard pin shake will exist.

(2) If the guard pin is broken or is too short, a new pallet assembly must be installed. If bent in the horizontal, it must be repositioned. If too long, it must be stoned down to correct length.

p. Broken or Bent Banking Pins.

(1) A broken or bent banking pin will throw the escapement out of adjustment and stop the watch. To determine this condition, remove movement from case and remove balance cock and balance assembly. Observe the action of the pallet fork as it strikes the banking pin at either side. See if they are positioned correctly. If the banking pins are too close, the escapement will not unlock; if they are too far apart, the watch will run erratically or will stop.

(2) If a banking pin is broken, replace it. If bent, it must be repositioned.

q. Broken, Bent, or Worn Escape Wheel Tooth.

(1) If an escape wheel tooth is broken or bent, the watch will stop, run erratically, or stop and go. To determine this condition, remove movement from case and remove balance cock and balance assembly. Move the pallet from side to side, causing the escape wheel to revolve. Note the condition of each tooth as it drops and locks on each pallet jewel.

(2) If an escape wheel tooth is broken or bent, replace the wheel.

r. Broken, Chipped, or Cracked Train Wheel Jewels or Bearing.

(1) If any of the train wheel jewels are broken, chipped, or cracked, or bearings are worn excessively, the watch will run erratically or will stop. To determine the cause, remove movement from case and remove hands, dial, and cannon pinion. Rotate balance by hand and observe the action of the escapement. If it is not free, it will indicate that a binding exists in the train. Check the pillar plate and bridge jewels to see if they are damaged. Check to see if bearings are worn. If

this condition cannot be observed with the train assembled, disassemble and inspect.

(2) Replace damaged jewels. If bearings are removable, replace them; if they are of the permanent type, close the holes then broach them out to correct size.

s. Broken or Bent Train Wheel Pinions, Leaves, and Pivots.

(1) Broken or bent train wheel pinions, leaves, or pivots, will cause the train to stop completely, run erratically, or stop and go. If a pivot is broken, it will allow the wheel to fall out of contact with the adjacent pinion and bind the train. If the pinion leaves are broken or bent, it will bind when it contacts the adjacent wheel. To determine the cause, remove movement from case and remove hands and dial. Check jewels and bearings on the pillar plate and bridges to see that the pivots are in their respective holes. Check each wheel with a feeler or tweezers and see if the wheel will move away from its jewel or bearings. In case of a broken or bent leaf, it will be necessary to disassemble the train to make a more complete inspection.

(2) A pinion with broken or bent pivot or leaves must be replaced with a new wheel assembly.

t. Broken or Bent Train Wheel or Teeth.

(1) A broken or bent train wheel or wheel tooth will stop the watch and cause a bind on the adjacent wheel or pinion when contact is made. To determine this condition, remove movement from case and disassemble for a complete inspection.

(2) A broken train wheel must be replaced. A bent train wheel may be straightened.

u. Broken or Bent Mainspring Barrel Teeth.

(1) A broken or bent tooth on the mainspring barrel will cause a bind when it contacts the center arbor pinion, causing the watch to stop. To determine this condition, remove movement from case and release the unused power of the mainspring. Remove ratchet wheel, mainspring barrel bridge, and mainspring barrel to inspect the barrel teeth.

(2) A broken or bent tooth on the mainspring barrel necessitates replacing the barrel with a new one.

v. Dirt in Movement.

(1) The accumulation of dirt in a watch will be gradual and cause the watch to lose time. It will also cause the oil to gum up and stop the watch. This condition may be determined by removing the movement from the case and inspecting it for dirt accumulation.

(2) To remedy this condition, disassemble, clean, and oil the watch.

TROUBLE SHOOTING, ADJUSTMENT, AND REPAIR

20. CROWN UNSCREWS.

a. If the crown unscrews in normal use, it may be caused by the threads being stripped on the stem or crown, stem rusted on the inside mechanism, the clutch or winding pinion binding, or the cannon pinion too tight or binding in the dial train or setting wheel. To determine the cause, remove movement from the case and remove the hands and dial. Examine threads on stem and crown with an eye loupe. To determine the other causes, disassemble the winding and setting mechanism, and inspect for broken or rusted parts.

b. To correct any of these conditions, replace defective parts.

21. STEM PULLS OUT.

a. If the stem pulls out, check for loose setting lever screw or stripped threads. Check the setting lever for broken parts, wear, or stripped threads. Check stem for size, or shoulder for being too small. Check recesses in barrel bridge for wear and for loose or bent bridge. To determine this condition remove movement from case and remove hands and dial. If the error cannot be observed, disassemble the winding mechanism.

b. Worn or broken parts of the winding mechanism must be replaced. If recesses in barrel bridge or pillar plate are worn, a new stem will have to be made to fit, since new bridges or pillar plates are not available as spare parts.

22. WATCH CAN BE WOUND BUT NOT SET.

a. This condition may be caused by an improperly engaged clutch; broken clutch teeth; broken or worn setting lever; minute wheel slipping out of mesh with setting wheel or cannon pinion due to broken, worn, or loose stud of either wheel; teeth sheared off hour or minute wheel; cannon pinion broken or loose, causing it to shift out of mesh with minute wheel; or by a broken clamp assembly. To determine the cause, remove movement from case and remove hands and dial. Engage the setting mechanism and rotate it to check for above conditions.

b. Any parts that are worn or broken in the setting mechanism must be replaced. If the minute wheel, setting wheel, and cannon pinion are not meshed, straighten the studs until proper mesh is obtained. If the cannon pinion is too loose, it may be tightened; or if it is too tight, it may be broached out to fit properly.

23. WATCH WILL SET BUT NOT WIND.

a. This may be caused by a broken mainspring, broken clutch lever spring, broken click or click spring, sheared or stripped teeth on the ratchet wheel, crown wheel, winding pinion, cannon pinion, loose barrel cover, hook on barrel worn or barrel arbor broken, or stripped screws which cause parts to become loose and out of adjustment. To determine the cause, remove movement from case, wind the watch and check the click and click spring, and crown and ratchet wheels, and check the screws retaining these parts. Remove hands and dial, wind the watch, and note operation of the winding mechanism. Check the power assembly by removing the ratchet wheel and lifting the barrel assembly out; check the barrel cap to see that it fits snugly into its recess. Remove barrel cap and check the mainspring to see that it is not broken and is properly hooked on the barrel at the outer end and on the arbor at the inner end.

b. Replace worn or broken parts; replace screws which have worn or stripped threads.

24. WATCH WILL NOT WIND OR SET.

a. The cause will be a broken clutch lever, clutch lever spring, or the stem broken below the bottom shoulder. To determine this, remove movement from case and remove hands and dial. Check the clutch lever, clutch lever spring, and the stem below the bottom shoulder.

b. To correct this condition, replace broken, worn, or rusty parts.

25. WATCH IS HARD TO SET.

a. This cause may be due to rusty parts, cannon pinion being too tight, minute wheel stud bent, a bent tooth on any of the wheels in the setting mechanism, or a weak clutch lever spring. To determine the cause, remove movement from case and remove hands and dial. With the clutch in setting position, rotate dial train and check for any of the above conditions.

b. To correct condition, replace broken, worn, or rusty parts. Straighten the minute stud, if bent; if stud is loose, replace it.

26. WATCH HARD TO WIND.

a. This may be due to bent stem, movement not cased properly, crown too small or knurling worn off, or rusty parts. To determine cause, inspect crown for size and condition. Rotate crown and, by feeling, note whether or not stem is binding at any point. Check to see that the movement is properly seated in the rebate of the case. Remove movement from case. Remove hands and dial to check winding mechanism and for rusty parts.

b. To correct condition, replace a small or worn crown; replace a bent stem. Reseat movement if improperly seated in case. Replace all rusty parts.

TROUBLE SHOOTING, ADJUSTMENT, AND REPAIR

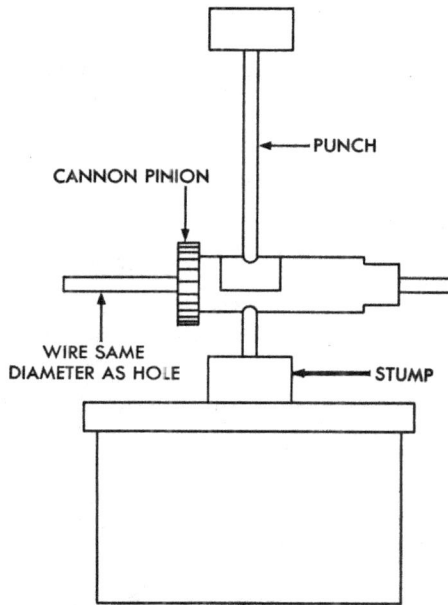

Figure 29 — Tightening Cannon Pinion With Staking Tool

27. STEM SLIPPING IN SETTING POSITION.

a. The cause may be improper depthing of the sleeve in pendant, sleeve worn, weak, or broken, stem shoulder worn, or setting spring too strong. To determine the cause, pull crown out to setting position and rotate it to see if it slips. Remove crown, sleeve, and stem assembly from the pendant and check to see if sleeve is worn, weak, or broken. Check stem shoulder for wear. Remove movement from case; remove hands and dial to check setting spring.

b. If stem slips in setting position, adjust the sleeve in or out to correct the trouble. If the sleeve is worn, weak, or broken, replace it. If stem shoulder is worn, replace it. If the setting spring is too strong, replace with a weaker spring.

28. WATCH DOES NOT WIND TIGHT.

a. This indicates that the mainspring slips off arbor hook or barrel hook. To determine the cause, remove movement from case and remove ratchet wheel screw and ratchet wheel. Remove barrel bridge. Remove barrel assembly and snap out barrel cap. Inspect mainspring to see that it is hooked at both ends.

b. If mainspring or either the barrel hook or arbor hook are broken or badly worn, replace them with new parts.

29. WATCH WILL RUN ONLY A FEW HOURS.

a. This indicates that the mainspring is not the proper one for this watch.

b. To correct this condition, replace the mainspring with one of correct size.

30. WATCH GAINS TIME EXCESSIVELY.

a. This condition may be caused by oil on the hairspring, hairspring caught on regulator pins or a screw missing from the balance wheel.

b. If the hairspring has oil on it, remove the balance cock and balance assembly and clean the parts following the procedure as outlined in paragraph 16. If the hairspring is caught on the regulator pins, it must be repositioned. If a screw is missing from the balance wheel, replace it with one of the same weight as the opposite screw. Check the balance for poise (par. 36).

31. WATCH WILL NOT INDICATE PROPER TIME.

a. If the watch runs, showing proper balance action, but does not indicate the correct time, remove the bevel and check the hands to see if they are loose on their respective settings. Pull stem out to setting position and rotate it to see if the cannon pinion is too loose.

b. If the hands do not fit tightly on their arbors or pipes, adjust or replace them. If the cannon pinion is too loose, tighten or replace it (fig. 29).

32. WATCH BAND BROKEN OR WORN.

a. This condition can be determined by observation. Remove band from wrist watch. Insert small screwdriver in hole in side of case lug and pull out strap at the same time. Check spring bar for proper tension. Check lugs for enlarged holes.

b. To replace band, insert spring bar in band loop. Insert one end of spring bar in hole lug and depress spring bar spring on opposite end until bar snaps into place. Pull band slightly to make sure spring bar is secure at both ends. When replacing watch bands, attach buckle end at 12 o'clock end of case.

33. BUCKLES.

a. Buckles are removed in the same manner as wrist bands. To replace a buckle, insert tongue in slot of watch band. Slide spring

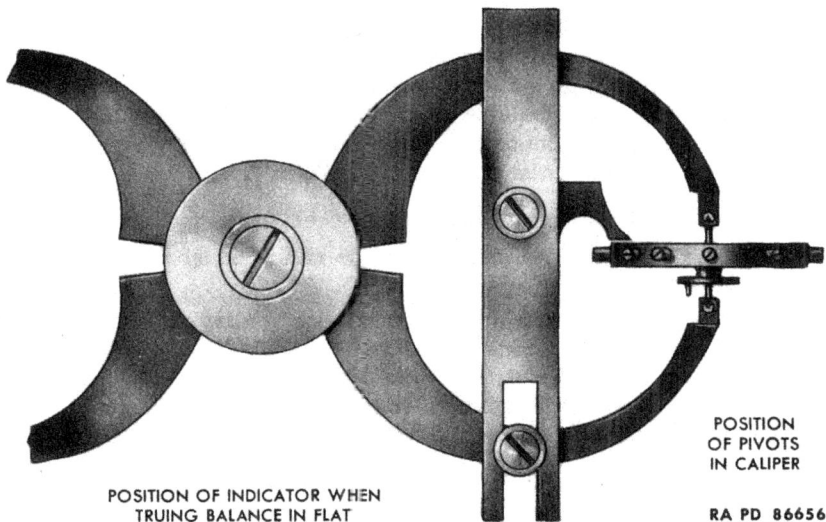

POSITION
OF PIVOTS
IN CALIPER

POSITION OF INDICATOR WHEN
TRUING BALANCE IN FLAT

RA PD 86656

Figure 30 — Method of Holding Calipers for Truing Balance in Flat

bar through band loop and tongue. Insert end of spring bar and snap into place.

34. MAGNETISM.

a. Magnetism will cause a watch to gain time, to lose time, or if heavily magnetized to stop. To correct this condition, remove back of case and place a compass over center of balance wheel, with the movement lying on a movement block, train side up. If watch is magnetized, the compass needle will have a jerky motion and will not come to rest. If no magnetism is present, the compass needle will come to a complete rest. Most ordnance watches in use today are equipped with an antimagnetic balance assembly which greatly reduces this malfunction. Place the compass on the barrel bridge and move it back and forth. If the mainspring is magnetized, it will cause a definite pull on the magnetic needle and cause it to move.

b. To eliminate magnetism, place watch in demagnetizer, switch on current by pressing button, and draw watch out slowly (a distance of about 18 inches) while the current is on. Test watch again. If magnetism is still present, repeat the above procedure until compass needle lies at complete rest. Never move the watch toward the demagnetizer with the current on, as this allows the watch to become magnetized. Never attempt to demagnetize a hairspring when it is out of the movement.

35. BALANCE UNTRUE.

a. **General.** An untrue balance may stop the watch by rubbing against the balance cock, center wheel, or pallet bridge; it will also make it difficult to poise, as well as hard to time. The proper place to begin truing a balance is of utmost importance; if a wrong start is made, it may take several times as long to finally get it true. Always begin by truing the balance in the flat.

b. **Balance Untrue in Flat.**

(1) The first point to examine is the condition of the two rims directly over the arms (for equal height).

(2) The proper position and firmness of holding calipers are of great importance when truing a balance. The calipers should be held at an angle of about 45 degrees. Hold the balance toward the eye, with the back end of the calipers resting firmly on the bench, and support the front end with the thumb. Set the indicator so there is a distinct space of light between it and the flat of the rim, directly over one of the arms. Note the amount of light and turn the balance so that the opposite rim is under the indicator. This will immediately show whether or not one rim is lower than the other. NOTE: *It is especially important to hold the head and indicator steady while making this examination. Always keep the calipers closed firmly on the balance staff.*

(3) If the light is not equal over both arms, sight under the balance and see if it is possible to detect which arm is up or down from level. This will determine which arm is to be worked on first; work on the rim that shows the greatest variation from true, over the entire surface. After making this decision, turn the balance to the right so that the rim to be worked on will be clear of the indicator. Hold the calipers firmly in the flat truing position, place wrench or tweezers over rim at the arm, and bend either up or down as necessary. Bending the rim through practice may be successfully done by using the thumb and forefinger of the right hand; this will eliminate the chance of roughing the balance. Place indicator over the rim above the arm and examine it again; repeat the procedure until rim is leveled.

(4) After successfully leveling both rims at the arms, set indicator slightly beyond the arm over the rim. Turn balance slowly and examine the light between indicator and rim over the entire length out to the cut of free end. The first indication of either more or less light will decide the point to begin truing the rim up or down. The important point is that the examination and truing should be started at the end of the rim which is joined at the arm. In the case of long sloping kinks or bends, the fingers should be placed beyond the point where the slope begins. If placed at the exact point, the tension would cause the actual bending to extend too far back of where it is wanted.

TROUBLE SHOOTING, ADJUSTMENT, AND REPAIR

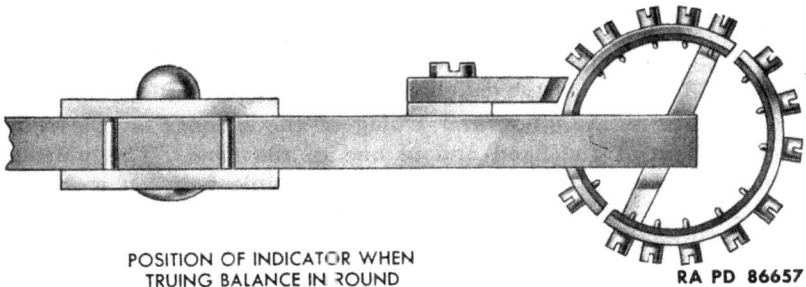

POSITION OF INDICATOR WHEN
TRUING BALANCE IN ROUND

RA PD 86657

Figure 31 — Method of Holding Calipers for Truing Balance in Round

When one rim has been trued, the opposite wheel should be handled in the same manner, always beginning from end attached to arm. Truing one rim will sometimes disturb the other, so it is necessary to go over each rim a second or third time before any attempt is made to true balance in the round.

(5) The final examination of the balance in the flat should be made by slanting the calipers back on the bench slightly, so that the light between the indicator and the rim can be plainly seen. Hold calipers steady in left hand and open them slightly so that the balance is just free enough to spin when touched with a camel's-hair brush. While it is slowly spinning, observe the top edge of the rim with a double-eye loupe and see if any waver can be noticed. If not, the balance truing in the round is next in order. NOTE: *A very important point in the examination of the balance in the flat while spinning, is the fact that the balance screws are not always in line or of an even diameter. The eye must be trained to observe the flat of the rim only, because although the irregularity of the screws causes a wavy appearance, the rims may be perfectly true.*

c. **Balance Untrue in Round.**

(1) After the rims have been well trued in the flat, truing of the round may be started. Included with the calipers are bending wrenches. These should be used as they have advantages over tweezers, pliers, or the fingers for general use. The leverage obtained through the use of this wrench gives an opportunity of placing it between screws and, with a slight bending, removes large or small kinks almost instantly. A wide slot wrench may be used when the balance screws are closely assembled. In using these wrenches, there is less danger of roughing the balance rim or screws than if tweezers or pliers are used.

(2) The proper position for holding calipers when truing balance in round is similar to that in flat. They should be held firmly on

the bench with end holding balance toward the eye. The angle at which they are held can be changed to suit the convenience of the repairman. In most cases, when the proper position of the setting is assumed, the angle of the calipers should be about 45 degrees.

(3) The examination and truing of the balance in the round should begin at the fixed end of one of the rims. The indicator should be placed so that light is plainly visible between it and the rim (fig. 31). The indicator should also be just enough away so that there will be no danger of its rubbing on the balance screws. Begin at the short segment extending beyond the arm, and move the balance slowly, so the free or cut end will advance toward the indicator. If the light is not exactly the same at all points, turn the balance so rim to be bent is away from indicator. Place bending wrench on the rim at the point where the first indication of change in light was noticed. After making the bend, examine with the indicator from the very beginning of the rim, continuing until the rim is trued. Never overlook the importance of setting the indicator. Begin the examination at the end of the rim attached to the arm each time a bend is made. In making a bend in the round, place wrench slightly nearer the arm than the exact point where the bend begins. This is contrary to truing in the flat for, in the flat, the tweezers or fingers are placed just beyond where the bend begins.

(4) When one rim has been trued, proceed to the next and use the same methods as with the first rim. In making bends, hold wrench level so that throwing the flat out of true will be avoided as much as possible. In case the bends in truing the round are made with an upward or downward twist, it will require extra bending to get the flat true again. Each time the flat is trued again, it will be necessary to check the round. This is called "touching up" and final results can be reached after about the second touching up. For final examination, loosen calipers and allow balance to spin slowly. Train eye to observe the rim only and not the screws.

36. POISING BALANCE.

a. The balance wheel must be poised after it has been trued. In closely rated position watches, such as railroad grade, poising of the balance is of utmost importance in order to obtain fine timing results. A balance that is out of poise will affect the arc of motion while running. A heavy point at the bottom of the balance wheel, when held in a vertical position, will show a losing rate in the first half of a 24-hour period or during its long arcs of motion. If the heavy point is at the top of the balance wheel, it would show position variations in the reverse.

b. It is well to remember that while poising a balance, reducing the weight will result in a gaining rate. Increasing the weight will

TROUBLE SHOOTING, ADJUSTMENT, AND REPAIR

result in a losing rate, so, therefore, the mean time rate should be considered before weight of balance is altered. In case the rate was a gaining one continually, weight can be slightly increased directly opposite the heavy point of the balance. If it showed a losing rate, weight can then be slightly reduced at the heavy point.

c. The necessary tools needed for poising a balance are: poising tool, balance screw undercutters, balance screwdriver, screw-head file, balance screw scale, assortment of timing washers, and balance screws.

d. The actual work of poising is accomplished by placing the balance wheel on the poising tool (or truing calipers if poising tool is not available) so as to have the most extreme end of each pivot supported. This is done with the rollers attached and hairspring removed, and with balance wheel in a vertical position. In this manner, the balance wheel is suspended freely and force of gravity will cause the heaviest part of the balance rim to turn to the lowest point. The screw which is at the lowest point indicates the heavy part of the balance, so this screw must be undercut. Hold balance firmly and remove this screw. Place screw in undercutters of its approximate size and undercut slightly by turning the screw. Replace screw and check. If after undercutting a screw, the weight shifts to the opposite side of the balance, it shows that too much weight has been removed.

e. A balance wheel which is badly out of poise will indicate such an error by the heavy screw falling rapidly to the low point. In a case of this type, it is advisable to add a timing washer to the screw opposite the heavy screw. To undercut the heavy screw would require removing too much weight. This will also maintain the original weight of the balance as nearly as possible. Another important factor is, if the balance wheel is supplied with timing screws, their position from the balance rim should be noted. If they are turned out so that very few threads remain, it is advisable to add timing washer to the light side of the balance when poising. This will allow the timing screws to be turned inward during the timing process. However, if the screws are turned in close to the balance rim, weight may be reduced from the heavy side, allowing the timing screws to be turned outward during the timing process.

f. The methods which can be used to reduce weight are: The screws may be undercut, the screw-head file may be drawn through the screw slot slightly, or the heavy screw can be removed and replaced with one of the same weight as the opposite screw. To increase weight, add timing washers to light screw, or exchange light screw for one that is of a weight equal to its opposite screw.

g. If the work of poising appears satisfactory, a final test may be applied by turning the balance wheel slowly with a camel's-hair brush and stopping it at each quarter of its circumference, beginning with

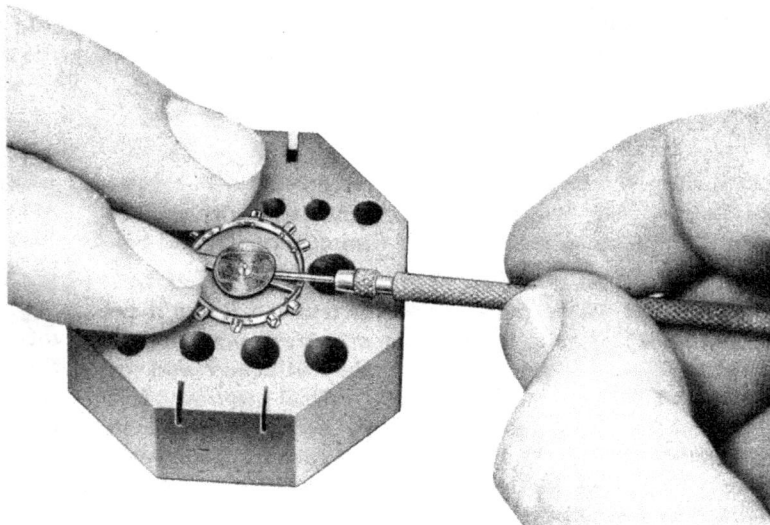

RA PD 86919

Figure 32 — Removing Hairspring From Balance Staff

the roller pin at the top. To have accomplished a good job of poising, the balance wheel should remain at rest and at the place it has been stopped. For a finer position adjusted watch, the balance wheel may be tested at every eighth part of its circumference. If the balance wheel remains at rest at all eight places it is stopped, it is considered in perfect poise. While testing the balance, if it is found that at some points it does not remain at rest, work must be resumed until the error has been eliminated.

37. HAIRSPRING.

a. In order to obtain the fine timing results of a well-poised balance, it is essential that the hairspring be true, with its center of gravity coinciding with the center of gravity of the balance wheel. This will cause the short and long arcs of the balance to be made in equal time, thereby making the hairspring isochronal. Hairspring errors are mostly found to be caused by careless handling during the cleaning process. If, when cleaning the balance assembly, the hairspring has become bent, tangled, or pulled up in a slight cone shape, it must be straightened and trued before attempting any timing adjustments. To straighten and true a hairspring requires skill and a great deal of patience, and it is only through continual trials that both will be acquired.

TROUBLE SHOOTING, ADJUSTMENT, AND REPAIR

b. To straighten a badly bent hairspring, it is best to remove it from the balance staff and lay it on a flat piece of glass. To remove hairspring, hold balance firmly on an anvil and insert a small screwdriver under hairspring collet. Turn screwdriver very carefully (fig. 32). This will slide the collet off the staff. While spring is lying on glass, examine carefully beginning at collet, and following around coil by coil until first bend or departure from true is detected. With a pair of tweezers, hold spring just ahead of bend; with a second pair of tweezers, bend hairspring close to first pair of tweezers in opposite direction of bend or departure. Follow around coils further and correct errors in a like manner until outside end of hairspring is reached.

c. After reshaping hairspring in the round is completed, the flat is then trued. Hold hairspring up edgeways to the light; begin from the collet end and examine spring, noting where it first departs from the flat. With tweezers, correct by bending in opposite direction to which it departs from the flat; then proceed to next point and so on until outer end of spring is reached. When straightening is complete, attach to balance cock. Beginning from the collet, divide the spaces between each coil evenly, and center the spring so that center of collet will rest directly above the balance pivot hole. The outer coil or overcoil should rest between the regulator pins without bearing against either of them. If the overcoil is properly adjusted, the regulator may be moved between both extremes and the regulator pins will slide around the coil without causing the collet to move away from the center. Before actual work is started on a hairspring, it should be closely inspected. In a good many instances, a hairspring which appears badly bent when closely inspected will be found to have but one or two bends. These bends may be corrected without too much difficulty and the hairspring can be properly adjusted.

d. A hairspring may be found to be cone-shaped all the way from the collet, or only part way. In the case of its being all the way from the collet, it may be made flat by placing the collet on a large broach or a round file and pulling the stud down in the reverse direction. If partly coned, hold the last flat coil with a pair of tweezers and pull the stud down with a second pair of tweezers, thus causing the hairspring to lie flat. After completing all corrections, the hairspring must be replaced on the balance cock and center as described above.

e. When making corrections on a hairspring, touching it with the fingers should be avoided, as this may cause rust. When rust begins its attack upon any point of the hairspring, there will be a constant loss of time and the hairspring must be replaced.

ORDNANCE MAINTENANCE — WRIST WATCHES, POCKET WATCHES, STOP WATCHES, AND CLOCKS

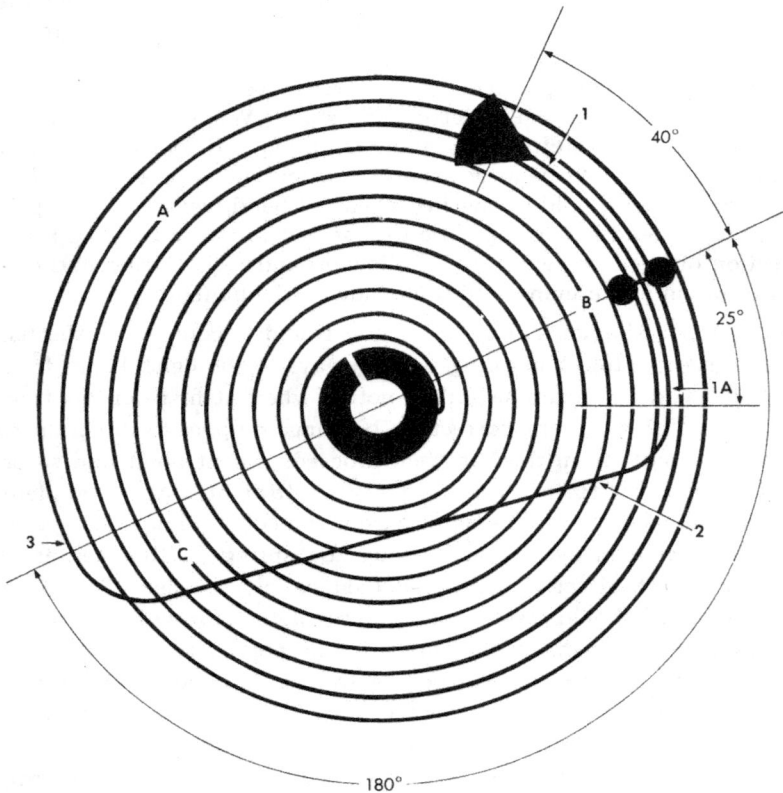

HIGH OR LOW AT **A**—BEND AT **2**
HIGH OR LOW AT **B**—BEND AT **3**
HIGH OR LOW AT **C**—BEND AT **1** OR **1A**

RA PD 86926

Figure 33 — Leveling Hairspring With Balance Assembly
Installed in Watch

38. ADJUSTMENT OF HAIRSPRING WITH BALANCE ASSEMBLY INSTALLED IN WATCH.

a. After the balance assembly has been installed and if the hairspring is out of flat and not centered, it can be trued up while in the watch (figs. 33 and 34). All adjustments must be made on the overcoil of the hairspring and are performed with tweezers or leveler.

b. Inspect the spring for flat. If it is out of flat, it can be made level by bending the overcoil in one of the three positions as indicated in figure 33.

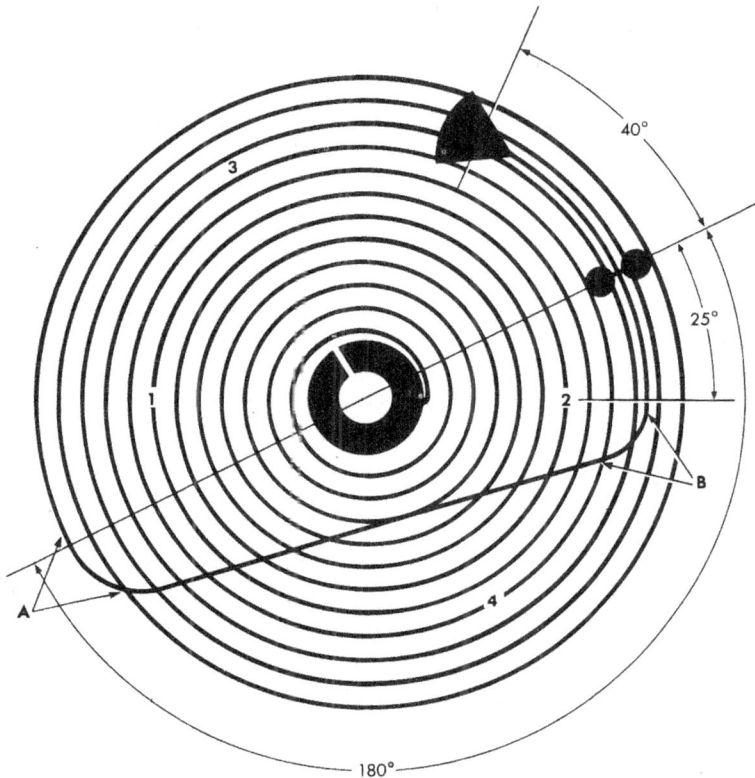

TO CLOSE OR OPEN COILS AT **1** AND **2**,
OPEN OR CLOSE POSITIONS **A**

TO CLOSE OR OPEN COILS AT **3** AND **4**,
OPEN OR CLOSE POSITIONS **B**

RA PD 96452

*Figure 34 — Centering Hairspring With Balance Assembly
Installed in Watch*

c. Check the centering of the hairspring. See that it is vibrating freely and evenly. If it is not centered, it can be brought to center by opening and closing points "A" and "B" of the overcoil as outlined in figure 34.

d. Inspect the watch for correct beat (par. 39).

39. SETTING UP ESCAPEMENT.

a. The escapement is set up properly at manufacture and under normal conditions rarely needs adjustment. However, if the watch is subjected to severe shock such as dropping, etc., adjustment of the escapement may be necessary. Listed below is a step-by-step procedure for inspection and setting up the escapement.

(1) Check the end shake and side shake of the escape wheel, pallet assembly, and balance assembly. The end shake of these assemblies should be equal, and the side shake not excessive.

(2) Check the length of the roller jewel. With the watch in the dial down position, the bottom of the roller jewel must not rub on the guard pin (fig. 7). It should also be perpendicular to the impulse roller and center in the crescent of the safety roller.

(3) Adjust the banking pins so that the roller jewel clears the fork of the pallet with a minimum of freedom. At the same time, check the length and angle of the point of the guard pin. This angle should be 90 degrees. Roll the balance around until the guard pin is in contact with the polished surface of the safety roller. The clearance between these two should be approximately one-half the clearance between the roller jewel and the horns of the pallet. A new pallet assembly must be installed if the guard pin is too short.

(4) At this point, with the power off the train and the balance in place, the watch must be checked for beat. Observe the position of the pallet as it rests. It should be centered between the banking pins. It can be brought to center by removing the balance and very carefully turning the hairspring a slight amount in the same direction that the pallet is off.

(5) Observe the amount of lock and slide of the pallet stones on the escape wheel teeth. This should not exceed one-quarter the width of the impulse face of the pallet stone and, in most cases, can be refined to one-fifth the width. If there is lock but no slide on one stone, the adjustment is made by drawing the *opposite* stone in toward the balance assembly. If there is too much slide on one stone, the adjustment is made by moving the *opposite* stone toward the escape wheel.

(6) Check the safety action of the escapement. This is accomplished by assembling the balance to the movement and slowly leading the balance around until an escape wheel tooth drops from one stone and another tooth is arrested on the opposite stone. At this point, test the shake of the pallet assembly and examine the tooth of the escape wheel to make sure it is still at rest on the locking face of the pallet stone. If the tooth unlocks at this point, the escapement is unsafe. The possible remedy would be to set the pallet stones a trifle deeper, or to move the roller jewel forward to eliminate the play that occurs at this point.

TROUBLE SHOOTING, ADJUSTMENT, AND REPAIR

40. TIMING.

a. Wind watch fully and set with an accurate timepiece. Allow to run for 24 hours with the dial up, then note rate of gain or loss. Rewind watch fully and allow to run with dial down for 24 hours and again note the rate of gain or loss. Any variation between these horizontal positions must be corrected. While running in a horizontal position, less friction exists due to the balance oscillating on the end of only one pivot. This is responsible for the long arcs of motion which result in a slower and truer rate. In the vertical positions, the arcs of motion are short, due to excessive friction of the balance wheel oscillating on the sides of both balance staff pivots. Before the vertical positions are adjusted it is essential that both horizontal positions are of equal rate.

b. There are a number of faults that will cause a variation between running with the dial up or down. They are listed as follows:

(1) Dirt or thick oil in one or both balance hole jewels, due to improper cleaning and pegging of jewels.

(2) Burred or marred balance pivot.

(3) End of one balance pivot flat or rough.

(4) Ends of balance pivots of different form.

(5) Balance pivot bent.

(6) Hairspring rubbing on balance arm, stud, or regulator pins.

(7) Hairspring concave or convex instead of perfectly level.

(8) Overcoil rubbing under balance cock.

(9) Overcoil rubbing center wheel (supplied on some models only).

(10) Balance pivots fitting too tight in jewels.

(11) One balance pivot having excessive side shake and the opposite pivot being close fitting.

(12) Escape or pallet pivot bent or damaged.

(13) Balance end stone pitted or out of flat.

(14) Overcoil rubbing outside coil at point where it curves over spring.

(15) Balance arm touching pallet bridge.

(16) Balance screw touching balance bridge.

(17) Safety roller rubbing plate or jewel setting. (This is due to a loose cap jewel or a short pivot.)

(18) Fork rubbing impulse roller.

(19) Roller jewel pin (long) rubbing on guard (dart) pin.

(20) Pivot out of oil.

c. When the fault has been found and corrected, the watch must be tested again in both horizontal positions for 24 hours each. If no variation occurs, the arcs of motion in both horizontal positions are then of equal length. However, if there still is a variation, a closer check must be made until the fault is found and corrected.

d. After equalizing both horizontal positions, the arcs of motion of the vertical positions must be adjusted to equal the rate made by the horizontal positions. Before making adjustments, the watch must be tested for 24 hours in each of three positions, one horizontal and two vertical. The two vertical positions are tested in opposite quarters. This shows the rates of the short arcs of motion and determines if any error exists in the poise of the balance. Wind watch fully and set with a timepiece that is accurate. Allow to run 24 hours in dial up position, rewind, and allow to run in the vertical position with pendant (or crown) up for 24 hours; then, after rewinding, with pendant down. The rate of each position must be noted. After completing the three-position test, the rates noted may be somewhat as follows: dial up—6 seconds fast for 24 hours; pendant up—4 seconds slow for 24 hours; and pendant down—26 seconds slow for 24 hours. This rate shows that with pendant up, it is 10 seconds slower than with the dial up; and with the pendant down, it is 32 seconds slower than with the dial up. The mean for this rate is 21 seconds, this being the amount the short arcs are slow. The hairspring coils do not open and close equally in both vertical positions, due to an improperly formed overcoil which does not hold the hairspring concentrically. To correct this error, first determine which way the hairspring is off center, then reform the overcoil until the hairspring is concentric and appears to be vibrating uniformly in both vertical positions. If appearance is satisfactory, again test three positions for 24 hours each, and repeat alterations if necessary until rates are equal. When the rates of the vertical positions are equal, the arcs of motion are equal.

e. After completing the three-position test, the rates noted may be somewhat as follows: dial up—3 seconds fast for 24 hours; pendant up—11 seconds fast for 24 hours; and pendant down—5 seconds slow for 24 hours. This shows that, with pendant up, it is 8 seconds faster than with dial up; and with pendant down, it is 8 seconds slower than with dial up. The mean of the two vertical positions is equal to that of the horizontal. The difference between pendant up and pendant down shows a slight error in poise. The losing rate, when in pendant down position, signifies a heavy point at the top of the balance when running in that position. To bring to adjustment, screw in the mean time screw of the pendant down position a quarter turn closer to the balance rim. In the event that the screw is too close to the rim, unscrew the mean time screw of the pendant up

TROUBLE SHOOTING, ADJUSTMENT, AND REPAIR

position a quarter turn. Although both of these methods will bring the same results, the one to be used depends entirely upon what distance the screws are from the rim. If there are no mean time screws, a timing washer must be added under the quarter screw of the pendant up position. Each time adjustments are made to the balance, the watch must again be tested in three positions until the rates are equal.

f. Subparagraphs a, b, and c, above, have described a four-position adjustment. This amount is sufficient for ordinary wrist watches and pocket watches. When properly adjusted, these will be found to keep quite accurate time. For higher grade watches, such as railroad grade, a six-position adjustment is required: two horizontal positions and four vertical positions. The vertical positions are: pendant up, pendant down, pendant left, and pendant right. For the six-position adjustment, the mean of the four vertical rates is also determined by using the horizontal rate as the unit of comparison. After the mean has been determined, the adjustments are made accordingly and in the same manner as described above. After proper adjustments are made to equal all the rates, the watch is ready for final regulations.

g. Final regulations are the last minute regulations made by moving the regulator either toward fast or slow, as required. A watch that is regulated while resting on a rack and under even temperature cannot be considered to be accurately timed. It will have to be regulated again when it is being worn. While a watch is worn, it is subject to changes of temperature and quick jolts which will make a difference in the timing. For this reason, final regulations are made in coordination with the type of use it is given by the wearer.

h. A stop watch is regulated after testing it with a master timepiece for 30-minute intervals. A message center clock is set up in the position it is to be used, and synchronized with a master timepiece. Allow the clock to run for 24 hours. If there is a variation between it and the master timepiece, move the regulator as required. If the clock shows a gain in time, move the regulator to the side of the balance cock marked SLOW and vice versa.

i. After a general overhaul of watches, cleaning, changing staffs, truing and poising balance, and truing hairspring, it is often necessary to make corrections of several minutes a day in the mean time. In order to make it more convenient for the repairman, most manufacturers have provided two or four mean time screws (timing screws) in the balance rims. A complete turn in or out in opposite pairs of these screws, and sometimes considerably less, is all that is required to bring the watch in time. It is not only necessary that these screws be turned in opposite pairs, but also that they should both be turned an equal distance. The reason for this is that if one

ORDNANCE MAINTENANCE — WRIST WATCHES, POCKET WATCHES, STOP WATCHES, AND CLOCKS

screw was turned in or out more than its opposite screw, it would disturb the poise of the balance and would result in the watch showing variations in vertical positions. In the event the balance is not supplied with mean time screws, timing washers are added to the quarter screws in opposite pairs to slow the rate. If the rate is slow, the quarter screws in opposite pairs are exchanged for a pair of lighter screws, both of equal weight. To allow maximum movement of regulator for final regulation, all adjustment is made with the mean time screws while the regulator index is in the center of its movement.

j. Temperature Compensation. This is essential in a watch, to compensate for variations brought about by climatic changes which affect the balance assembly. Most of the ordnance watches have the solid monometallic balance, which is not affected when exposed to temperature changes. The others are of the bimetallic split-balance type, and are affected by temperature changes which are compensated for by balance screws. Usually there are twice as many holes in a balance as there are screws. Therefore, if the rate of the watch varies in different temperatures, this variation can be compensated for by moving the screws in opposite pairs closer or farther away from the open end of the balance. The following method can be used successfully in shifting screws to compensate for temperature changes: watches losing in heat compared to cold—shift screws (opposite pairs) toward open ends of balance; watches gaining in heat compared to cold—shift screws (opposite pairs) away from open ends of balance.

41. TIMING MACHINE.

a. A timing machine, used in fifth-echelon watch repair, is a device for recording the action of a watch on calibrated chart paper. The drum on which the chart is wrapped rotates exactly five times per second. The recording mechanism produces a dot on the chart paper every time the watch "ticks." The record produced consists of a sequence of these dots made from left to right on the chart.

b. The chart paper is 2 inches wide and is designed to reduce the 24-hour performance of a watch to the full width of the paper. The time required for this 24-hour record to be completed is 30 seconds. The chart paper is ruled in such a manner that each division represents a time error of 5 seconds in 24 hours and, for convenience in reading large errors, every sixth line is of double width and represents an error of 30 seconds in 24 hours. Records which slope upward from left to right indicate a gaining rate and, conversely, records which slope downward from left to right indicate a losing rate.

c. The watch is held in place in the timing machine by a compression spring clamp. Enclosed in this clamp is a sensitive plate

TROUBLE SHOOTING, ADJUSTMENT, AND REPAIR

which picks up the impulse from the escapement, and its volume is amplified by adjusting the volume control knob. The impulse is transmitted through a tuning fork which, in turn, actuates a stylus that prints the impulse on the chart paper. The watch should be checked in several positions as described in paragraph 40. This is made possible by turning the spring clamp to any desired position.

d. If the error in performance of a watch does not exceed that shown in paragraph 13 j, and as recorded on the chart paper, no further adjustment is required. By determining the amount of gain or loss in time as recorded on the chart paper, adjustment, if necessary, can be kept to a minimum.

e. Figures 35 to 45, inclusive, are examples of typical recordings on the timing machine. To aid in interpreting the various examples, the following explanations should be studied carefully in connection with the figures concerned. CAUTION: *The timing machine, if used by an inexperienced repairman for diagnosing watch troubles, may indicate errors which are nonexistent. Do not use this machine for diagnostic purposes.*

(1) FIGURE 35. Record "A" represents a watch which is exactly on time. Record "B" represents a watch which is gaining 15 seconds per 24-hour day. Record "C" represents a watch which is losing 30 seconds per 24-hour day. Record "D" is a record prepared in 15 seconds and shows a loss of 30 seconds per 24-hour day.

(2) FIGURE 36. This record represents a watch which is gaining 1,560 seconds, or 26 minutes, per 24-hour day.

(3) FIGURE 37. A perfectly adjusted escapement in a watch will produce only one line on the chart paper. However, many watch movements produce records consisting of a double line of dots as shown in this figure. Record "A" shows the distance between these two lines as a direct measure of the difference in time between the "tick and tock" and the "tock and tick" in the watch. When the watch is in perfect beat, this separation may be caused by excessive slide in the escapement. In general, it is safe to assume that if the two lines are parallel, as shown in record "B," the watch will be acceptable.

(4) FIGURE 38. Many watches have balance and hairspring assemblies which are out of true dynamic poise and consequently have differences in rate in various vertical positions. Records "A," "C," and "E" show that this watch is in an acceptable condition. Records "B" and "D" show that the watch is out of balance in these two particular positions. If the watch is not affected in the three positions of "A," "C," and "E," and the recordings of "B" and "D" are such that these two positions do not exceed the accepted limits for this grade of watch, the watch may be declared acceptable.

ORDNANCE MAINTENANCE — WRIST WATCHES, POCKET WATCHES, STOP WATCHES, AND CLOCKS

(5) FIGURE 39. Records "A," "B," and "C" show three positions of a watch in which the regulator pins may be excessively far apart. The horizontal rate is approximately correct, the pendant down and up rates are slow. Records "D," "E," and "F" show the same three positions after the regulator pins have been closed until the action of the hairspring between them is proper. This has the effect of making the watch run faster in all positions but the change in the vertical position rates is greater than the change in the horizontal rate. This has the effect of bringing the position error within acceptable limits. Records "D," "E," and "F" show that the watch is gaining 3 minutes in 24 hours in the horizontal position. Rate correction may now be made by adding balance weights rather than by regulator pin manipulation.

(6) FIGURE 40. Much of the ordinary trouble encountered in watches is traceable directly to the hairspring, particularly with regard to its relation to the regulator pins and also to defects in the escapement. Record "A" may indicate that the spring bears harder and longer against one of the pins. Record "B" may show that one of the pins is bent at an angle. Records "B" and "C" may indicate improper locking of the escapement. Record "B" may show trouble in the receiving stone of the pallet. Record "C" may indicate trouble in the discharge stone of the pallet. Record "D" shows good hairspring and good escapement adjustment but may indicate that the movement could be improved by putting in beat. This would bring the lines closer together as in record "E."

(7) FIGURE 41. Some watches will have isochronal error. Changes in power delivered to the escapement will make characteristic records which may tie exactly to that part in the train which is causing the trouble. If the fourth wheel, which normally makes one complete revolution per minute, is out-of-round, or has a bent arbor or pivot causing an eccentric motion, the changes in power will cause a change in the rate of the watch, thereby possibly producing a curved record as shown in this figure. The second hand binding or rubbing on the dial on one side may also produce this type of record. The degree of curve is directly proportional to the magnitude of error.

(8) FIGURE 42. This record indicates changes in power which may be due to dirt or binding in the train or occasionally to the mainspring binding in the barrel. This condition is extremely serious and can be corrected only by completely rechecking the train and mainspring.

(9) FIGURE 43. Records "A," "B," and "C" may indicate that the escape wheel is out-of-round or has a mar or bur on its pinion. This condition may cause a change 10 times per minute. Record "A" may indicate the escape wheel out-of-round or not exactly centered

TROUBLE SHOOTING, ADJUSTMENT, AND REPAIR

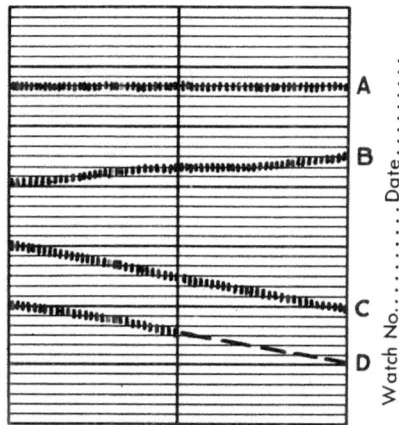

RA PD 86938

Figure 35 — Typical Recordings — Solid Part of "D" Is a 15-second Record and Each Line It Crosses Is Read as 10 Seconds When Taken as a 24-hour Rate

in its arbor. Record "B" may indicate that the pinion alone is defective but that the escapement is not affected. Record "C" may indicate that the pivot or arbor is at fault. Record "D" indicates that the escape wheel has a mutilated tooth but that adjustment is otherwise acceptable.

(10) FIGURE 44. Record "A" shows a condition of overbanking, or excessive balance motion. Record "B" shows the same watch after the mainspring has been replaced.

(11) FIGURE 45. Record "A" may indicate a watch having a loose pallet stone on the discharge side. Record "B" may indicate a watch having a loose banking pin on the receiving side. In addition to these possible faults, the record may show that excessive slide in the escapement is producing a ragged record. The upper or lower line of the record may be an indication of which side to reduce the slide on. The lines will be nearest together, in general, in that position when the balance is over the pallet and escape wheel, and the separation will be greatest in the position directly opposite that point with the records in the horizontal positions somewhere in between. Make all adjustments to the escapement in the position which brings the lines on the chart nearest together.

42. INSPECTION DURING DISASSEMBLY.

a. **General.** Inspection of a watch during disassembly will facilitate replacement of defective parts and permit adjustments before parts are cleaned and assembled.

ORDNANCE MAINTENANCE — WRIST WATCHES, POCKET WATCHES, STOP WATCHES, AND CLOCKS

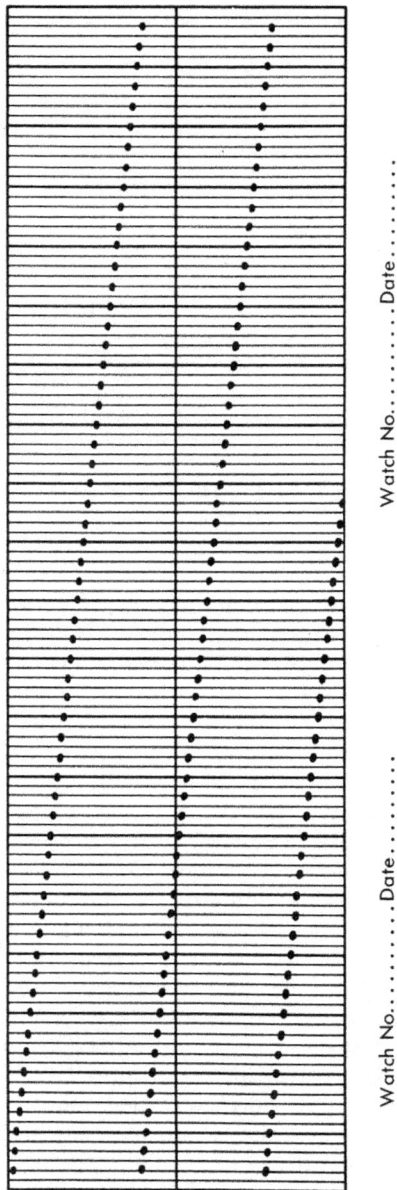

RA PD 86939

Figure 36 — Very Fast Rate, 26 Minutes per Day

TROUBLE SHOOTING, ADJUSTMENT, AND REPAIR

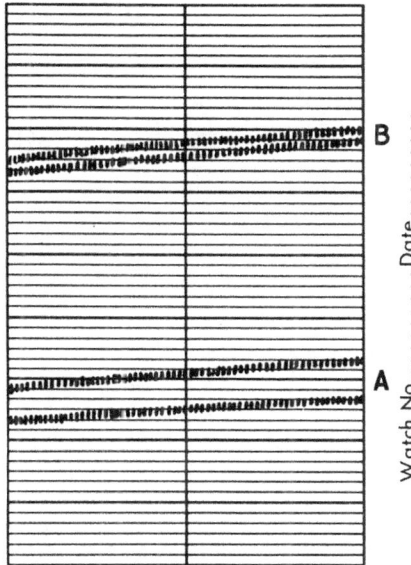

RA PD 86940

Figure 37 — Watches Producing Two Lines Instead of One — Either Line Is Used for Reading the Rate — Both Watches Shown Are 15 Seconds per Day Fast

b.   Pocket and Wrist Watches.

(1)   HANDS.   Check the fit of the minute, hour, and second hands to their respective bearings.

(2)   CASE—POCKET WATCH.   Check sleeve for rust or broken leaves.   Check winding arbor for rust or worn shoulder.

(3)   BALANCE ASSEMBLY.   Check for bent, worn, or cut pivots, and broken or chipped jewels.   Check the fit of the hairspring collet and stud, and the fit of balance regulator to balance cock.   Check position and fit of roller table to the balance staff; check for loose, chipped, or out-of-position roller jewel (jewel pin).

(4)   DIAL.   Check position of the dial in relation to the hour wheel pipe and second hand pivot; check condition of dial feet.

(5)   DIAL TRAIN WHEELS.   Check for broken teeth on hour wheel, minute wheel, setting wheel, and cannon pinion.   Check fit of hour wheel to the cannon pinion, and minute wheel to its stud.

(6)   ESCAPEMENT ASSEMBLY.   Check side and end shake of pallet arbor.   Check for bent or burred pivots, broken or bent guard pin, and loose or chipped pallet jewels.

75

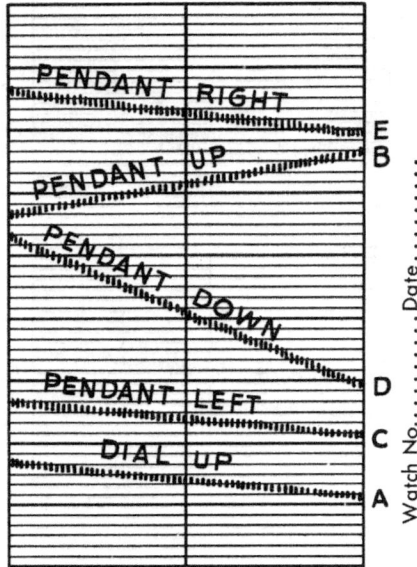

RA PD 86941

Figure 38 — Out-of-Poise Balance

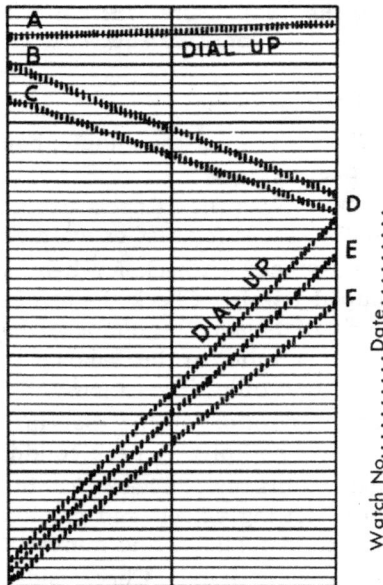

RA PD 86942

Figure 39 — Effect of Changing Regulator Pin Separation

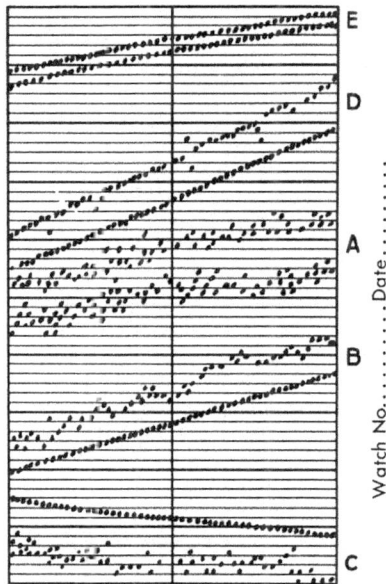

*Figure 40 — Result of Poor Adjustment of Hairspring and
Regulator Pins*

(7) WINDING AND SETTING MECHANISM. Check for stripped screws; broken or worn teeth on winding pinion, clutch, crown, or ratchet wheel; broken or worn setting or clutch levers; and weak or broken springs.

(8) PILLAR PLATE AND BRIDGES. Check for cracked or chipped jewels. If only a 7-jewel movement, check for worn pivot holes or bushings. Check condition of bridge screws, jewel assembly screws, and cap screws.

(9) TRAIN WHEELS. Check for worn or bent pivots. Check pinions for rust. Check wheels for bent or broken teeth and for trueness.

(10) MAINSPRING BARREL ASSEMBLY. Check teeth around barrel, fit of barrel cap, hook on barrel, and barrel arbor. See if mainspring is properly wound in barrel.

c. **Elgin Stop Watch.**

(1) FLY-BACK LEVER AND FLY-BACK LEVER SPRING. Check fit of upper and lower pivots on seconds wheel; fit should be close, with a minimum of side shake. If either of these pivots has excessive side shake, the sweep second hand will not return to zero point consistently. Check tips of fly-back lever. They should be adjusted with

77

ORDNANCE MAINTENANCE — WRIST WATCHES, POCKET WATCHES, STOP WATCHES, AND CLOCKS

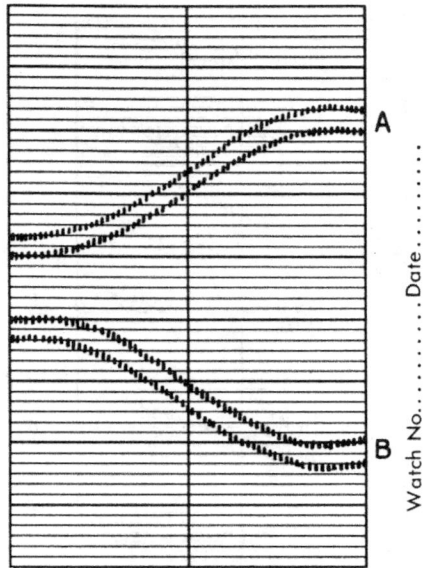

RA PD 86944

Figure 41 — Changes in Rate Caused by Defective Fourth Wheel or Binding of the Second Hand

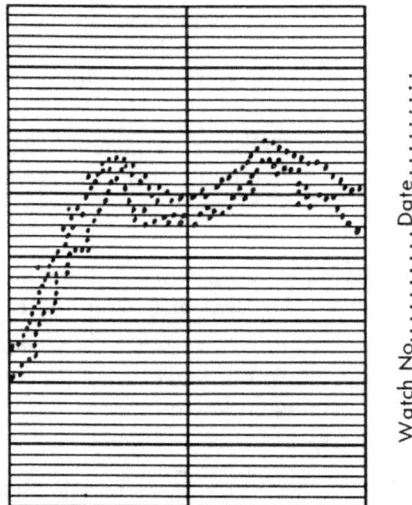

RA PD 86945

Figure 42 — Effect of Dirt, Binding of Parts, or Similar Irregular Frictions

TM 9-1575
42

TROUBLE SHOOTING, ADJUSTMENT, AND REPAIR

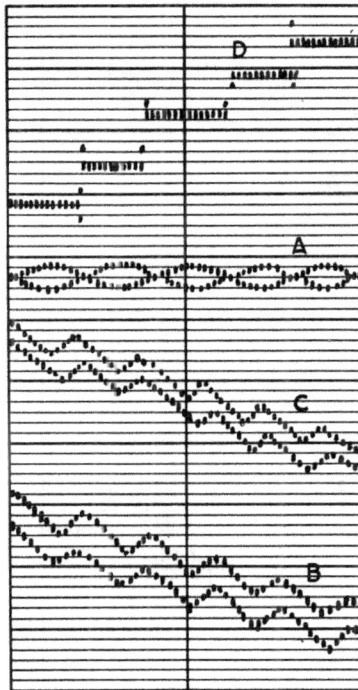

RA PD 86946

Figure 43 — Defective Escape Wheel Recordings

tips resting in heart cam without freedom in neutral position. The tip of fly-back lever must be polished. Check tension of fly-back lever spring.

(2) SECONDS WHEEL FRICTION SPRING AND SECONDS WHEEL. Check fork ends; they should lie directly over center wheel bearing to avoid friction against side of seconds wheel arbor. The tips of the spring are slightly turned upward to avoid excessive drag or oil adhesion. Check seconds wheel for proper end shake.

(3) MINUTE REGISTER WHEEL AND PAWL. Check minute register wheel for correct position. Place fly-back lever in zero position and check the register pawl to see if it lies directly in the center of the two teeth of the minute register wheel.

(4) CONNECTING PINION LEVER AND SPRING. Check the connecting lever. The connecting pinion which drives the seconds wheel is held in place by the connecting lever. The connecting lever spring bearing against the lever presses the connecting pinion into the fine

79

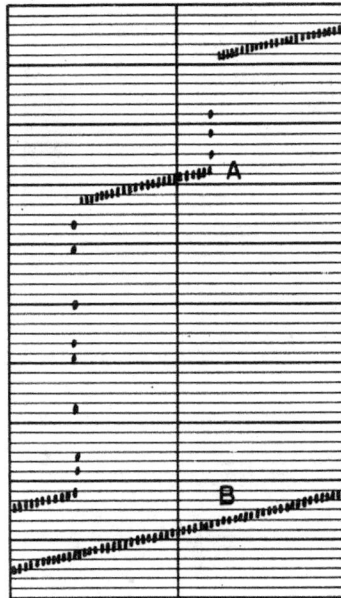

RA PD 86947

Figure 44 — Excessive Balance Wheel Motion, Before and After Correction

teeth of the seconds wheel, driving the wheel and second hand. The tension of the connecting lever spring against the connecting lever must be sufficient to hold the connecting pinion in contact with the seconds wheel. If the spring tension is too great, the pressure of the connecting pinion against the seconds wheel will cause the watch to stop. If the tension is too light, it will allow the connecting pinion to slip by the teeth of the center seconds wheel, and the hands will show a losing rate.

(5) ACTUATING CAM AND CAM SCREW. Check fit of cam to plate. The cam is an important factor, as all lever motions originate from this cam. The cam must fit closely but freely to the plate and be without any side shake. If side shake exists, eliminate it. There are three sizes of screws issued as an aid to obtaining proper fit.

(6) HANDS. Check fit of hands. The minute register hand and sweep second hand must fit tightly. *Loose hands are a source of trouble* and often confuse the repairman, who will look for trouble in the timer mechanism when the real trouble is due to the fact that the seconds hand is loose on its socket, or the socket is loose on its pivot.

(7) ACTUATING CAM PAWL. Check the actuating cam pawl and make certain that it passes over the ratchet teeth. The spring at-

TROUBLE SHOOTING, ADJUSTMENT, AND REPAIR

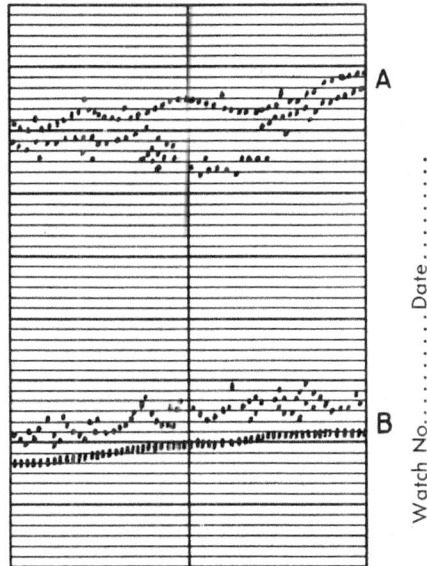

RA PD 86948

Figure 45 — Ragged Records Due to Defective Locking of Escape Wheel

tached to the cam pawl may be tensioned to secure safe locking of the ratchet teeth and cam pawl. There are three types of springs in use. Be sure the spring used is the correct one.

(8) INTERMITTENT LEVER SPRING. Check tension of the intermittent lever spring. It should be sufficient to give safe action of the intermittent wheel assembly.

(9) PARTS TO BE OILED. Check the following points for oil and see that a very limited amount of oil is used at each point: actuating cam shoulder, actuating cam index teeth, cam pawl bearing, cam hook pin on actuating lever, actuating lever screw shoulder, actuating lever spring tip, connecting lever and fly-back lever posts, intermittent lever post tip of recording pawl, tip of fly-back lever, contacting heart cam, and tip of fly-back lever arm.

(10) PARTS NOT TO BE OILED. The following parts are not to be oiled, as oil adhesion has proven detrimental and the danger of damage from friction or wear is negligible: pivots for seconds or minute register wheel connecting pinion, tip of friction spring, connecting lever spring, intermittent lever spring, and castle teeth on cam. NOTE: *Inspection of the remainder of the movement is the same as for the pocket and wrist watches.*

43. INSPECTION OF POCKET AND WRIST WATCHES DUR-ING ASSEMBLY.

a. **Train Wheels and Barrel Assembly.** Check freedom of train. Check mesh between wheels and pinions. Check for correct side and end shake of wheels and barrel arbor pivots.

b. **Winding and Setting Mechanism.** Check smoothness of operation. In setting position, check fit of cannon pinion to center arbor for tightness and smoothness of operation. In winding position, check smoothness of winding mechanism.

c. **Escapement Assembly.** Check freedom of movement, jewel pin shake, guard pin shake, lock, slide, drop, impulse, and draw on every tooth of the escape wheel.

d. **Balance Assembly.** Check for correct end and side shake of staff; balance should run free and not strike on any adjacent parts. Check clearance of hairspring between balance cock and balance. Check to make sure hairspring is flat, round, and centered to balance cock. When lying at rest, space between each coil should be uniform and jewel pin on line of centers (fig. 6). Check overcoil or outer coil for proper position between regulator pins. Check clearance between roller table and pallet fork. Check clearance between roller jewel pin and guard pin. Check for proper safety action.

e. **Hour Wheel and Dial.** Check hour wheel pipe for fit to cannon pinion. Check play between hour wheel and dial. See that dial foot screws hold dial flush against top of pillar plate. Check dial position in relation to the hour wheel pipe and second hand pivot; they should aline in the direct center of their respective holes.

f. **Hands.** Check to see that hands are in correct position as shown in figure 25.

g. **Case.** Check position of movement in case for free and smooth operation of winding mechanism. See that crown does not rub on case or pendant. Check for snug fit of movement in case. Check to see that case screws do not allow movement to shake.

h. **Accessories.** Make sure that the rubber shock absorber, leather thong, wrist band, and buckle are in a serviceable condition.

44. INSPECTION OF ELGIN STOP WATCH.

a. **General.** The inspection of the stop watch movement is the same as for pocket and wrist watches (par. 43) up to the stop works mechanism.

b. **Actuating Cam and Cam Screw.** Check fit of cam to pillar plate. The cam must fit closely to the plate without side shake.

c. **Actuating Cam Pawl.** Check the actuating cam pawl to see that it passes over the ratchet teeth. See that the spring on the cam

TROUBLE SHOOTING, ADJUSTMENT, AND REPAIR

pawl is tensioned to secure safe locking of the ratchet teeth and cam pawl.

d. Intermittent Wheel Assembly and Lever Spring. Check fit of intermittent wheel assembly on its post. Check tension of intermittent lever spring. It should be sufficient to give safe action of the intermittent wheel assembly.

e. Seconds Wheel Friction Spring and Seconds Wheel. Check the seconds wheel friction spring to see that it is directly over the center wheel bearing and does not rub against the sides of the seconds wheel arbor. Check tension of spring ends against the flat shoulder of the seconds wheel arbor; it must be so tensioned that when the watch is running, the seconds hand advances $\frac{1}{5}$ second for each vibration of the balance. If tension is excessive it may cause the watch to stop. See that the seconds recording wheel has sufficient end shake. Check to see that the driver under the seconds wheel contacts the intermittent wheel once every revolution.

f. Minute Register Wheel and Pawl. Check minute register wheel for correct position. Place fly-back lever in zero position, and adjust register pawl so that it lies directly in the center of the two teeth of the minute register wheel. The tension of the pawl must be light, yet enough so that the minute wheel is carried forward one tooth, the pawl holding the wheel securely in position for the next count. If the tension of the pawl is too severe, it will retard free action of the train and may cause stoppage or loss of power throughout the train, resulting in a short balance arc.

g. Fly-back Lever and Fly-back Lever Spring. Check fit of fly-back lever on post and check tips of fly-back lever. They should be adjusted with tips resting in the heart cam without freedom in neutral position. The tip of the fly-back lever must be polished, and the upper finger must be contacting the minute register heart cam. Check fly-back lever spring for correct tension against the fly-back lever.

h. Connecting Pinion, Lever, and Spring. The tension of the connecting lever spring against the connecting lever must be sufficient to hold the connecting pinion in contact with the seconds wheel. If the spring is tensioned too much, the pressure of the connecting pinion against the seconds wheel will cause the watch to stop. If the tension is too light, it will allow the connecting pinion to slip by the teeth of the seconds wheel and the hands will show a losing rate.

i. Actuating Lever, Hooked Cam, and Lever Spring. Check to see that the actuating lever is in position so that when the stem and crown is pushed in, it will operate the hooked cam, which shifts the actuating cam one tooth. See that the actuating lever spring is in position against the hooked cam, returning it to neutral position when the stem and crown is released.

CHAPTER 2

POCKET AND WRIST WATCHES

Section I

CHARACTERISTICS OF POCKET AND WRIST WATCHES

45. CHARACTERISTICS.

a. Pocket Watches. All pocket watches currently used are standard American manufacture, 16 size, of the open-face type, mounted in either a snap or screw back and bezel type case, or a combination of both.

b. Wrist Watches. Wrist watches are all standard American manufacture and are 10½ ligne, 8/0, and 6/0 size. They are all of the open-face type and are now being issued in waterproof cases.

Section II

HAMILTON POCKET WATCH, 16 SIZE, 21-JEWEL, RAILROAD GRADE, MODEL 992B

46. IDENTIFICATION.

a. Hamilton Pocket Watch. Only one Hamilton pocket watch is issued. It is 21-jewel, 16 size, Railroad grade, model 992B, with the prefix "OE" ahead of the serial number on the exterior back of the case. The case is of the screw back and bezel type; the dial is white porcelain, with black arabic numerals to indicate the hours, and small black numerals on the outer ring of the dial indicating each minute, with each 5-minute graduation indicated by a red numeral. The hour, minute, and second hands are of blued steel.

47. DISASSEMBLY OF HAMILTON POCKET WATCH, 16 SIZE, 21-JEWEL, RAILROAD GRADE, MODEL 992B.

a. Remove Rubber Shock Absorber (fig. 47). Remove rubber shock absorber by slipping it off the watch and sliding it along the leather thong.

b. Remove Bezel (fig. 49). Remove bezel by unscrewing counterclockwise.

c. Remove Hands (figs. 48 and 50). Cut a V-slot in a piece of paper and slide it under hands to protect dial. Remove hands with hand remover.

84

HAMILTON POCKET WATCH, 16 SIZE, 21-JEWEL,
RAILROAD GRADE, MODEL 992B

FRONT   BACK

RA PD 78870

*Figure 46 — Hamilton Pocket Watch, 21-jewel, 16 Size,
Railroad Grade — Front and Back*

d. Remove Back Cover. Remove the back cover by unscrewing it (fig. 51).

e. Release Unused Power of Mainspring (fig. 52). Release the unused power of the mainspring by holding the crown with the thumb and index finger; then disengage the click with a screwdriver and allow the crown to turn between the thumb and finger, which unwinds the mainspring.

f. Remove Case Screws. Place watch on a movement block of proper size with train side up and remove the two case screws (fig. 53).

g. Remove Movement From Case Band Assembly (figs. 54 and 55). Hold case band firmly between the right thumb and finger, with train side up. With the thumb and middle finger of the left hand on the contour of the case, push movement down with the left index finger and pull the movement away from the case band in a tilted position. Make sure that balance wheel does not hook on case band.

h. Remove Dial. Back out dial foot screws from contour of pillar plate two turns; remove dial and screw dial foot screws back into position so they will not be lost (fig. 56).

i. Remove Hour Wheel. Remove hour wheel with tweezers (fig. 57).

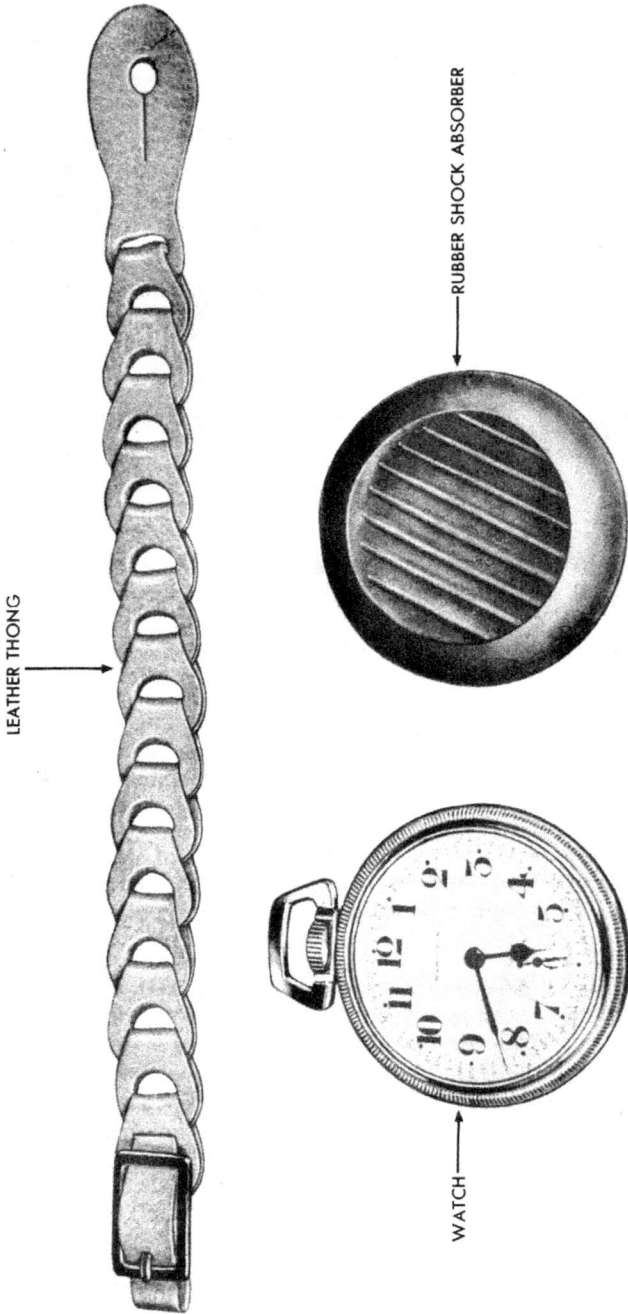

RA PD 77418

RUBBER SHOCK ABSORBER

LEATHER THONG

WATCH

Figure 47 — Watch With Rubber Shock Absorber and Leather Thong Removed

HAMILTON POCKET WATCH, 16 SIZE, 21-JEWEL,
RAILROAD GRADE, MODEL 992B

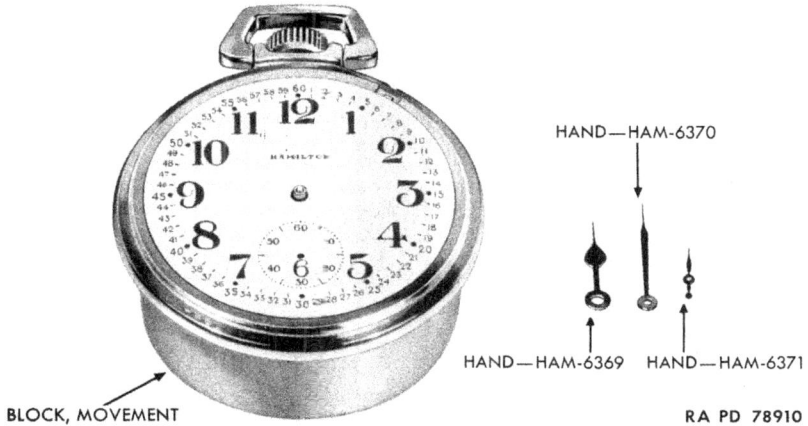

Figure 48 — Hamilton Pocket Watch — Hands Removed

Figure 49 — Hamilton Pocket Watch — Bezel Removed

j. **Remove Cannon Pinion.** Remove cannon pinion with a pin vise. Pull cannon pinion straight upward to prevent bending or breaking center wheel arbor (fig. 58).

k. **Remove Balance Cock and Balance Assemblies** (fig. 59). Place the movement train side up on the movement block. Loosen

ORDNANCE MAINTENANCE — WRIST WATCHES, POCKET WATCHES, STOP WATCHES, AND CLOCKS

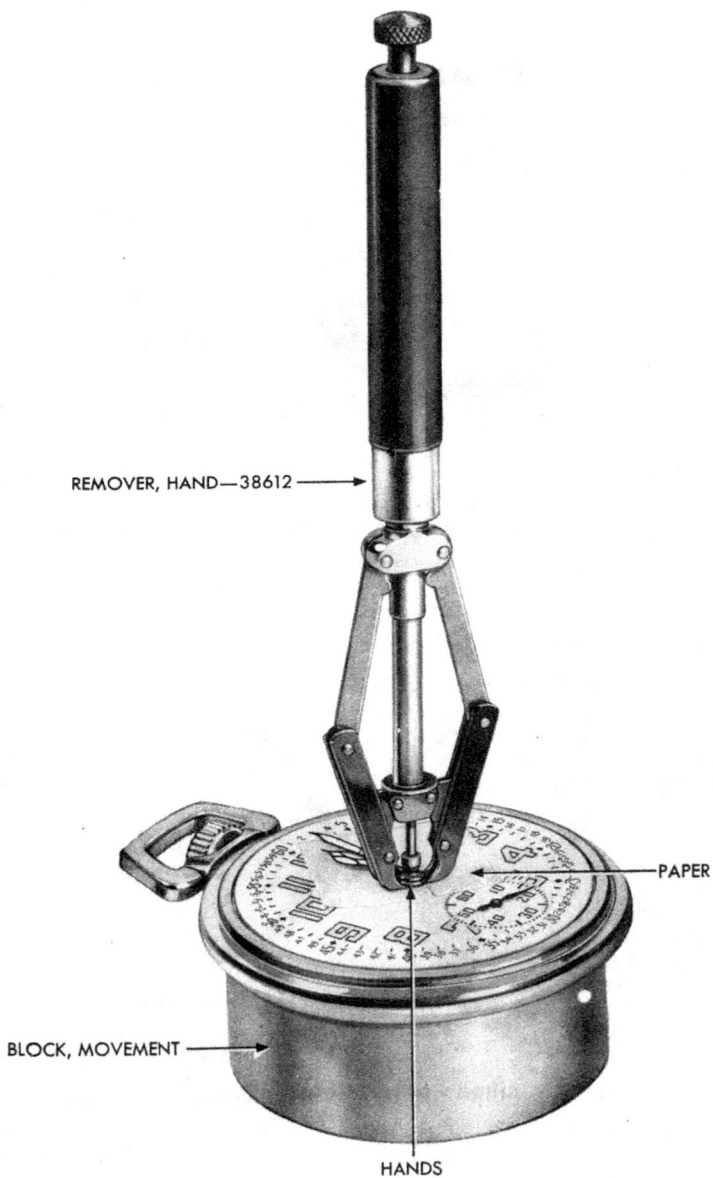

Figure 50 — Removing Hands With Hand Remover

RA PD 79005

HAMILTON POCKET WATCH, 16 SIZE, 21-JEWEL, RAILROAD GRADE, MODEL 992B

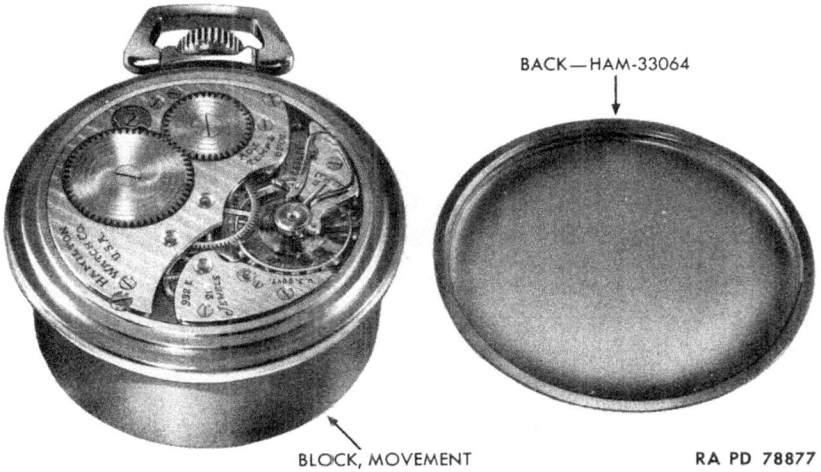

BACK—HAM-33064

BLOCK, MOVEMENT

RA PD 78877

Figure 51 — Hamilton Pocket Watch — Back Removed

RA PD 86932

Figure 52 — Releasing Power of Mainspring

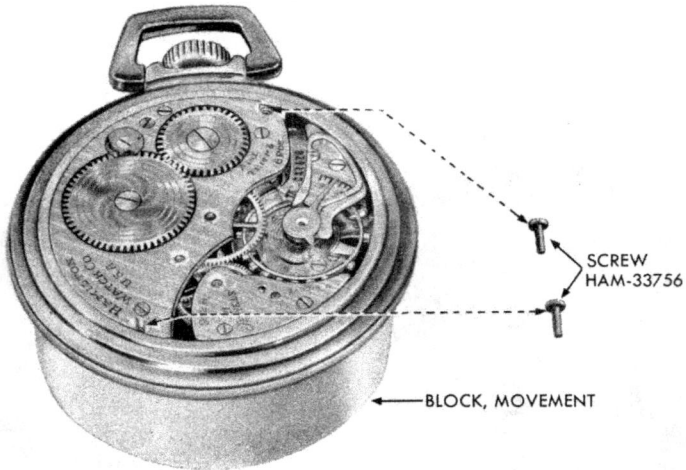

SCREW
HAM-33756

BLOCK, MOVEMENT

RA PD 78873

Figure 53 — Hamilton Pocket Watch — Case Screws Removed

RA PD 78872

*Figure 54 — Hamilton Pocket Watch — Removing Movement From
Case Band Assembly*

HAMILTON POCKET WATCH, 16 SIZE, 21-JEWEL, RAILROAD GRADE, MODEL 992B

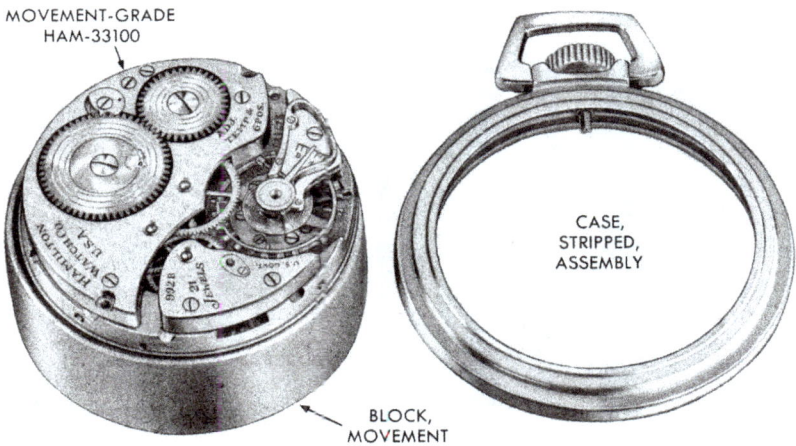

Figure 55 — Hamilton Pocket Watch — Movement Removed From Case Band Assembly

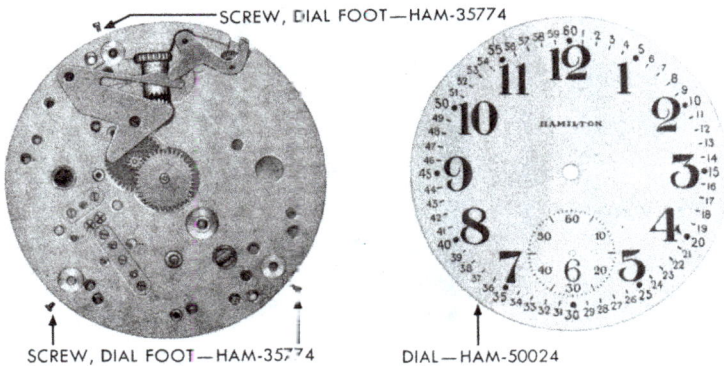

Figure 56 — Hamilton Pocket Watch — Dial Removed

the hairspring stud screw and, with the tweezers, free hairspring stud from the balance cock. Remove balance cock screw and remove balance cock. If the balance cock is tight, insert screwdriver in slot underneath the balance cock and pry it loose. Remove balance assembly with tweezers. Secure hairspring stud screw in place to avoid losing it. Remove two regulator spring screws from balance cock and remove regulator spring assembly. Invert balance cock on bench and remove two upper end stone cap assembly screws to release the end stone cap assembly and regulator assembly.

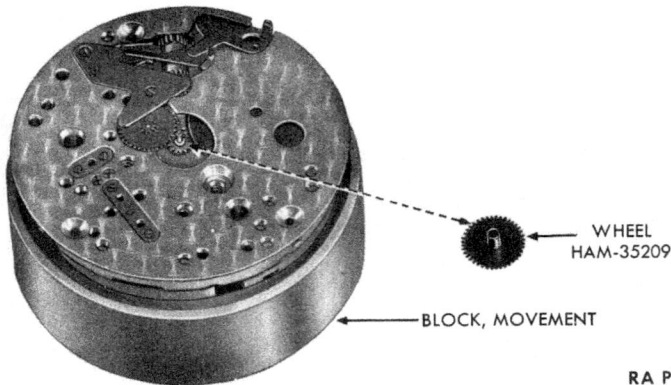

WHEEL
HAM-35209

BLOCK, MOVEMENT

RA PD 78881

Figure 57 — Hamilton Pocket Watch — Hour Wheel Removed

BLOCK, MOVEMENT

PINION—HAM-35215

RA PD 78894

Figure 58 — Hamilton Pocket Watch — Cannon Pinion Removed

l. **Remove Pallet Bridge and Pallet Assembly** (fig. 60). Remove two pallet bridge screws and remove pallet bridge assembly. Remove upper end stone pallet cap screw and remove end stone cap assembly. Remove pallet assembly with tweezers.

m. **Remove Click and Ratchet Wheel Assemblies** (fig. 61). Remove ratchet wheel click screw, ratchet wheel click, and click spring. Remove ratchet wheel screw and ratchet wheel.

n. **Remove Bridges** (fig. 64). Remove winding wheel screw, holding wheel from turning with a screwdriver. Lift off winding wheel. Remove barrel bridge screws and remove barrel bridge; if the

HAMILTON POCKET WATCH, 16 SIZE, 21-JEWEL, RAILROAD GRADE, MODEL 992B

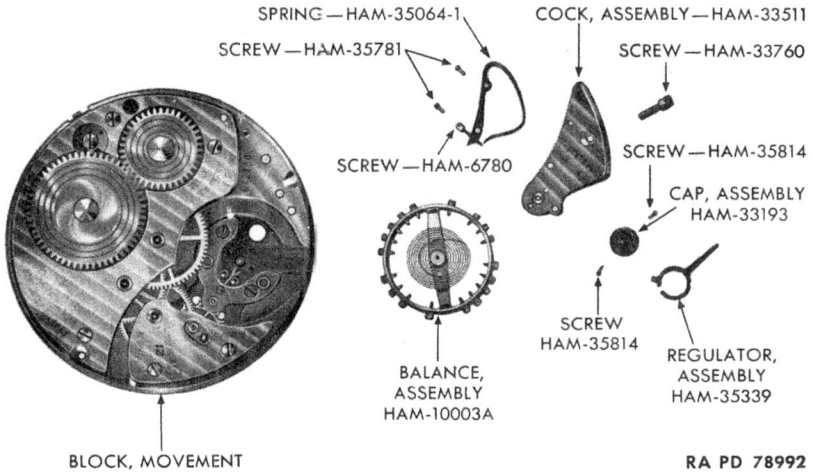

SPRING—HAM-35064-1
SCREW—HAM-35781
COCK, ASSEMBLY—HAM-33511
SCREW—HAM-33760
SCREW—HAM-6780
SCREW—HAM-35814
CAP, ASSEMBLY HAM-33193
SCREW HAM-35814
BALANCE, ASSEMBLY HAM-10003A
REGULATOR, ASSEMBLY HAM-35339
BLOCK, MOVEMENT
RA PD 78992

Figure 59 — Hamilton Pocket Watch — Balance Cock and Balance Assembly Removed

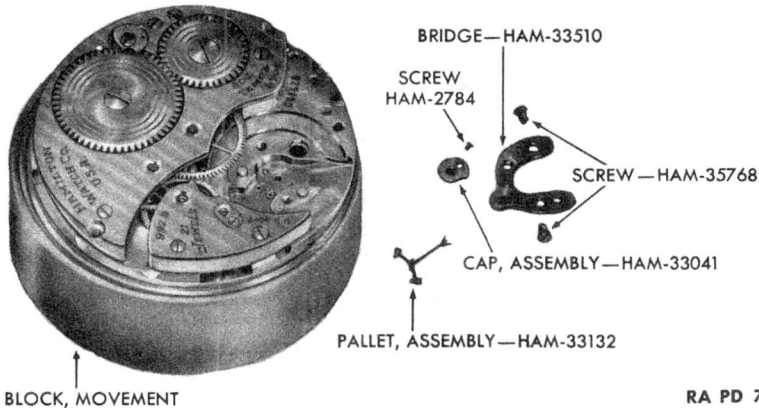

BRIDGE—HAM-33510
SCREW HAM-2784
SCREW—HAM-35768
CAP, ASSEMBLY—HAM-33041
PALLET, ASSEMBLY—HAM-33132
BLOCK, MOVEMENT
RA PD 78973

Figure 60 — Hamilton Pocket Watch — Pallet Bridge and Pallet Assembly Removed

bridge is tight, insert a screwdriver in the slots in the pillar plate and pry loose. After removing the barrel bridge, remove the lower winding wheel assembly. Remove the upper end stone cap assembly. Remove train bridge assembly screws and remove train bridge in same manner.

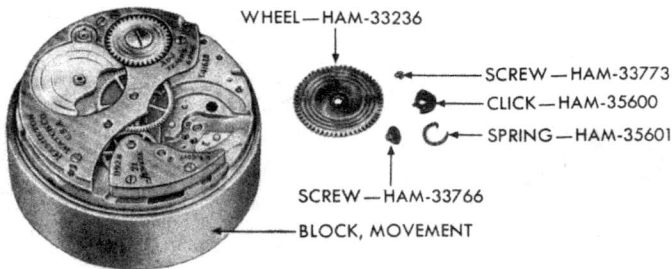

RA PD 78977

Figure 61 — Hamilton Pocket Watch — Ratchet Wheel and Click Assembly Removed

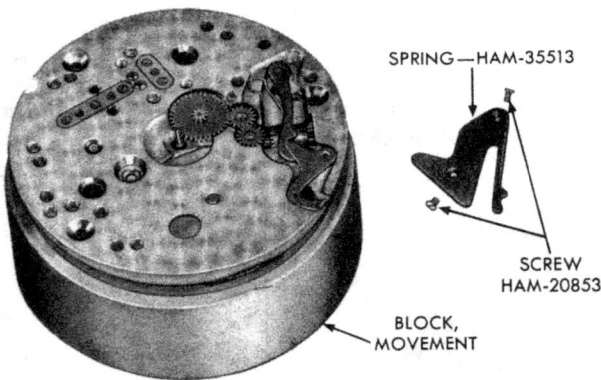

RA PD 78890

Figure 62 — Hamilton Pocket Watch — Setting Cap Spring Removed

o. **Remove Train Wheels and Barrel Assemblies** (fig. 65). Using tweezers, remove the center, third, fourth, and escape wheels. Remove barrel assembly. Insert end of screwdriver in slot of winding arbor clip, place end of index finger over clip, and lift screwdriver upward to remove clip.

p. **Remove Setting Cap Spring** (fig. 62). Remove setting cap spring screws and setting cap spring.

q. **Remove Winding and Setting Assembly** (fig. 63). Remove winding wheel by lifting off with tweezers; then remove two setting wheels. Remove clutch lever spring; in doing so, place the end of the index finger over the clutch lever stud to prevent the spring from snapping off and being lost. Remove clutch lever. Turn movement

HAMILTON POCKET WATCH, 16 SIZE, 21-JEWEL,
RAILROAD GRADE, MODEL 992B

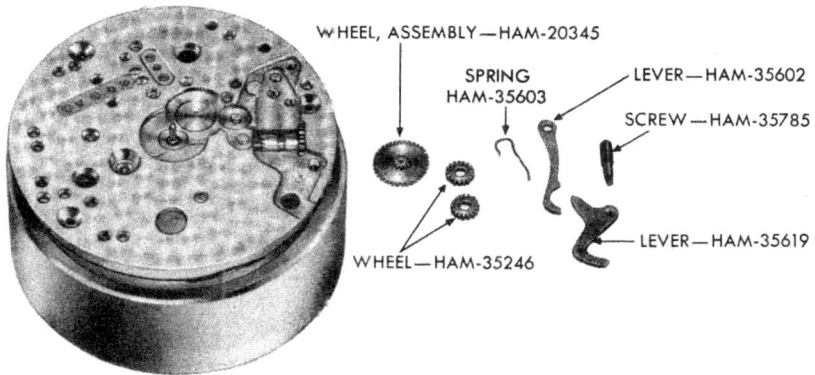

*Figure 63 — Hamilton Pocket Watch — Winding and Setting
Assembly Removed*

on movement block and unscrew shipper lever screw and the shipper
lever will drop off.

r. **Remove Winding Arbor and End Stone Cap Assemblies**
(fig. 66). Slide winding arbor off pillar plate; winding and setting
clutch and winding pinion can then be removed. Remove lower balance cap assembly screws and remove the lower escape and pallet cap.
This completes the disassembly of the movement, stripping it down
to the pillar plate and leaving only the hole jewel assemblies and
banking screws in place.

s. **Remove Mainspring From Barrel** (fig. 71). Hold the mainspring barrel between the thumb and index finger, while the barrel is
supported on the anvil, and place a screwdriver of the proper size
within the slot provided in the cap and pry off the cap. Remove
barrel arbor, grasp the inside coil of the mainspring with tweezers,
and pull it out of the barrel slowly, letting it uncoil as it comes out
of the barrel. Refrain from handling mainspring with bare fingers as
much as possible.

t. **Remove Stem, Crown, and Bow** (fig. 66). Grasp the square
of the winding stem between the smooth portion of flat-nosed pliers
and hold while the crown is unscrewed. This allows the winding
stem to be pulled out of the pendant. Remove bow with bow contracting pliers only if necessary.

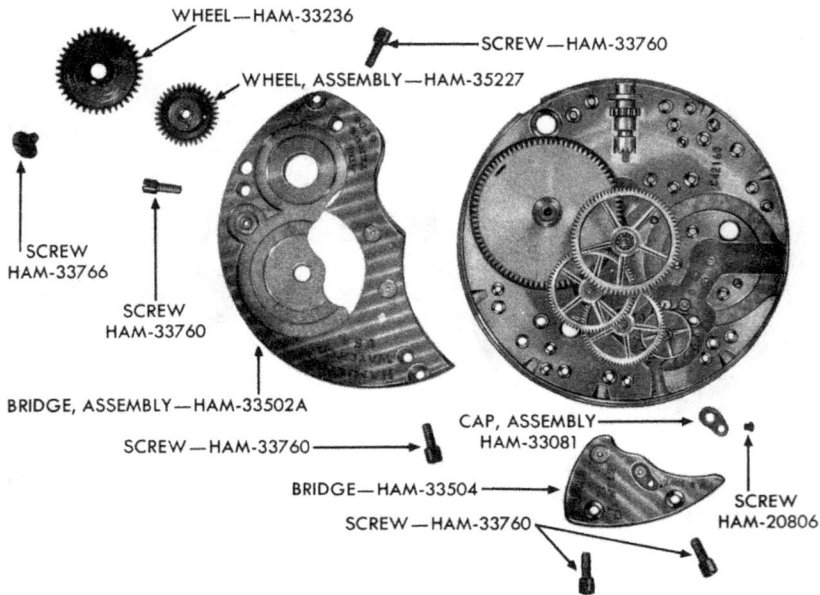

Figure 64 — Hamilton Pocket Watch — Barrel and Train Bridge
Assemblies Removed

48. ASSEMBLY OF HAMILTON POCKET WATCH, 16 SIZE, 21-JEWEL, RAILROAD GRADE, MODEL 992B.

a. Wind in Mainspring (figs. 68, 69, and 70). Select proper mainspring winder and wind mainspring into it slowly; insert mainspring winder in barrel, hook end of mainspring on the barrel hook, and press plunger to transfer mainspring into barrel. Insert barrel arbor and replace barrel cap, snapping it into its recess.

b. Replace Winding Arbor (fig. 66). Place pillar plate on movement block, train side up. Assemble the winding arbor assembly by placing the winding pinion and the winding and setting clutch on winding arbor. Insert it into the pillar plate at its proper location, replace winding arbor clip, and snap it into the recess of the arbor and slot of the pillar plate. Replace lower balance pallet and escape assemblies and secure in place with cap screws.

c. Replace Train Wheels and Barrel Assembly (fig. 65). Place barrel assembly on the pillar plate. Replace escape, fourth, third, and center wheels.

d. Replace Bridges (fig. 64). Assemble the lower winding wheel and the winding wheel on the barrel bridge. Place lower winding

HAMILTON POCKET WATCH, 16 SIZE, 21-JEWEL,
RAILROAD GRADE, MODEL 992B

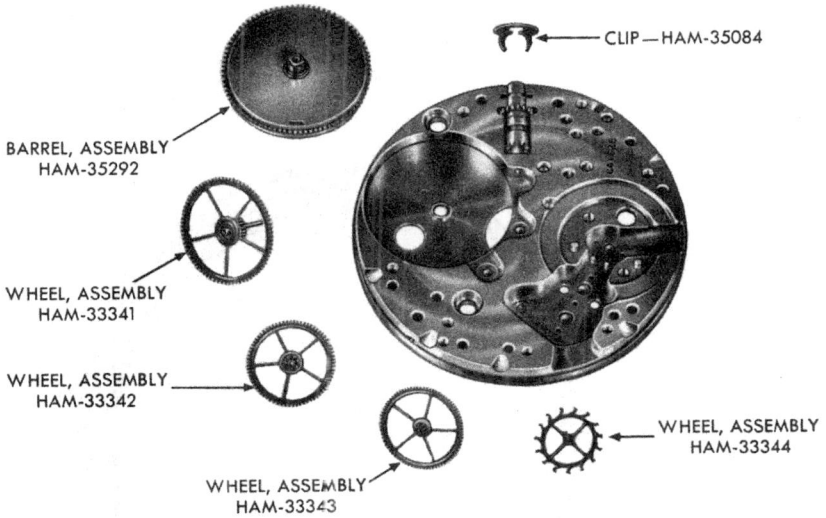

CLIP—HAM-35084

BARREL, ASSEMBLY
HAM-35292

WHEEL, ASSEMBLY
HAM-33341

WHEEL, ASSEMBLY
HAM-33342

WHEEL, ASSEMBLY
HAM-33344

WHEEL, ASSEMBLY
HAM-33343

RA PD 78900

*Figure 65 — Hamilton Pocket Watch — Train Wheels and Barrel
Assembly Removed*

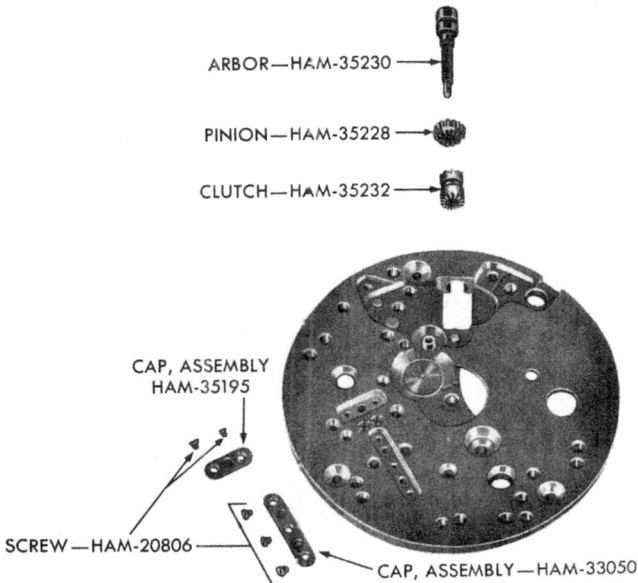

ARBOR—HAM-35230

PINION—HAM-35228

CLUTCH—HAM-35232

CAP, ASSEMBLY
HAM-35195

SCREW—HAM-20806

CAP, ASSEMBLY—HAM-33050

RA PD 78921

*Figure 66 — Hamilton Pocket Watch — Winding Arbor and End Stone
Cap Assembly Removed*

97

ORDNANCE MAINTENANCE — WRIST WATCHES, POCKET WATCHES, STOP WATCHES, AND CLOCKS

RA PD 84362

CASE - HAM-33073

STEM - HAM-33085

BOW - HAM-33067

CROWN - HAM-33069

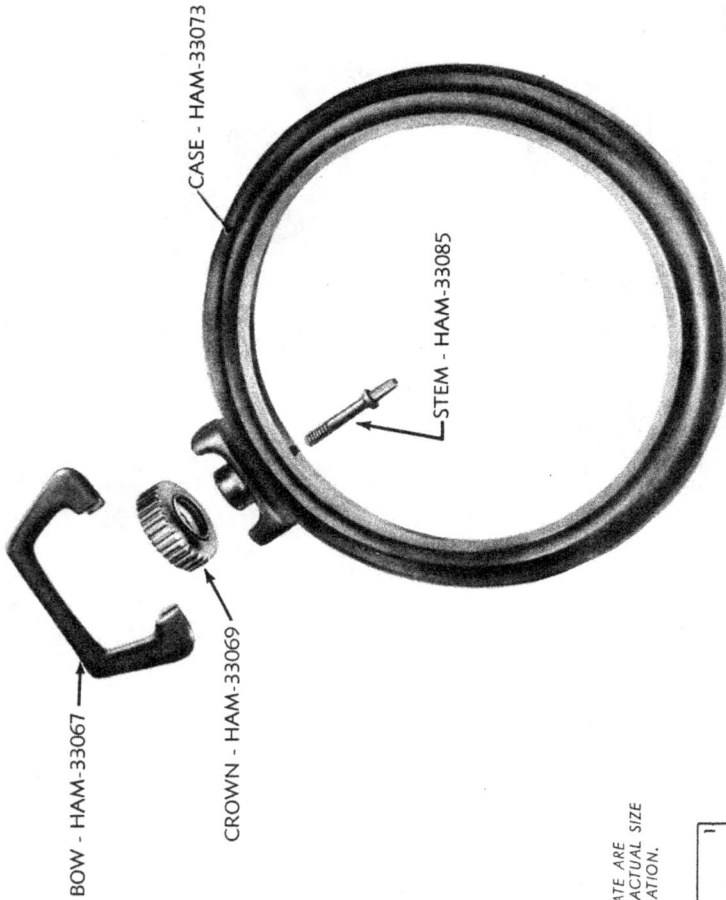

THE PARTS IN THIS PLATE ARE
ENLARGED TO 1-1/2 TIMES ACTUAL SIZE
FOR EASIER IDENTIFICATION.

INCH

Figure 67 — Hamilton Pocket Watch — Case With Bow, Crown, and Stem Removed

HAMILTON POCKET WATCH, 16 SIZE, 21-JEWEL,
RAILROAD GRADE, MODEL 992B

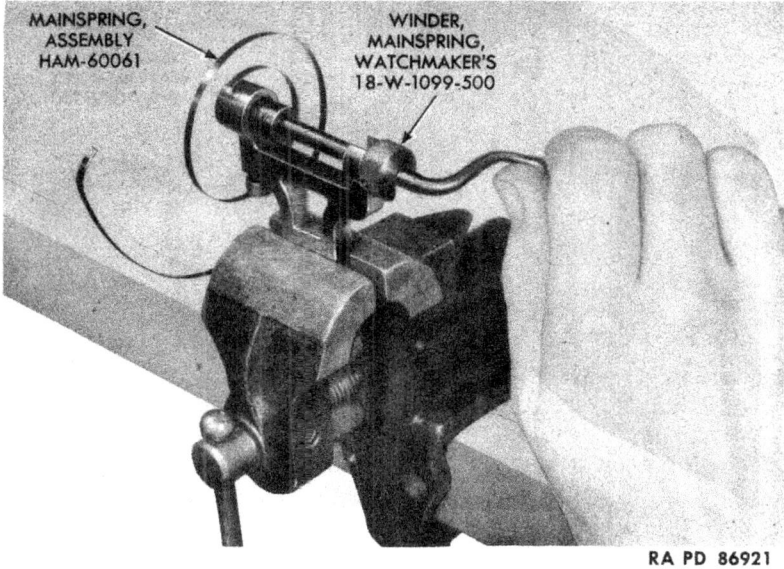

RA PD 86921

Figure 68 — Winding Mainspring in Mainspring Barrel

wheel underneath in its proper location. Place winding wheel on top of barrel bridge, fitting it on the stud set into the lower winding wheel. Secure upper and lower winding wheels together with winding wheel screw. Replace barrel bridge assembly, alining the pivots of the center wheel and third wheel in their respective pivot holes. Secure barrel bridge in place with bridge screw. Replace upper escape end stone cap assembly on train bridge and secure with cap screw. Replace train bridge assembly, alining fourth wheel and escape pivots in their respective holes, and secure bridge with bridge screws.

e. **Replace Winding and Setting Mechanism** (fig. 63). Invert the movement, placing it dial side up on the movement block. Place shipper lever in position on pillar plate. Cover end of index finger of the left hand with watchmaker's paper and hold the shipper lever in position. Grasp the movement and invert it; replace the shipper lever screw and secure. Replace movement on movement block with dial side up. Push the winding and setting clutch in toward the center of the pillar plate. Place the clutch lever on its stud on the pillar plate and aline the stud under the clutch lever so that it will fall into the recess of the clutch. Replace clutch lever spring on its stud. Hold the clutch lever spring in position with one screwdriver and pull the

ORDNANCE MAINTENANCE — WRIST WATCHES, POCKET WATCHES, STOP WATCHES, AND CLOCKS

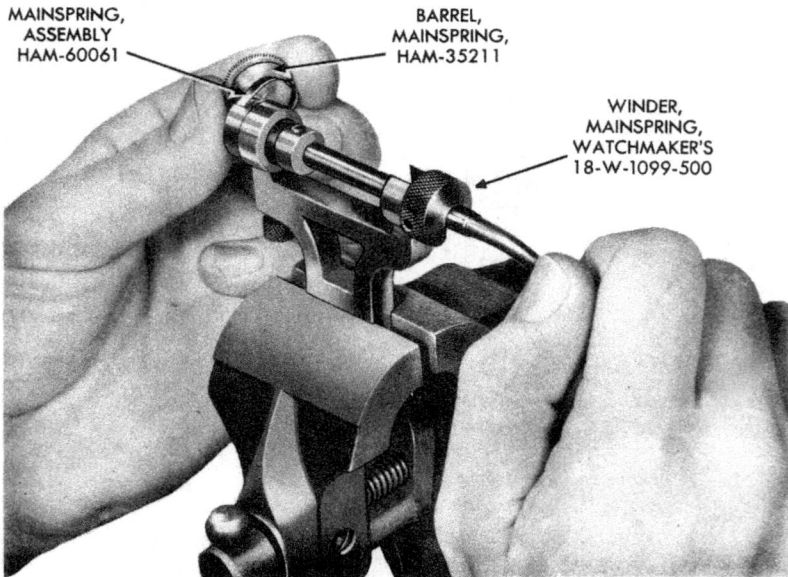

Figure 69 — Transferring Mainspring From Winder Into Barrel

end of the spring back until it falls into place back of clutch lever. Place setting and minute wheels on their respective studs.

f. Replace Setting Cap Spring (fig. 62). Replace setting cap spring and secure in place with setting spring screws. The end of the setting spring should be held behind the shipper lever in order to hold it in setting and winding position.

g. Replace Winding Assembly (fig. 61). Invert movement on movement block and replace click spring, allowing it to rest in the hole in the pillar plate. Place click over its stud, with bent end of click spring resting in the hole in click. Replace click screw and secure. Replace ratchet wheel, fitting it on the square of the mainspring barrel arbor. Replace screw and secure. At this point, an examination must be made to check freedom of the train. Do this by winding the mainspring one full turn with the key winder; if wheels of train backlash on reaching the end of the winding, the train has perfect freedom. If they stop abruptly or slow down and gradually stop, a bind exists and must be corrected.

h. Replace Pallet and Pallet Bridge (fig. 60). Replace pallet assembly. Replace upper pallet end stone cap assembly on pallet bridge and secure in place with cap screw. Replace bridge and care-

HAMILTON POCKET WATCH, 16 SIZE, 21-JEWEL,
RAILROAD GRADE, MODEL 992B

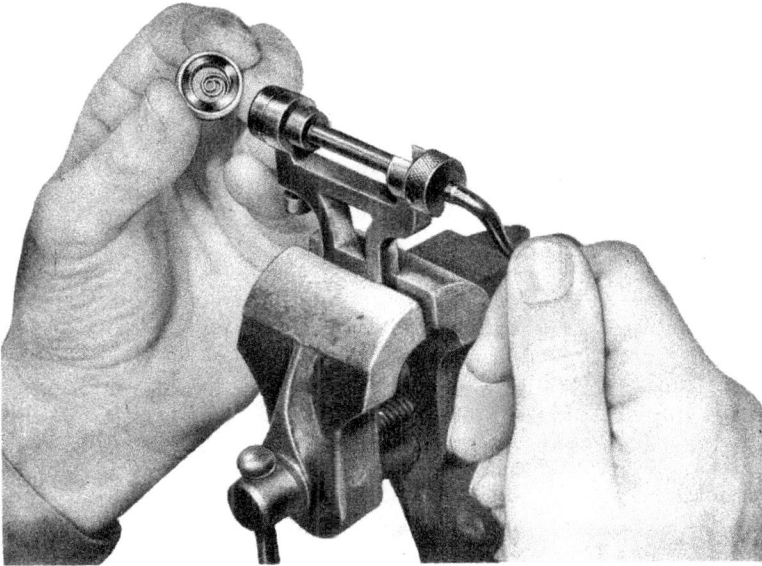

Figure 70 — Mainspring Wound in Barrel

fully aline the pallet arbor pivot in its hole. Replace pallet bridge screws and secure. Check freedom of the pallet assembly. NOTE: *The action of the pallet and escape wheel must be checked by winding the mainspring two turns.*

i. **Replace Balance and Balance Cock** (fig. 59). Place upper end stone cap assembly on bench with polished surface down. Invert the balance cock and place it on end stone cap assembly. Aline the screw holes, replace end stone cap assembly screws, and secure. NOTE: *Upper end stone assembly cap screws have highly polished ends.* Invert the balance cock. Replace regulator assembly, allowing it to snap in place around the end stone cap assembly. Replace regulator spring assembly, with the spring on one side of the regulator, and the regulator spring regulating screw on the other side resting against the regulator. Invert the balance cock and loosen the hairspring stud screw. Grasp the balance wheel assembly with tweezers and insert hairspring stud in hole in balance cock, allowing the overcoil of the hairspring to be placed between the regulator pins simultaneously. Secure hairspring stud screw. Grasp balance cock assembly with tweezers and invert carefully in order not to distort the hairspring. Place balance wheel under the center wheel, engaging roller

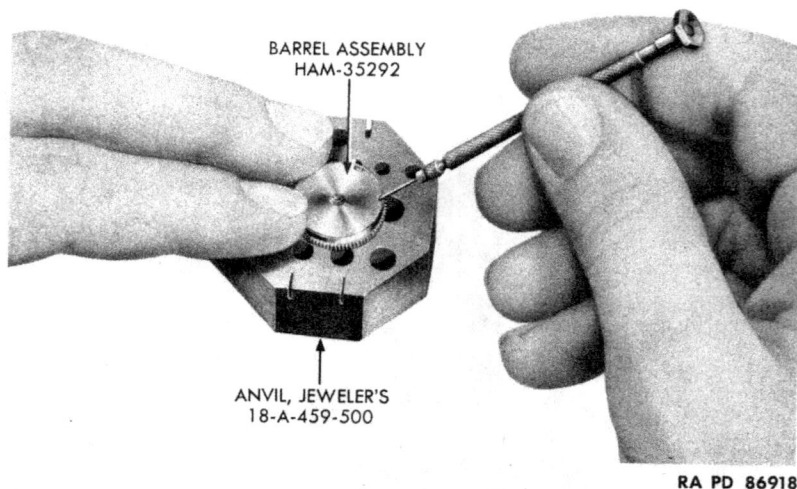

BARREL ASSEMBLY
HAM-35292

ANVIL, JEWELER'S
18-A-459-500

RA PD 86918

Figure 71 — Removing Mainspring Barrel Cap

jewel pin in slot of pallet fork, and cautiously set balance cock in place. Replace balance cock screw and secure.

j. Replace Cannon Pinion (fig. 58). Replace cannon pinion.

k. Replace Hour Wheel (fig. 57). Replace movement on movement block, dial side up. Replace hour wheel with tweezers, engaging teeth with the minute wheel pinion.

l. Replace Dial (fig. 56). Back dial foot screws out three turns and replace dial, securing it in place by tightening the foot screws.

m. Replace Stem and Crown (fig. 67). Insert the stem in pendant from the inside of case band. Hold square of stem between smooth portion of flat-nosed pliers and screw on crown securely.

n. Replace Movement in Case Band (fig. 54). Grasp case band by the pendant. With the dial side up, hold movement in a tilted position, allowing the stem to enter the winding arbor. Lower the movement into the case band, being careful not to hook the balance wheel on the case band as it is seated in place.

o. Replace Case Screws (fig. 53). Replace case screws and secure. Before tightening case screws, make sure that movement is centered and no binding exists in the stem.

p. Replace Hands (fig. 70). Replace seconds hand; replace hour hand with the point at the twelfth hour and the minute hand in the same manner.

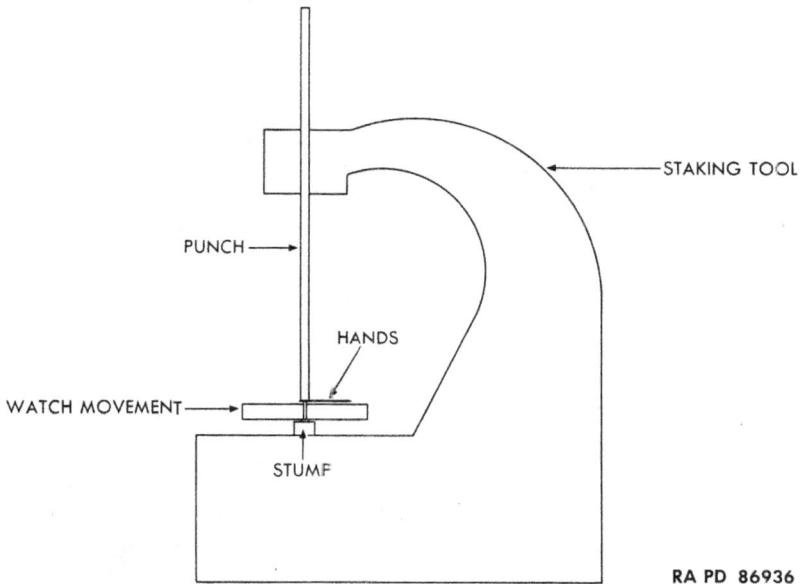

Figure 72 — Replacing Hands, Using Staking Tool

q. Replace Case Back. Replace back of case and screw into place.

r. Replace Bezel. Replace bezel and screw into place.

s. Replace Rubber Shock Absorber. Slide shock absorber over leather thong and replace on watch by inserting the pendant in the slot and sliding the shock absorber over the case.

Section III

ELGIN POCKET WATCH, 16 SIZE, 7- OR 17-JEWEL

49. IDENTIFICATION.

a. Elgin Pocket Watches. There are two models used, the 7-jewel and the 17-jewel. Both watches are 16 size, mounted in a combination case with a hinged snap type back and snap bezel. The 7-jewel watch has the prefix "OA" before the serial number and the 17-jewel has the prefix "OC." Both watches have porcelain dials with the hour graduations outlined in black and filled with radium luminous material. The dial of the 7-jewel watch has red arabic numerals on

ORDNANCE MAINTENANCE — WRIST WATCHES, POCKET WATCHES, STOP WATCHES, AND CLOCKS

7-JEWEL

17-JEWEL

RA PD 78860

Figure 73 — Elgin Pocket Watches, 7- and 17-jewel, 16 Size —
Front and Back

ELGIN POCKET WATCH, 16 SIZE, 7- OR 17-JEWEL

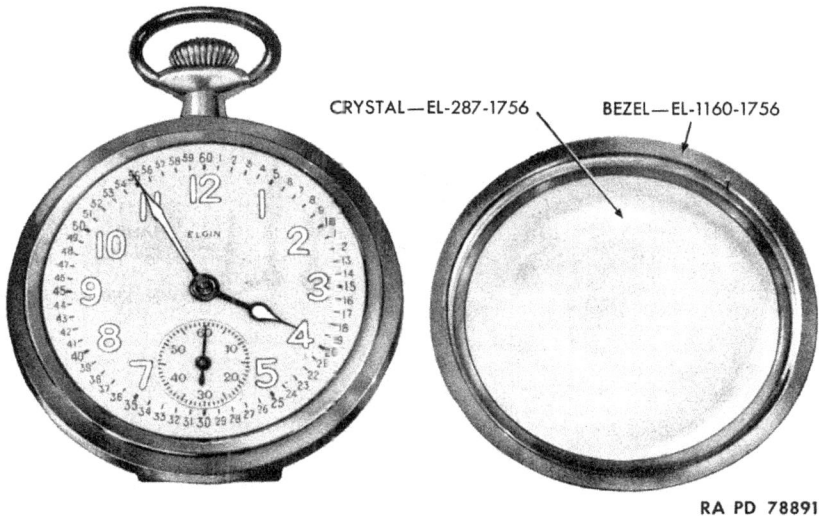

CRYSTAL—EL-287-1756   BEZEL—EL-1160-1756

RA PD 78891

Figure 74 — Elgin Pocket Watch — Bezel Removed

the outer circle of the dial which indicate each 5-minute graduation, whereas the 17-jewel watch has small arabic numerals to indicate each minute graduation. The hour and minute hands are also coated with radium luminous material, making it possible to tell time in the dark. Both watches are stem wound and stem set.

50. DISASSEMBLY OF ELGIN POCKET WATCH, 16 SIZE, 7- OR 17-JEWEL.

a. **Remove Rubber Shock Absorber** (fig. 47). Remove rubber shock absorber by slipping it off the watch and sliding it along the leather thong.

b. **Remove Bezel** (fig. 74). Insert case opener in slot of bezel and pry it off.

c. **Remove Hands.** Cut a V-slot in a piece of paper and slide it under the hands to protect the dial. Remove hands with hand remover (fig. 50).

d. **Open Back Covers.** Insert case opener in slot, and pry open back cover and dust cover in the same manner.

e. **Release Unused Power of Mainspring.** Release unused power of mainspring by holding the crown with thumb and index finger; disengage click with a small screwdriver and allow the crown to turn slowly between fingers, thus releasing power of the mainspring.

ORDNANCE MAINTENANCE — WRIST WATCHES, POCKET WATCHES, STOP WATCHES, AND CLOCKS

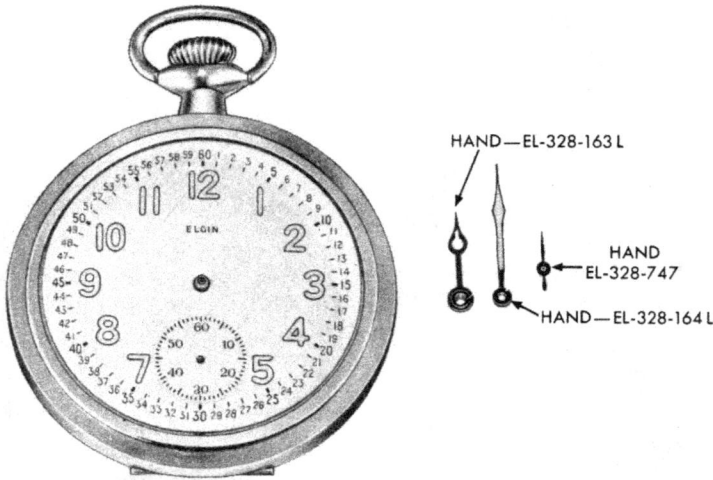

HAND—EL-328-163 L

HAND
EL-328-747

HAND—EL-328-164 L

RA PD 78887

Figure 75 — Elgin Pocket Watch — Hands Removed

f. Remove Case Screws (fig. 77). Place watch on movement block of proper size, with train side up, and remove the two case screws.

g. Remove Movement From Case Band Assembly (fig. 78). Pull stem out to setting position. Hold case band firmly with thumb and finger, train side up. With thumb and middle finger of the left hand on the contour of the case, push movement down with the left index finger and pull the movement away from the case band in a tilted position. Make sure balance wheel does not hook on case band.

h. Remove Dial (fig. 79). Back out dial foot screws two turns. Remove dial and screw dial foot screws back into position to prevent losing them.

i. Remove Hour Wheel (fig. 80). Remove hour wheel with tweezers.

j. Remove Cannon Pinion (fig. 81). Remove the cannon pinion with a pin vise. Pull cannon pinion straight upward to prevent bending or breaking the center wheel arbor.

k. Remove Balance Cock and Balance Assemblies. Invert movement on movement block, train side up. Loosen hairspring stud screw with a screwdriver. Free stud from balance cock. Remove balance cock screw and remove balance cock. Remove balance assembly with tweezers. Remove upper end stone cap assembly screws; then remove upper end stone cap assembly setting. Pry off regulator

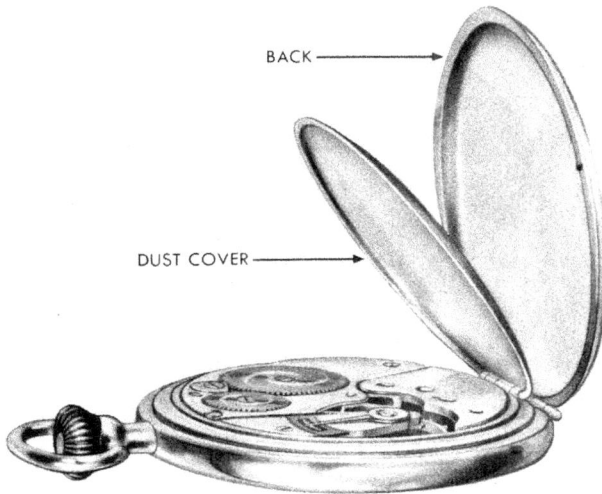

RA PD 78963

Figure 76 — Elgin Pocket Watch — Case Back Opened

assembly from cock dome with a screwdriver. Remove two regulator index screws and remove regulator index.

l. **Remove Pallet Bridge and Pallet Assembly** (fig. 83). Remove pallet bridge screw and pallet bridge. Remove pallet assembly with tweezers.

m. **Remove Ratchet Wheel and Click Assemblies** (fig. 83). Remove ratchet wheel click screw; remove ratchet wheel click and click spring. Remove ratchet wheel screw and ratchet wheel.

n. **Remove Setting Spring and Setting Spring Cam** (fig. 85). Invert movement on movement block and remove setting spring cam screw and setting spring cam. Remove setting spring screw and setting spring.

o. **Remove Winding and Setting Subassemblies and End Stone Cap Assembly** (fig. 86). Remove clutch lever screw and clutch lever. Remove minute wheel clamp screws, then remove minute wheel clamp and minute wheel. Remove lower end stone cap assembly screws and end stone cap assembly.

p. **Remove Bridges** (fig. 87). Remove crown wheel screw, left-hand thread crown wheel, and washer. Remove barrel and train bridge screws and bridges. If bridges are tight, loosen by pushing up

SCREW — EL-662-392-G

SCREW — EL-662-392-G

RA PD 78902

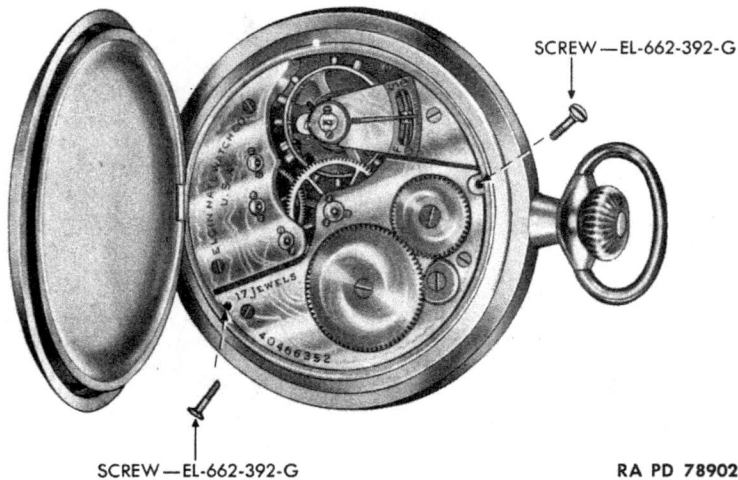

Figure 77 — Elgin Pocket Watch — Case Screws Removed

on steady pins from top of pillar plate, until space will permit insertion of a screwdriver between plate and bridge to pry bridge free.

q. Remove Train Wheels and Barrel Assembly (fig. 88). Using tweezers, remove, in order, the center, third, fourth, and escape wheels. Remove barrel assembly.

r. Remove Winding Arbor and Setting Lever Assembly (fig. 89). Grasp winding arbor sleeve with tweezers and lift it off plate. Strip assembly by removing winding pinion, winding and setting clutch, and winding arbor. Remove setting lever screw and setting lever. Remove setting lever cam. This completes disassembly of the movement, stripping it down to the pillar plate and leaving only the hole jewel assemblies and banking screws in place. NOTE: *If a 7-jewel movement, this procedure will leave the bushings of the train wheel pivots in their places.*

s. Remove Mainspring From Barrel (fig. 90). Hold the mainspring barrel between the thumb and index finger while the barrel is supported on an anvil. Place a screwdriver of the proper size within the slot provided in the cap and pry off the cap. Remove barrel arbor, grasp the inside coil of the mainspring with tweezers, and pull it out of the barrel slowly, letting it uncoil as it comes out of the barrel. NOTE: *Refrain from handling mainspring with bare fingers as much as possible.*

ELGIN POCKET WATCH, 16 SIZE, 7- OR 17-JEWEL

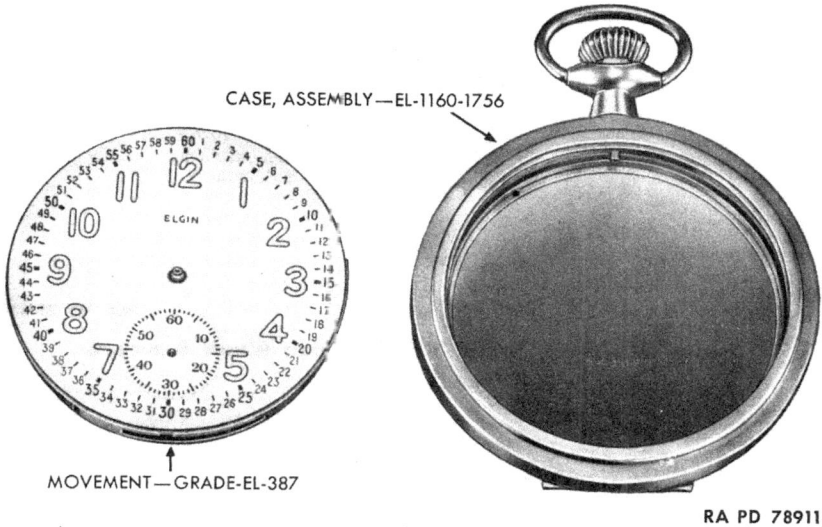

CASE, ASSEMBLY—EL-1160-1756

MOVEMENT—GRADE-EL-387

RA PD 78911

Figure 78 — Elgin Pocket Watch — Movement Removed From Case

DIAL, ASSEMBLY—EL-1234-1532L

RA PD 78922

Figure 79 — Elgin Pocket Watch — Dial Removed

t. **Remove Crown, Stem, and Sleeve** (figs. 91 and 92). Grasp the square of the winding stem between smooth portion of flat-nosed pliers and hold it while crown is unscrewed. Insert the proper size sleeve wrench over the stem into slots cut in sleeve, and unscrew until sleeve is free of pendant. To remove stem from sleeve, hold square of stem firmly and pull sleeve off threaded end.

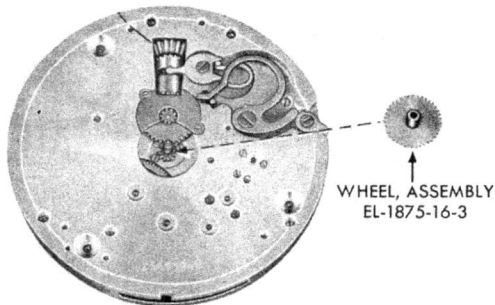

RA PD 78919

Figure 80 — Elgin Pocket Watch — Hour Wheel Removed

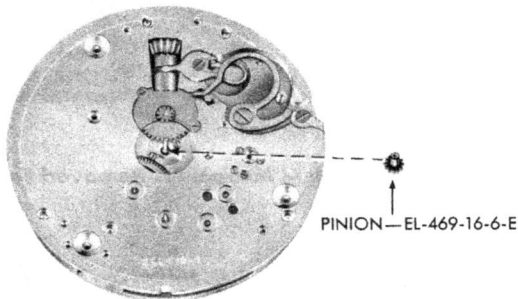

RA PD 78939

Figure 81 — Elgin Pocket Watch — Cannon Pinion Removed

51. ASSEMBLY OF THE ELGIN POCKET WATCH, 16 SIZE, 7- OR 17-JEWEL.

a. **Winding in Mainspring** (figs. 68, 69, and 70). Select proper mainspring winder and wind mainspring into it slowly. Insert mainspring winder in barrel, hook end of mainspring on barrel hook, and press plunger, transferring mainspring into barrel. Insert barrel arbor and replace barrel cap, snapping it into its recess.

b. **Replace Winding Bar** (fig. 91). Place pillar plate on movement block, train side up. Place winding and setting clutch, winding pinion, and winding arbor sleeve on winding arbor, and replace the assembly in its recess in the pillar plate. Replace setting lever cam assembly, inserting the stud of the cam in its hole in the pillar plate, and place the cam on its stud on the pillar plate. Replace the setting lever on its stud on the pillar plate with the stud of the setting lever placed in its slot in the pillar plate.

ELGIN POCKET WATCH, 16 SIZE, 7- OR 17-JEWEL

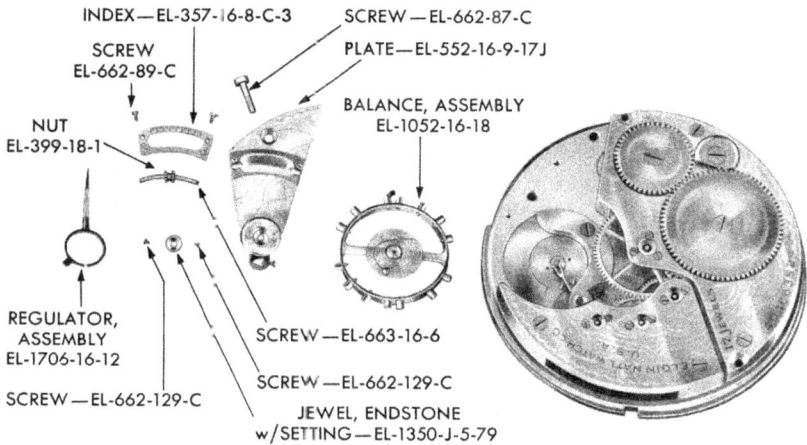

INDEX—EL-357-16-8-C-3
SCREW EL-662-89-C
NUT EL-399-18-1
REGULATOR, ASSEMBLY EL-1706-16-12
SCREW—EL-662-129-C
SCREW—EL-662-87-C
PLATE—EL-552-16-9-17J
BALANCE, ASSEMBLY EL-1052-16-18
SCREW—EL-663-16-6
SCREW—EL-662-129-C
JEWEL, ENDSTONE w/SETTING—EL-1350-J-5-79

RA PD 78897

Figure 82 — Elgin Pocket Watch — Balance Cock and Balance Assembly Removed

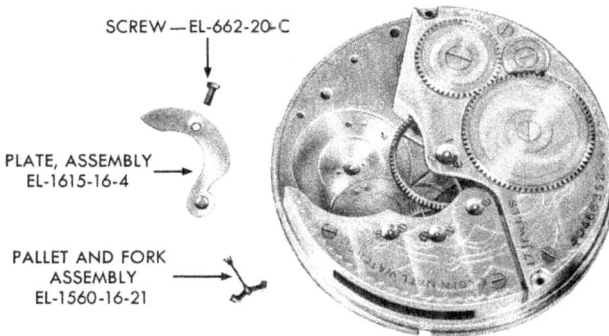

SCREW—EL-662-20-C
PLATE, ASSEMBLY EL-1615-16-4
PALLET AND FORK ASSEMBLY EL-1560-16-21

RA PD 78901

Figure 83 — Elgin Pocket Watch — Pallet Bridge and Pallet Assembly Removed

c. **Replace the Train Wheels and Barrel Assembly** (fig. 88). Place barrel assembly on the pillar plate; replace third wheel, escape wheel, fourth wheel, and center wheel.

d. **Replace Bridges** (fig. 87). Replace barrel bridge assembly, alining the pivot of the center wheel in its respective pivot hole in the barrel bridge. Secure the barrel bridge assembly in place with bridge screws. Replace train bridge assembly, alining the third,

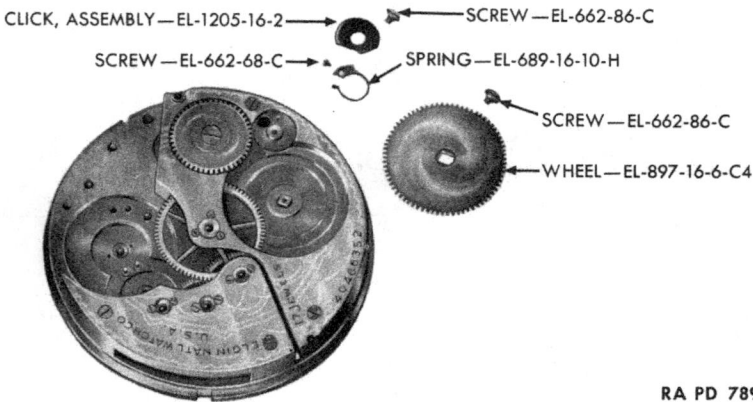

CLICK, ASSEMBLY—EL-1205-16-2

SCREW—EL-662-68-C

SCREW—EL-662-86-C

SPRING—EL-689-16-10-H

SCREW—EL-662-86-C

WHEEL—EL-897-16-6-C4

RA PD 78908

*Figure 84 — Elgin Pocket Watch — Ratchet Wheel and Click
Assemblies Removed*

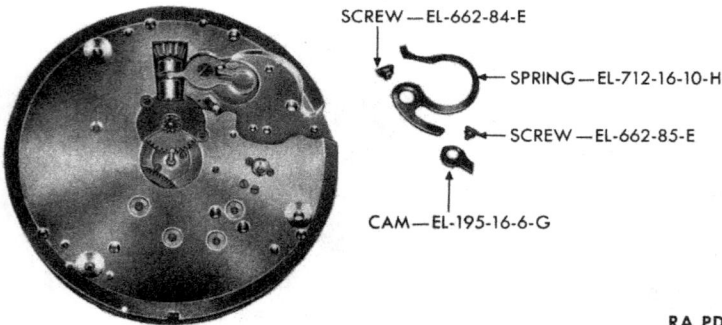

SCREW—EL-662-84-E

SPRING—EL-712-16-10-H

SCREW—EL-662-85-E

CAM—EL-195-16-6-G

RA PD 79006

Figure 85 — Elgin Pocket Watch — Setting Subassembly Removed

fourth, and escape wheel pivots in their respective holes. Secure train bridge assembly with bridge screws.

e. **Replace Winding and Setting Assembly and End Stone Cap Assembly** (fig. 86). Invert movement on movement block. Replace clutch lever, placing single end in the recess of the clutch and allowing the spring end to rest against stud of setting lever cam, which projects through hole in pillar plate. Secure with setting lever screw. Replace minute wheel and minute wheel clamp, and secure with minute wheel clamp screws. Replace lower balance end stone cap assembly above the balance hole jewel and secure in place with cap screws.

ELGIN POCKET WATCH, 16 SIZE, 7- OR 17-JEWEL

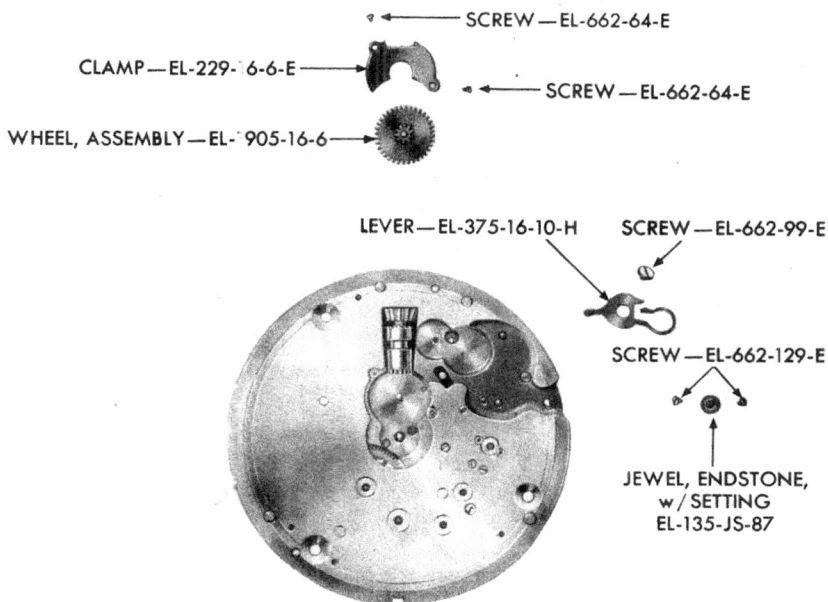

SCREW — EL-662-64-E

CLAMP — EL-229-6-6-E

SCREW — EL-662-64-E

WHEEL, ASSEMBLY — EL-905-16-6

LEVER — EL-375-16-10-H   SCREW — EL-662-99-E

SCREW — EL-662-129-E

JEWEL, ENDSTONE,
w / SETTING
EL-135-JS-87

RA PD 78981

Figure 86 — Elgin Pocket Watch — Wind and Setting
Assembly Removed

f. Replace Setting Spring and Setting Spring Cam (fig. 85). Replace setting spring and secure in place with screw, with end of spring resting against the setting lever stud which projects through the pillar plate. Replace setting spring cam and setting spring cam screw.

g. Replace Click, Ratchet Wheel, and Crown Wheel (fig. 84). Replace click spring on its stud and secure in place with screw. Replace click over click spring stud, placing stud of click in open end of click spring and secure in place with click screw. Replace crown wheel and crown wheel washer, and secure with crown wheel screw, turning it counterclockwise. Replace the ratchet wheel on the square of mainspring barrel arbor and secure in place with the ratchet wheel screw. At this point, check the freedom of the train by installing the movement within the case band and rotating the crown one turn. Observe the train to determine whether or not the wheels backlash. If the wheels backlash, the train has perfect freedom.

h. Replace Pallet and Pallet Bridge (fig. 83). Replace pallet and pallet bridge assembly, carefully alining the pallet arbor pivots. Secure in place with pallet bridge assembly screw. The action of the pallet and escape wheel must be checked by inserting the bench key into the winding arbor sleeve and winding two turns.

WASHER—EL-821-16-6-C

SCREW—EL-662-83-C

WHEEL—EL-886-16-7-C2

SCREW
EL-662-87-C

PLATE, ASSEMBLY
EL-1608-16-1

PLATE, ASSEMBLY
EL-1623-16-1

SCREW—EL-662-87-C

SCREW—EL-662-87-C

RA PD 79000

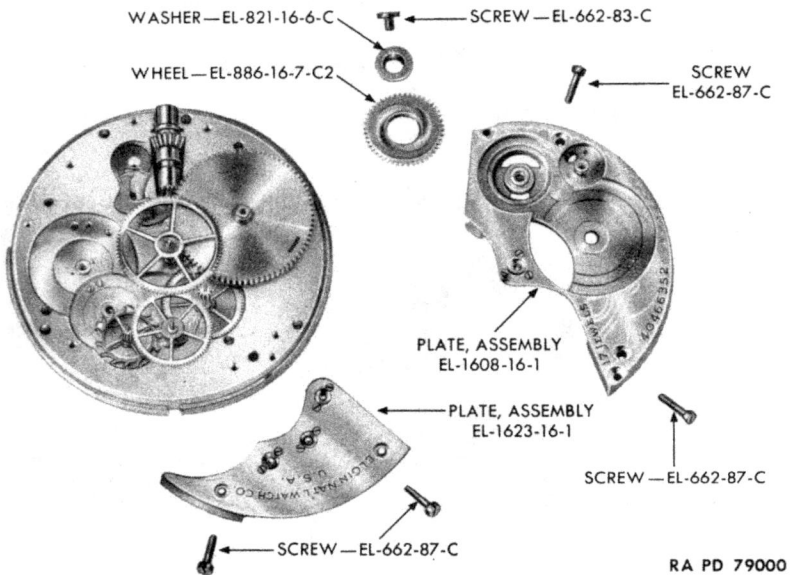

*Figure 87 — Elgin Pocket Watch — Barrel and Train Bridge
Assemblies Removed*

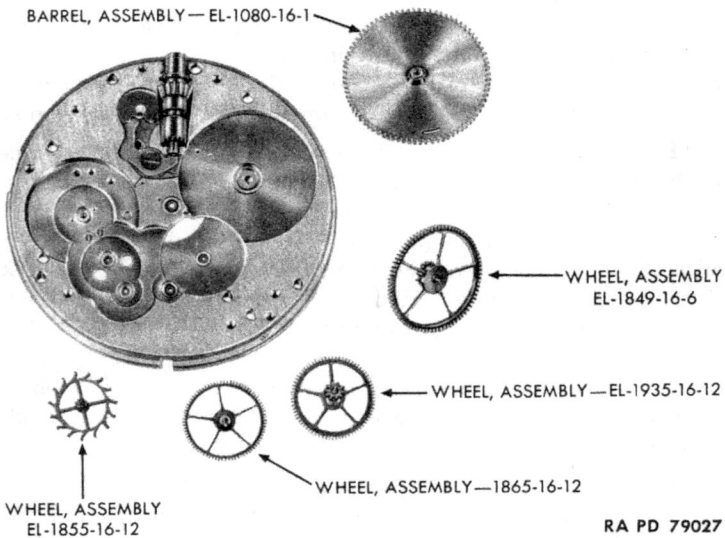

BARREL, ASSEMBLY — EL-1080-16-1

WHEEL, ASSEMBLY
EL-1849-16-6

WHEEL, ASSEMBLY—EL-1935-16-12

WHEEL, ASSEMBLY—1865-16-12

WHEEL, ASSEMBLY
EL-1855-16-12

RA PD 79027

*Figure 88 — Elgin Pocket Watch — Train Wheels and Barrel
Assembly Removed*

ELGIN POCKET WATCH, 16 SIZE, 7- OR 17-JEWEL

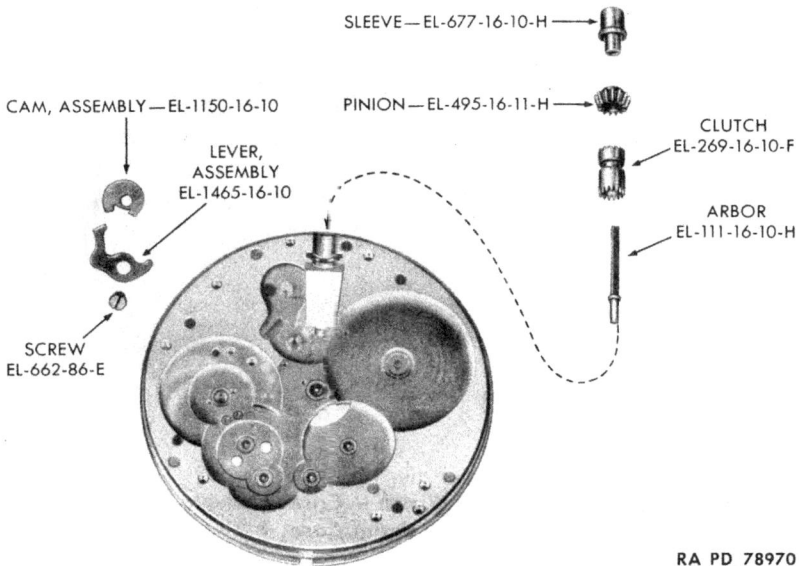

SLEEVE—EL-677-16-10-H

CAM, ASSEMBLY—EL-1150-16-10

PINION—EL-495-16-11-H

CLUTCH
EL-269-16-10-F

LEVER,
ASSEMBLY
EL-1465-16-10

ARBOR
EL-111-16-10-H

SCREW
EL-662-86-E

RA PD 78970

Figure 89 — Elgin Pocket Watch — Winding Arbor Assembly Removed

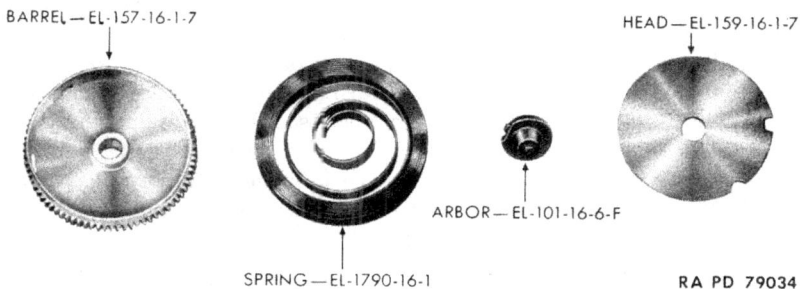

BARREL—EL-157-16-1-7

HEAD—EL-159-16-1-7

ARBOR—EL-101-16-6-F

SPRING—EL-1790-16-1

RA PD 79034

Figure 90 — Elgin Pocket Watch — Mainspring Barrel Assembly
Disassembled

i. **Replace Balance and Balance Cock** (fig. 82). Replace regulator index and secure in place with regulator index screws. Replace regulator assembly, allowing it to snap into place around the balance cock dome. Replace the upper end stone assembly and secure in place with two upper end stone cap assembly screws. Invert the balance cock and loosen the hairspring stud screw. Grasp balance

115

ORDNANCE MAINTENANCE — WRIST WATCHES, POCKET WATCHES, STOP WATCHES, AND CLOCKS

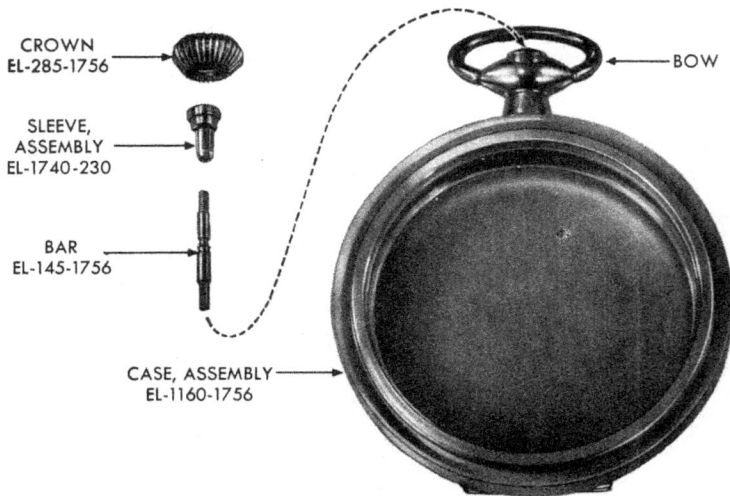

CROWN
EL-285-1756

SLEEVE,
ASSEMBLY
EL-1740-230

BAR
EL-145-1756

CASE, ASSEMBLY
EL-1160-1756

BOW

RA PD 78878

*Figure 91 — Elgin Pocket Watch — Crown, Sleeve, and Bar
Removed From Case*

wheel assembly with tweezers and insert hairspring stud in hole in
balance cock, allowing the overcoil of the hairspring to be placed between the regulator pins simultaneously. Secure hairspring stud
screw. Grasp balance cock assembly with tweezers and invert carefully in order not to distort the hairspring. Place balance under center wheel, engaging roller jewel pin in slot of pallet fork, and cautiously
set balance cock in place. Before securing balance cock, set balance
wheel vibrating and slowly tighten cock screw. If balance wheel
slows down or binds, balance cock is not seating properly or balance
pivots are not in proper place. Replace balance cock screw. Never
force balance assembly in place; if roller jewel pin is engaged in slot
of fork, balance wheel sets in its place freely.

j. **Replace Cannon Pinion** (fig. 81). Replace cannon pinion.

k. **Replace Hour Wheel** (fig. 80). Place movement on movement block, dial side up. Replace hour wheel with tweezers, engaging teeth with the minute wheel pinion.

l. **Replace Dial** (fig. 79). Back dial foot screws out three
turns and replace dial. Secure it by tightening dial foot screws.

m. **Replace Stem Sleeve and Crown** (figs. 91 and 92). Replace stem in sleeve, placing threaded end of stem through sleeve
from the end of the leaves. Replace sleeve in pendant of case band,
set with sleeve wrench, and check it for proper length. Grasp the

ELGIN POCKET WATCH, 16 SIZE, 7- OR 17-JEWEL

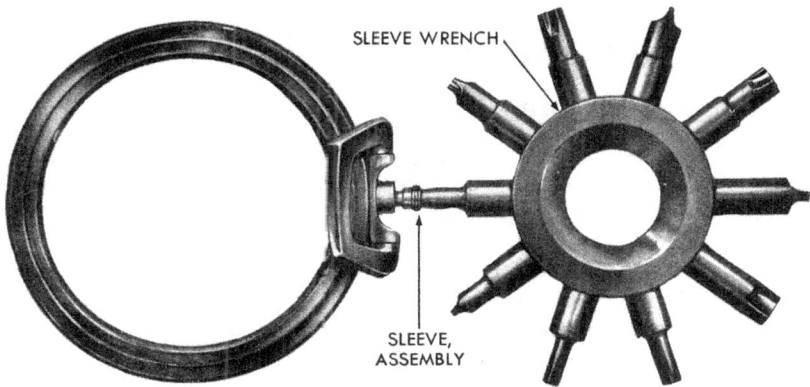

RA PD 78950

Figure 92 — Removing Stem and Sleeve With Sleeve Wrench

square end of stem with smooth portion of flat-nosed pliers and screw on crown.

n. Replace Movement in Case (fig. 54). Pull stem out of setting position. Grasp case band by pendant with the dial side up; hold movement in a tilted position as the stem enters the winding arbor and lower movement into case band, being careful not to hook balance wheel on case band as it is seated in place.

o. Replace Case Screws (fig. 77). Replace two case screws and secure. Before tightening the case screws, see that the movement is centered in the case and that no binding exists in the stem.

p. Replace Hands (fig. 75). Replace second hand. Replace hour hand with the point at the twelfth hour and replace minute hand in the same manner. Check hands for clearance at the dial and make sure they do not hook on each other when turned through a complete revolution.

q. Close Case Backs (fig. 76). Close both back covers by pressing until they snap shut.

r. Replace Bezel (fig. 74). Replace bezel on case band and snap it closed.

s. Replace Shock Absorber (fig. 47). Place crown through hole in shock absorber and slip it over the watch. Attach the leather thong.

Section IV

WALTHAM POCKET WATCH, 9- OR 17-JEWEL

52. IDENTIFICATION.

a. **Waltham Pocket Watches.** There are two models used, the 9-jewel and 17-jewel. Both watches are 16 size, mounted in open-faced screw back and bezel type case, with a short pendant. The ordnance markings on the exterior back of the case are "OA" for the 9-jewel, and "OC" for the 17-jewel. The dials on both watches have the manufacturer's name and the number of jewels indicated just below the twelfth-hour graduation. The dials are white porcelain with the hour graduations outlined in black and filled with radium luminous material. The hour and minute hands are also coated with radium luminous material, making it possible to tell time in the dark. Both watches are stem wound and stem set.

53. DISASSEMBLY OF THE WALTHAM POCKET WATCH, 16 SIZE, 9- OR 17-JEWEL.

a. **Remove Rubber Shock Absorber** (fig. 47). Remove rubber shock absorber by slipping it off the watch and sliding it along the leather thong.

b. **Remove Bezel** (fig. 94). Remove bezel by unscrewing it counterclockwise.

c. **Remove Hands** (fig. 95). Cut a V-slot in a piece of paper and slide it under the hands to protect the dial. Remove hands with hand remover.

d. **Remove Back Covers** (fig. 96). Remove back cover by unscrewing it counterclockwise. Insert a case opener under slot of dust cover and pry it off.

e. **Release Unused Power of Mainspring** (fig. 52). Release unused power of mainspring by holding crown with thumb and index finger. Disengage click with a small screwdriver and allow the crown to turn slowly between the fingers, releasing power of the mainspring.

f. **Remove Case Screws** (fig. 97). Place the watch on a movement block of the proper size, train side up, and remove the two case screws.

g. **Remove Movement From Case Band Assembly** (fig. 98). Pull stem out to setting position. Hold case band firmly with thumb and finger, train side up, and with the middle finger of the left hand on the contour of the case, push the movement down with the left index finger and pull the movement away from the case in a tilted

WALTHAM POCKET WATCH, 9- OR 17-JEWEL

WATCH, POCKET, WALTHAM
(9 JEWEL—16 SIZE)
1609-MOVEMENT

WATCH, POCKET, WALTHAM
(17 JEWEL—16 SIZE)
1617-MOVEMENT

FRONT   FRONT

BACK   BACK

WALTHAM—9 JEWEL   WALTHAM—17 JEWEL

RA PD 78918

*Figure 93 — Waltham Pocket Watches, 9- and 17-jewel, 16 Size —
Front and Back*

119

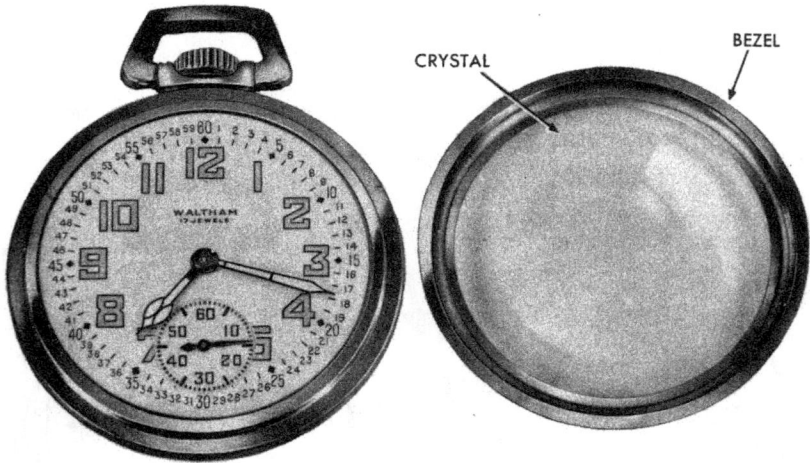

RA PD 78888

Figure 94 — Waltham Pocket Watch — Bezel Removed

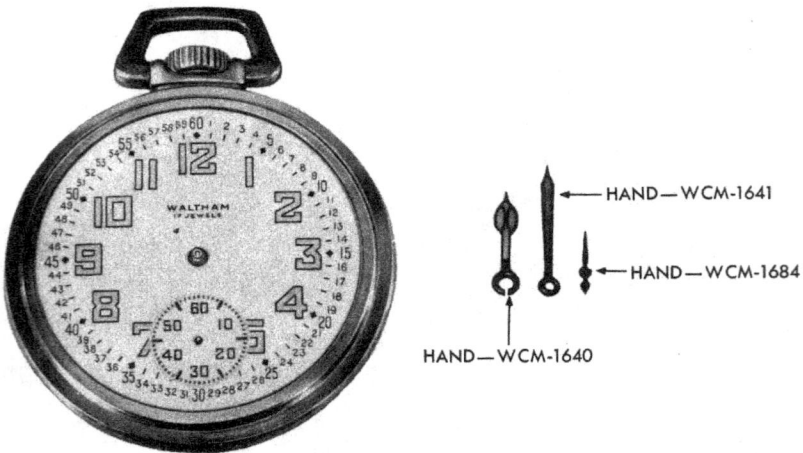

RA PD 78899

Figure 95 — Waltham Pocket Watch — Hands Removed

position. Make sure that the balance wheel does not hook on case band.

h. Remove Dial (fig. 99). Back out dial foot screws two turns from contour of pillar plate and remove dial. Screw dial foot screws back into position to prevent their being lost.

WALTHAM POCKET WATCH, 9- OR 17-JEWEL

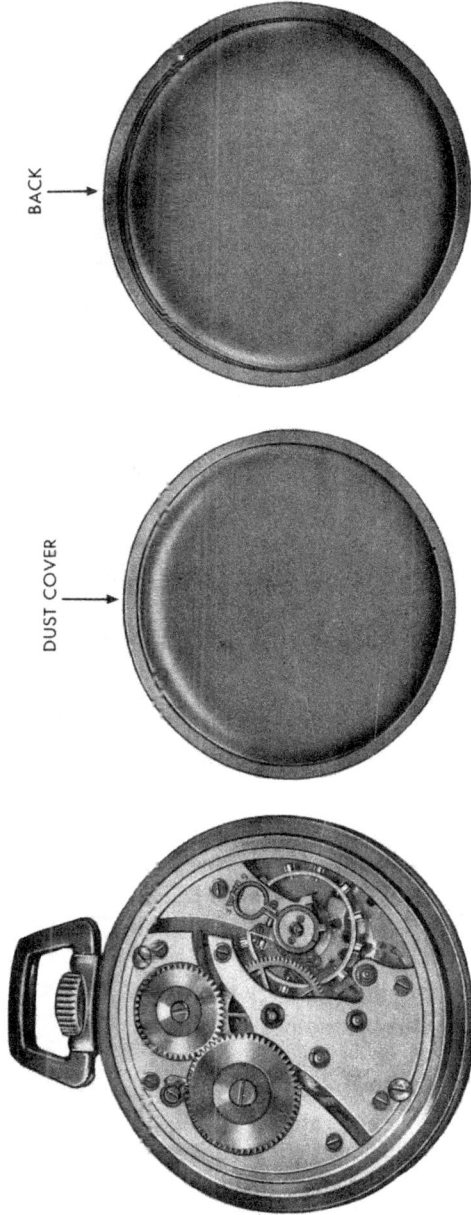

RA PD 78925

BACK →

DUST COVER →

Figure 96 — Waltham Pocket Watch — Back Covers Removed

ORDNANCE MAINTENANCE — WRIST WATCHES, POCKET WATCHES, STOP WATCHES, AND CLOCKS

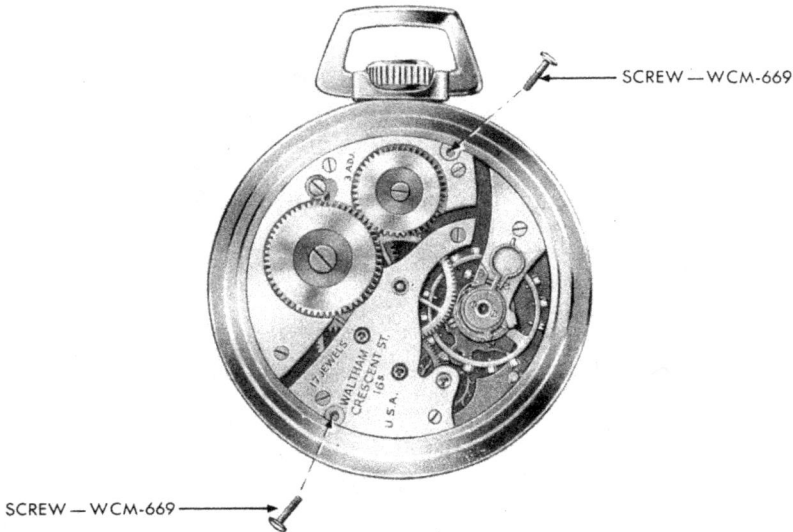

SCREW — WCM-669

SCREW — WCM-669

RA PD 78991

Figure 97 — Waltham Pocket Watch — Case Screws Removed

i. Remove Hour Wheel (fig. 100). Remove hour wheel with tweezers.

j. Remove Cannon Pinion (fig. 101). Remove the cannon pinion with a pin vise. The cannon pinion must be pulled straight upward to prevent bending or breaking the center wheel arbor.

k. Remove Balance Cock and Balance Assembly (fig. 102). Invert movement on movement block, train side up. Loosen hairspring stud screw and free hairspring stud with a small screwdriver. Remove balance cock screw and balance cock. Remove balance assembly with tweezers. Remove balance cock dome screws and remove dome with end stone. Remove regulator assembly.

l. Remove Pallet Bridge and Pallet Assembly (fig. 103). Remove pallet bridge screws and pallet bridge. Remove pallet assembly with tweezers.

m. Remove Ratchet Wheel and Click Assemblies (fig. 104). Remove ratchet wheel screw, ratchet wheel, and disk. Remove ratchet wheel click screw, click, and click spring.

n. Remove Setting Subassembly Including Lower End Stone Assembly (fig. 105). Remove setting wheel cap screw, setting wheel cap, and setting wheel. Remove minute wheel. Remove lower balance end stone cap screw and lower end stone cap assembly.

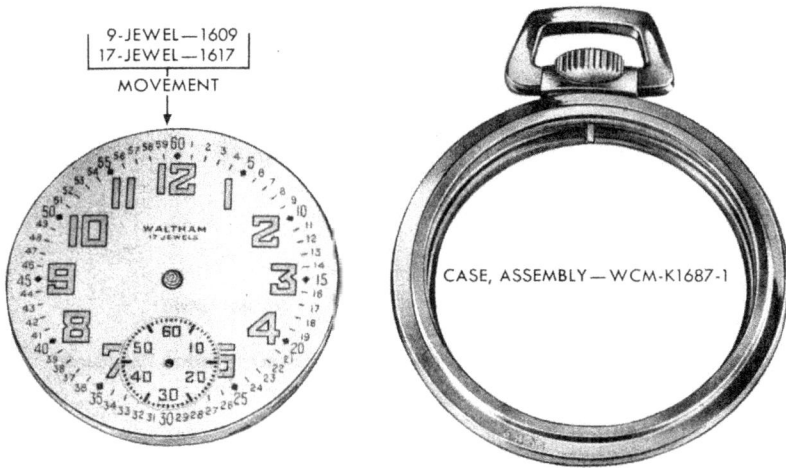

RA PD 78912

Figure 98 — Waltham Pocket Watch — Movement Removed From Case

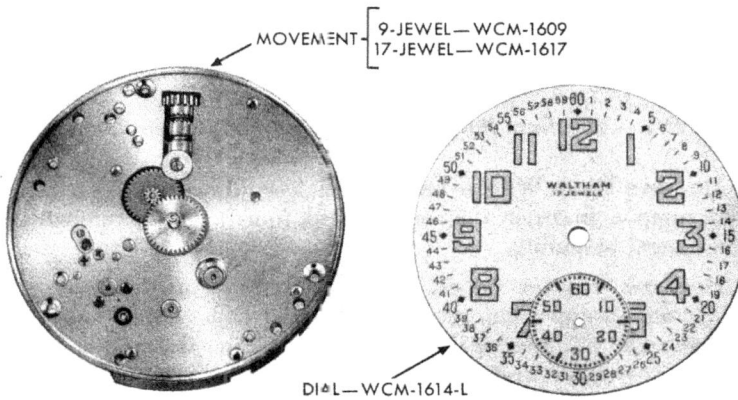

RA PD 78903

Figure 99 — Waltham Pocket Watch — Dial Removed

o. **Remove Bridges** (fig. 106). Remove crown wheel screw, crown wheel disk, stud, and crown wheel. Remove the barrel, and train bridge screws and bridges. If the bridges are tight, loosen by pushing on steady pins from top of pillar plate until space permits insertion of a screwdriver between plate and bridge to pry bridge free.

ORDNANCE MAINTENANCE — WRIST WATCHES, POCKET WATCHES, STOP WATCHES, AND CLOCKS

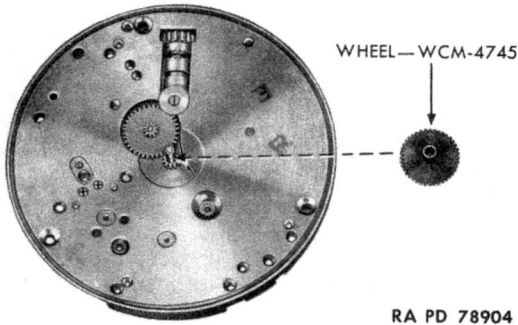

RA PD 78904

Figure 100 — Waltham Pocket Watch — Hour Wheel Removed

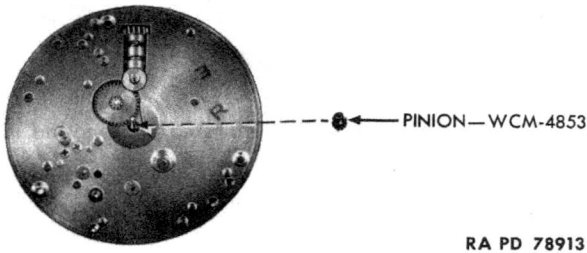

RA PD 78913

Figure 101 — Waltham Pocket Watch — Cannon Pinion Removed

p. **Remove Train Wheels and Barrel Assembly** (fig. 107). Using tweezers remove, in order, the center, third, fourth, and escape wheels. Remove barrel assembly.

q. **Remove Shipper Lever, Shipper Spring, and Shipper** (fig. 108). Remove shipper cap screw and shipper cap. Place end of left index finger over shipper spring to avoid losing it. Grasp one end of spring with tweezers and lift it upward, freeing spring. Remove shipper lever and shipper.

r. **Remove Winding Arbor Assembly** (fig. 109). Remove winding arbor assembly by grasping stem end with tweezers. Lift up and slide winding arbor assembly off pillar plate. Strip assembly by removing winding pinion, clutch, and setting plunger from the winding arbor. Insert tweezers in winding arbor bearing and pry it off pillar plate. This strips the movement down to the pillar plate, leaving only the hole jewel assemblies and the banking screws in place. If a 9-jewel movement, it will leave the bushings of the train wheel pivots in their place.

WALTHAM POCKET WATCH, 9- OR 17-JEWEL

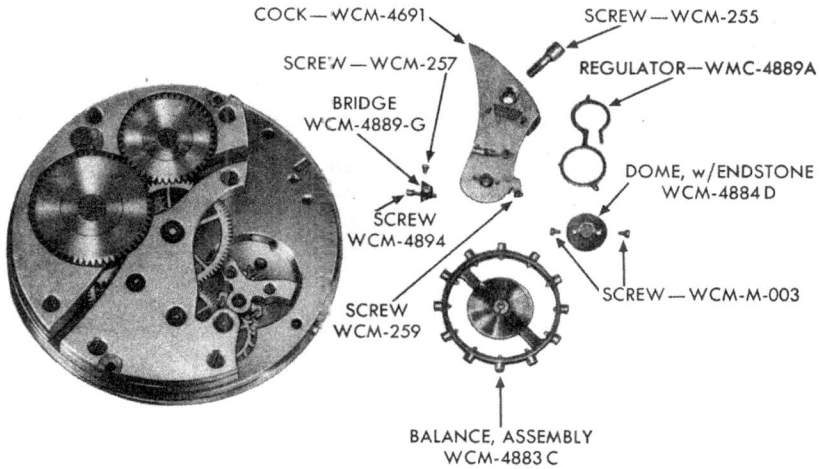

Figure 102 — Waltham Pocket Watch — Balance Cock and Balance Assembly Removed

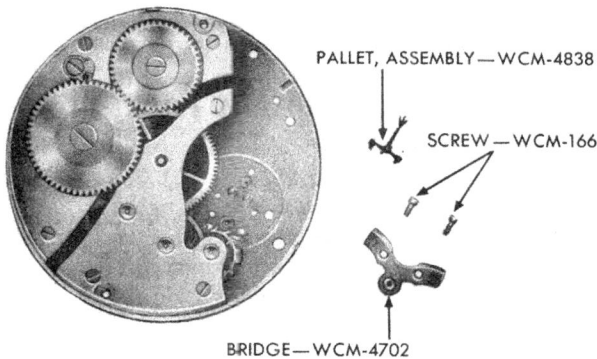

Figure 103 — Waltham Pocket Watch — Pallet Bridge and Pallet Assembly Removed

s. **Remove Mainspring From Barrel** (fig. 110). To disassemble the mainspring barrel assembly, remove the arbor; turn main wheel clockwise to release the hub from mainspring and lift off. Grasp inside coil of mainspring with tweezers and slowly let it uncoil as it comes out of the barrel. Refrain from handling mainspring with bare fingers as much as possible.

t. **Remove Crown, Stem, and Sleeve** (fig. 111). Grasp the square of the winding stem between smooth portion of flat-nosed pliers and

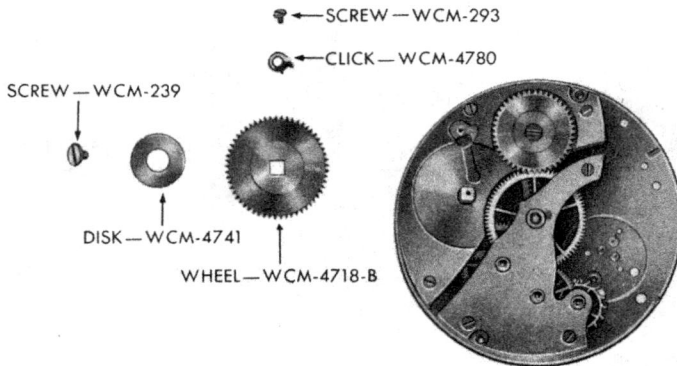

SCREW — WCM-293

CLICK — WCM-4780

SCREW — WCM-239

DISK — WCM-4741

WHEEL — WCM-4718-B

RA PD 79028

Figure 104 — Waltham Pocket Watch — Ratchet Wheel and Click Assemblies Removed

hold it while crown is unscrewed. Insert the proper size sleeve wrench in slots cut in sleeve; unscrew until sleeve is free of pendant. To remove stem from sleeve, hold square of stem firmly and pull sleeve off threaded end.

54. ASSEMBLY OF THE WALTHAM POCKET WATCH, 16 SIZE, 9- OR 17-JEWEL.

a. **Wind in Mainspring** (figs. 68, 69, and 70). Select proper mainspring winder and wind mainspring into it slowly. Insert mainspring winder into barrel, hook end of mainspring on barrel hook, and press plunger which transfers mainspring into barrel. Insert main wheel, hook inner end of mainspring on main wheel hub, replace arbor, and snap it into its square.

b. **Replace Winding Arbor** (fig. 111). Replace winding pinion and winding and setting clutch on the winding arbor. Insert setting plunger in winding arbor from the square end. Insert winding arbor in its proper place in the pillar plate, alining the curvature to conform with the mainspring barrel well in the pillar plate. Insert the winding arbor assembly in place on the pillar plate with the plunger end in the winding arbor bearing.

c. **Replace Shipper Assembly** (fig. 108). Replace shipper and shipper lever in their respective places on the pillar plate. Replace shipper lever spring, hooking one end on the shipper lever; hold it in place with one screwdriver, and spread the spring over the shipper with another screwdriver until it is in position. Replace shipper cap and secure in place with shipper cap screw.

WALTHAM POCKET WATCH, 9- OR 17-JEWEL

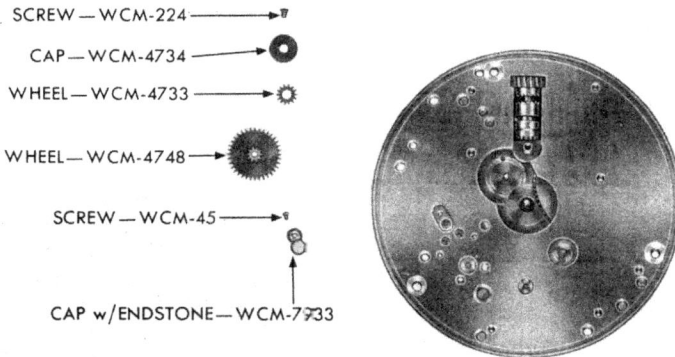

SCREW — WCM-224

CAP — WCM-4734

WHEEL — WCM-4733

WHEEL — WCM-4748

SCREW — WCM-45

CAP w/ENDSTONE — WCM-7733

RA PD 79014

Figure 105 — Waltham Pocket Watch — Setting Subassembly Removed

d. **Replace Train and Barrel Assembly** (fig. 107). Place barrel assembly on the pillar plate. Replace escape, fourth, third, and center wheels.

e. **Replace Bridges** (fig. 106). Replace barrel bridge and secure in place with bridge screws. Replace train bridge, alining train wheel pivots in their respective holes in the train bridge. Secure bridge with bridge screws. Replace crown wheel, crown wheel washer, and crown wheel disk, and secure with crown wheel screw.

f. **Replace Setting Assembly and Lower End Stone Cap Assembly** (fig. 105). Invert movement on movement block, dial side up. Replace setting wheel and setting wheel cap and secure with setting wheel cap screw. Replace lower balance end stone cap assembly and secure in place with cap screws.

g. **Replace Ratchet Wheel and Click Assembly** (fig. 104). Invert movement on movement block, train side up. Replace click and click spring and secure in place with click screw. Replace ratchet wheel, fitting it on the square of the mainspring barrel arbor. Replace ratchet wheel, fitting it on the square of the mainspring barrel arbor. Replace ratchet wheel disk and secure in place with ratchet wheel screw. Check freedom of the train.

h. **Replace Pallet and Pallet Bridge** (fig. 103). Replace pallet assembly. Replace bridge and carefully aline the pallet arbor pivot in its hole. Replace pallet bridge screws and secure. Check freedom of pallet assembly, temporarily installing the movement within the case band and rotating the crown two turns.

i. **Replace Balance and Balance Cock** (fig. 102). Replace balance cock dome with end stone assembly and secure with end stone

ORDNANCE MAINTENANCE — WRIST WATCHES, POCKET WATCHES, STOP WATCHES, AND CLOCKS

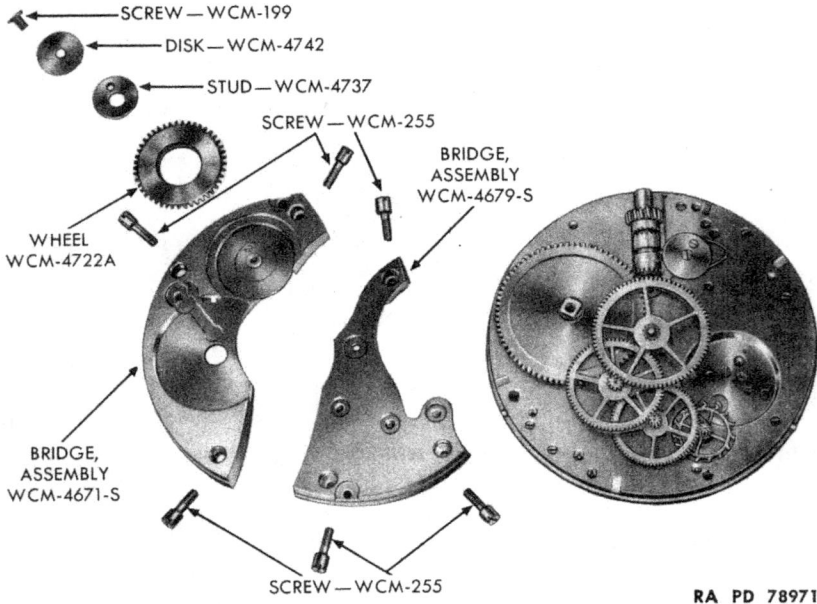

SCREW — WCM-199
DISK — WCM-4742
STUD — WCM-4737
SCREW — WCM-255
BRIDGE, ASSEMBLY WCM-4679-S
WHEEL WCM-4722A
BRIDGE, ASSEMBLY WCM-4671-S
SCREW — WCM-255

RA PD 78971

Figure 106 — Waltham Pocket Watch — Barrel and Train Bridge Assemblies Removed

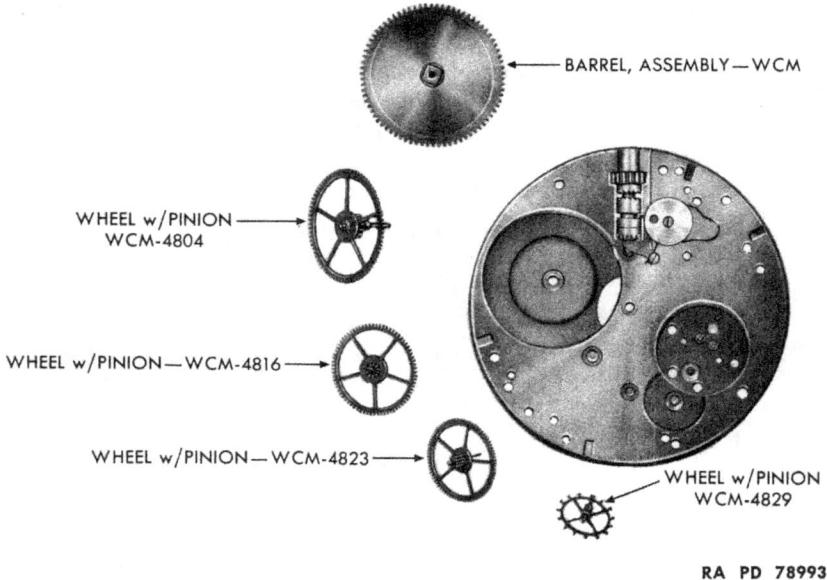

BARREL, ASSEMBLY — WCM
WHEEL w/PINION WCM-4804
WHEEL w/PINION — WCM-4816
WHEEL w/PINION — WCM-4823
WHEEL w/PINION WCM-4829

RA PD 78993

Figure 107 — Waltham Pocket Watch — Train Wheels and Barrel Assembly Removed

WALTHAM POCKET WATCH, 9- OR 17-JEWEL

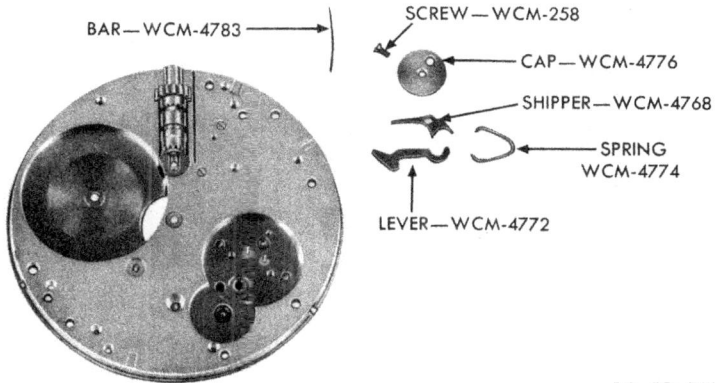

RA PD 78905

*Figure 108 — Waltham Pocket Watch — Winding and Setting
Assembly Removed*

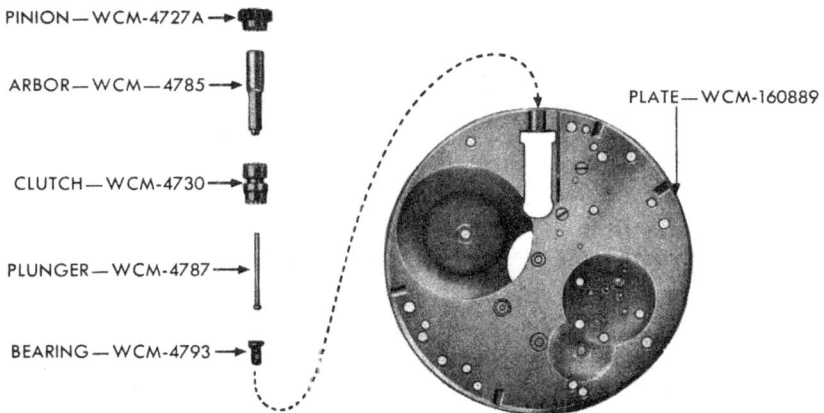

RA PD 79040

*Figure 109 — Waltham Pocket Watch — Winding Arbor Assembly
Removed*

cap screws. Replace regulator assembly, allowing it to snap in place
around the balance cock dome. Invert balance cock and loosen hairspring stud screw. Grasp balance wheel assembly with tweezers and
insert hairspring stud in place in balance cock, which allows the overcoil of the hairspring to be placed between the regulator pins simultaneously. Secure hairspring. Grasp balance assembly with tweezers
and invert carefully in order not to distort the hairspring. Place balance wheel under center and engage roller jewel pin in slot in pallet
fork. Cautiously set balance cock in place; before securing balance
cock, set balance wheel vibrating and slowly tighten cock screw. If

129

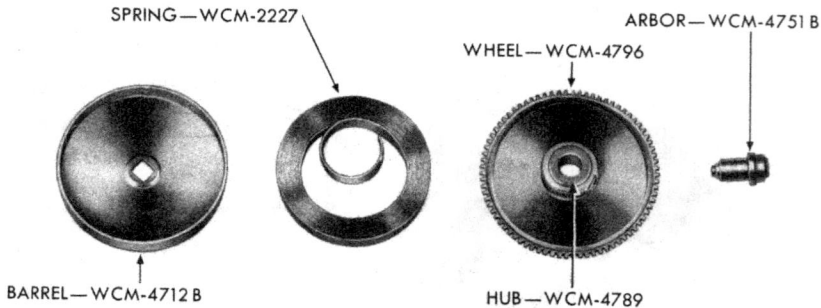

SPRING—WCM-2227

WHEEL—WCM-4796

ARBOR—WCM-4751 B

BARREL—WCM-4712 B

HUB—WCM-4789

RA PD 78917

Figure 110 — Waltham Pocket Watch — Mainspring Barrel Assembly
Disassembled

balance wheel slows down or binds, balance cock is not seating properly or balance pivots are not in proper place.   Never force balance assembly in place; if roller jewel pin is engaged in slot of fork, balance wheel will set in its place freely.

j.   Replace Cannon Pinion (fig. 101).   Replace cannon pinion.

k.   Replace Hour Wheel (fig. 100).   Replace hour wheel with tweezers.

l.   Replace Dial (fig. 99).   Back dial foot screws out three turns, replace dial, and aline it.   Tighten dial foot screws.

m.   Replace Stem Sleeve and Crown (fig. 111).   Replace bar in sleeve, placing threaded end of bar through sleeve from the end of the leaves.   Replace bar in pendant of case band and set with sleeve wrench.   Check bar for proper length.   Grasp the square end of stem with smooth portion of flat-nosed pliers and screw on crown.

n.   Replace Movement in Case Band (fig. 54).   Pull stem out to setting position.   Grasp case band by pendant with dial side up; hold movement in a tilted position as the stem enters the winding arbor and lower movement into case band, being careful not to hook balance wheel on case band as it is seated in place.

o.   Replace Case Screws (fig. 97).   Replace two case screws and secure.   Before tightening case screws, make sure that movement is centered in case and stem does not bind.

p.   Replace Hands (fig. 95).   Replace seconds hand.   Replace hour hand with the point at the twelfth hour and replace minute hand in the same position.   Check hands for clearance at the dial and make sure they do not hook each other when turned through one complete revolution.

HAMILTON WRIST WATCH, 6/0 SIZE, 17-JEWEL, MODEL 987A

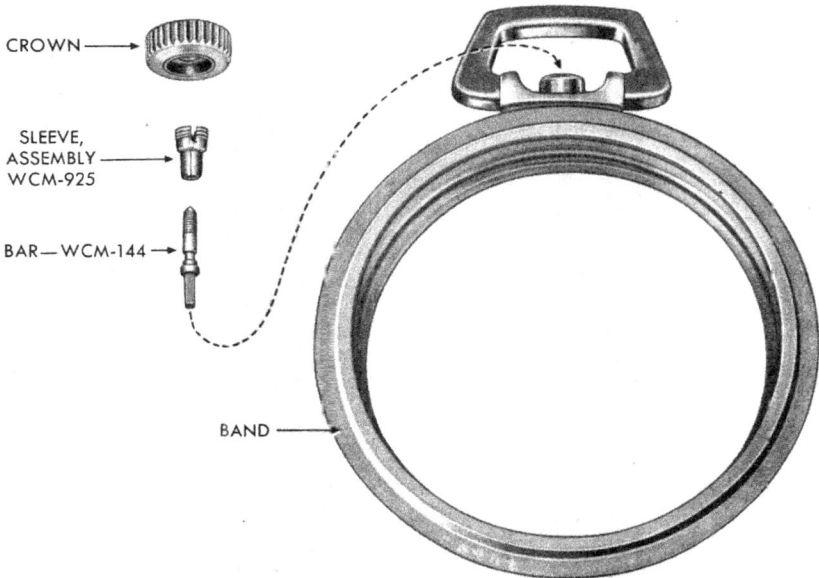

RA PD 78876

*Figure 111 — Waltham Pocket Watch — Crown, Sleeve, and Bar
Removed From Case Band Assembly*

q. **Replace Case Back** (fig. 96). Replace dust cover by snapping it into place, and replace back by screwing it into place.

r. **Replace Bezel** (fig. 94). Replace bezel and screw into place.

s. **Replace Rubber Shock Absorber** (fig. 47). Place crown through hole in shock absorber and slip it over the watch. Attach the leather thong.

Section V

HAMILTON WRIST WATCH, 6/0 SIZE, 17-JEWEL, MODEL 987A

55. IDENTIFICATION.

a. **Hamilton Wrist Watch.** There is one Hamilton wrist watch issued, the model 987A, 6/0 size, 17-jewel. This movement was originally issued in a cup-type case but is now issued in the waterproof type. The removal of the movement from the case covered in this section will deal only with the cup type. The ordnance marking on the exterior back of the case has the prefix "OD" before the serial

131

ORDNANCE MAINTENANCE — WRIST WATCHES, POCKET WATCHES, STOP WATCHES, AND CLOCKS

RA PD 78880

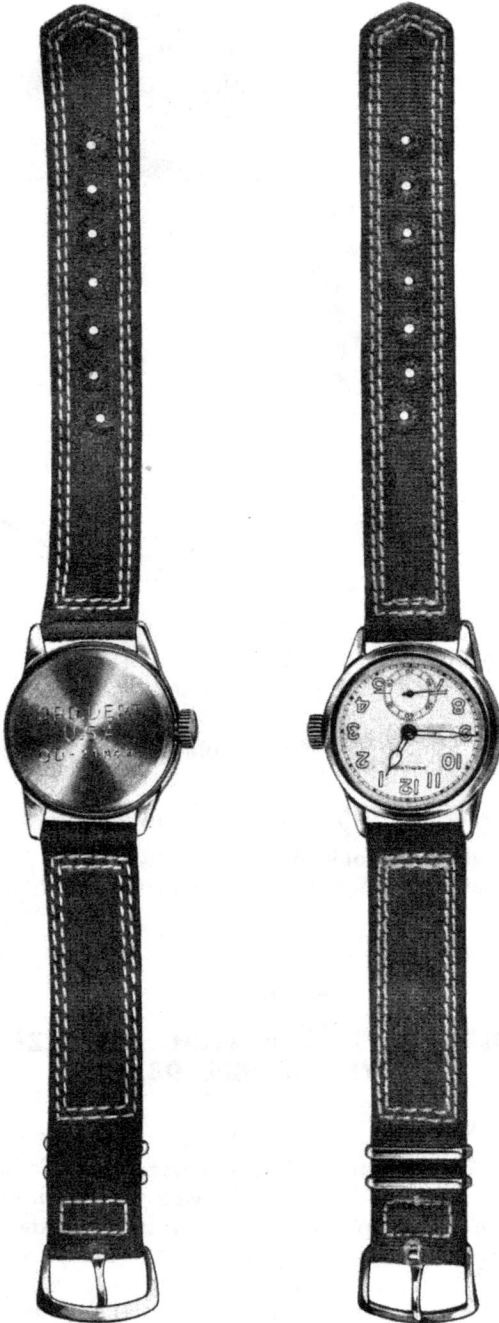

Figure 112 — Hamilton Wrist Watch, 17-jewel, 6/0 Size — Front and Back

HAMILTON WRIST WATCH, 6/0 SIZE, 17-JEWEL, MODEL 987A

Figure 113 — Hamilton Wrist Watch — Bezel Removed

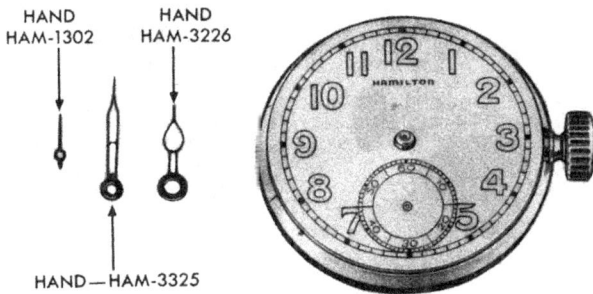

Figure 114 — Hamilton Wrist Watch — Hands Removed

number. The hour dial is graduated in minutes; and arabic numerals indicate the hours. The second dial orbit is graduated in seconds, with 10-second divisions indicated by numerals. The hour numerals and hour and minute hands are coated with radium luminous material for night use. The second hand is of blued steel.

56. DISASSEMBLE HAMILTON WRIST WATCH, 6/0 SIZE, 17-JEWEL, MODEL 987A.

a. **Remove Bezel** (fig. 113). Insert case opener in slot in bottom portion of case and pry off bezel.

b. **Remove Hands** (fig. 114). Cut a V-slot in a piece of paper and slide it under the hands to protect the dial. Remove hands with hand remover.

RA PD 78906

Figure 115 — Hamilton Wrist Watch — Movement Removed From Case

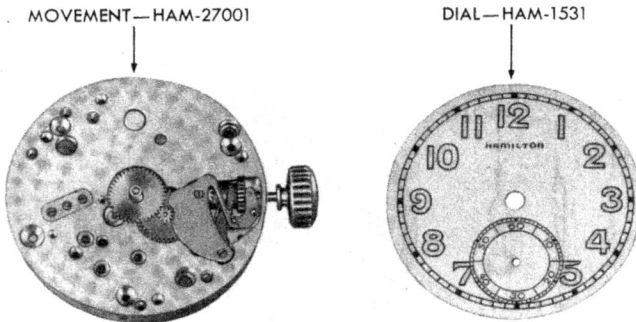

RA PD 79029

Figure 116 — Hamilton Wrist Watch — Dial Removed

c. **Remove Movement From Case** (fig. 115). Place edge of case opener under flange of movement and pry it loose at two sides. Remove movement, being careful not to hook balance wheel on case.

d. **Release Unused Power of Mainspring** (fig. 52). Release unused power of mainspring by holding crown with thumb and index finger. Disengage click with a small screwdriver and allow the crown to turn slowly between the fingers, releasing power of the mainspring.

e. **Remove Dial** (fig. 116). Back out dial foot screws two turns from contour of pillar plate and remove dial. Screw dial foot screws back into position to avoid losing them.

f. **Remove Hour Wheel** (fig. 117). Remove hour wheel with tweezers.

g. **Remove Balance Cock and Balance Assembly** (fig. 118). Invert movement on movement block, train side up. Loosen hairspring

HAMILTON WRIST WATCH, 6/0 SIZE, 17-JEWEL, MODEL 987A

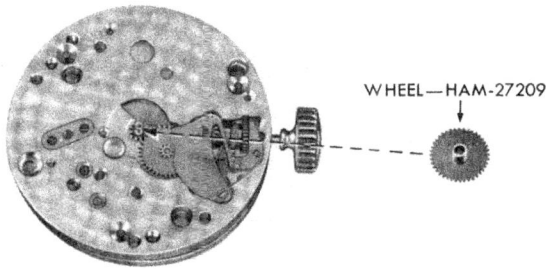

WHEEL—HAM-27209

RA PD 78951

Figure 117 — Hamilton Wrist Watch — Hour Wheel Removed

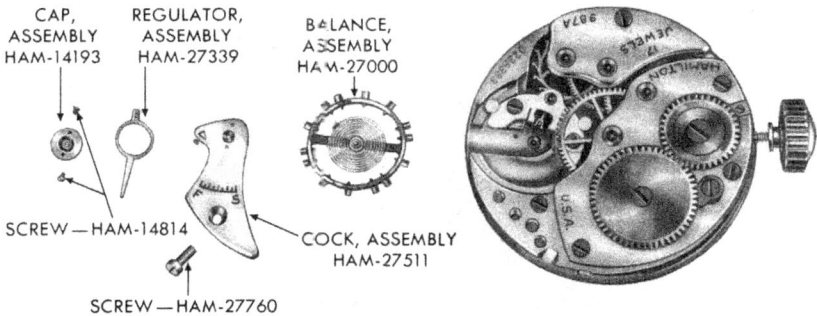

CAP,
ASSEMBLY
HAM-14193

REGULATOR,
ASSEMBLY
HAM-27339

BALANCE,
ASSEMBLY
HAM-27000

SCREW—HAM-14814

COCK, ASSEMBLY
HAM-27511

SCREW—HAM-27760

RA PD 79050

Figure 118 — Hamilton Wrist Watch — Balance Cock and Balance Assembly Removed

stud screw with a small screwdriver and free stud from balance cock. Remove balance cock screw and balance cock. If balance cock is tight, insert a screwdriver in slot underneath cock and pry it loose. Remove balance assembly with tweezers, securing stud screw to prevent its being lost. Invert balance cock on bench and remove upper balance end stone cap assembly screws; this permits removal of end stone cap assembly setting and regulator assembly.

h. **Remove Pallet Bridge and Pallet Assembly** (fig. 119). Remove pallet bridge screws and pallet bridge assembly. Grasp pallet assembly with tweezers and lift it out of movement.

i. **Remove Setting Cap Spring** (fig. 120). Invert movement on movement block and remove setting cap spring screw and setting cap spring.

j. **Remove Setting Mechanism and Lower End Stone Cap Assembly** (fig. 121). Remove minute and setting wheels. Remove

ORDNANCE MAINTENANCE — WRIST WATCHES, POCKET WATCHES, STOP WATCHES, AND CLOCKS

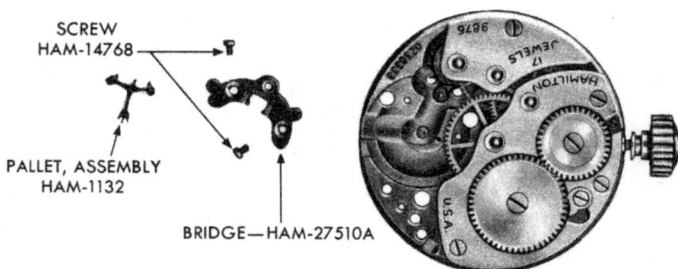

Figure 119 — Hamilton Wrist Watch — Pallet Bridge and Pallet Assembly Removed

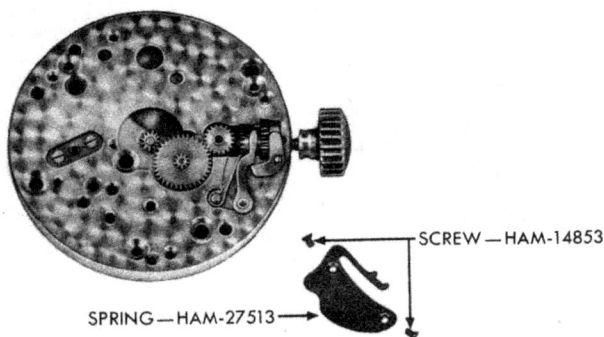

Figure 120 — Hamilton Wrist Watch — Setting Cap Spring Removed

clutch lever spring by placing the end of index finger over the clutch spring and stud to prevent it from being lost and then removing the clutch lever spring with tweezers. Remove the clutch lever. Place index finger on setting lever, invert movement, and unscrew setting lever screw until setting lever is released. Invert movement and remove setting lever. Pull out stem and crown; remove winding pinion and winding and setting clutch. Remove cannon pinion (fig. 121). Remove lower end stone balance assembly cap screws and lower end stone cap assembly.

   k. Remove Winding Wheels and Click Assembly (fig. 122). Remove winding wheel screw by turning clockwise. Remove winding wheel hub and winding wheel. Remove ratchet wheel screw and ratchet wheel. Remove click screw, click, and click spring. Note how the click spring is inserted in the recess of the click for reference in replacement.

HAMILTON WRIST WATCH, 6/0 SIZE, 17-JEWEL, MODEL 987A

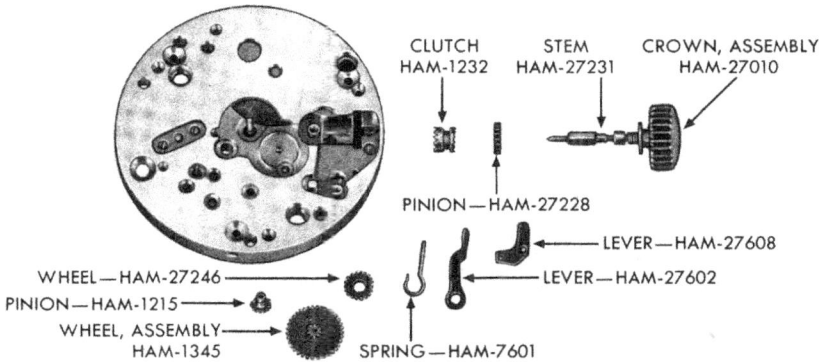

Figure 121 — Hamilton Wrist Watch — Setting Mechanism Removed

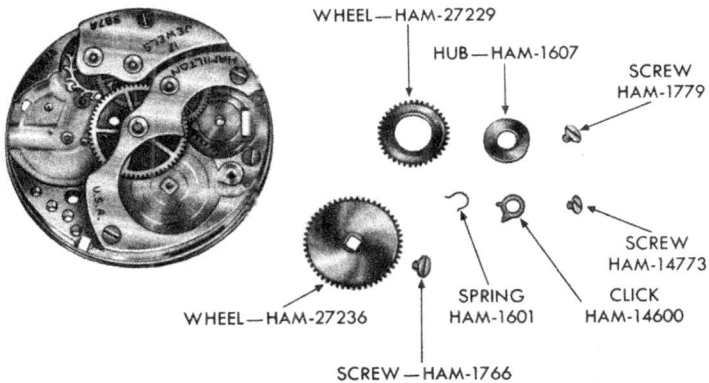

Figure 122 — Hamilton Wrist Watch — Winding Wheel and Click Assembly Removed

l. **Remove Bridges** (fig. 123). Remove barrel and train bridge assembly screws; then remove bridge assemblies. If the bridges are tight, insert a screwdriver in the slots provided in the pillar plate and pry loose.

m. **Remove Train Wheels and Barrel** (fig. 124). Remove center, third, fourth, and escape wheels. Remove barrel assembly.

n. **Remove Setting Lever Screw** (fig. 125). Lift setting lever screw off the pillar plate. This completes the disassembly of the movement, stripping it down to the pillar plate and leaving only the hole jewel assembly settings in place.

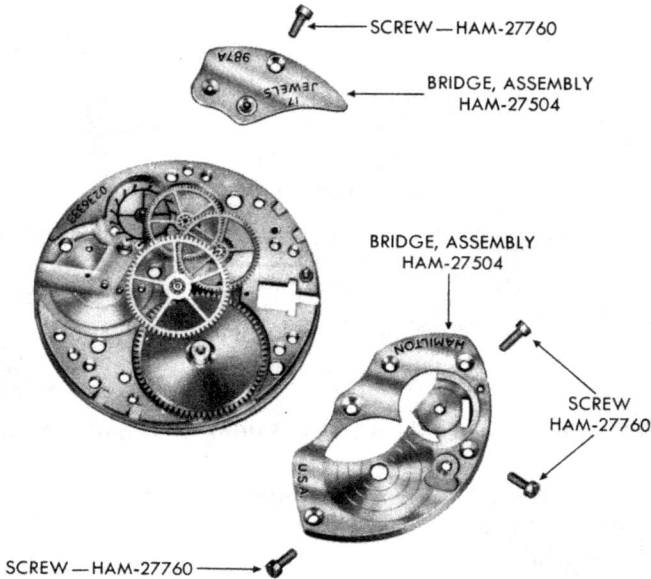

SCREW — HAM-27760

BRIDGE, ASSEMBLY
HAM-27504

BRIDGE, ASSEMBLY
HAM-27504

SCREW
HAM-27760

SCREW — HAM-27760

RA PD 79061

*Figure 123 — Hamilton Wrist Watch — Train and Barrel Bridge
Assemblies Removed*

o. **Remove Mainspring From Barrel** (fig. 71). Hold the main-spring barrel between thumb and index finger while the barrel is sup-ported on the anvil, and place a screwdriver of the proper size within the slot provided in the cap and pry off the cap. Remove barrel arbor, grasp the inside coil of the mainspring with tweezers, and pull it out of the barrel slowly, letting it uncoil as it comes out. Refrain from handling mainspring with bare fingers as much as possible.

57. ASSEMBLY OF THE HAMILTON WRIST WATCH, 6/0 SIZE, 17-JEWEL, MODEL 987A.

a. **Wind in Mainspring** (figs. 68, 69, and 70). Select proper mainspring winder and wind mainspring into it slowly. Insert main-spring winder in barrel, hook end of mainspring on barrel hook, and press plunger which transfers mainspring into barrel. Insert barrel arbor and replace barrel cap, snapping it into its recess.

b. **Replace Setting Lever Screw** (fig. 125). Place pillar plate on proper size movement block and replace setting lever screw in its hole.

HAMILTON WRIST WATCH, 6/0 SIZE, 17-JEWEL, MODEL 987A

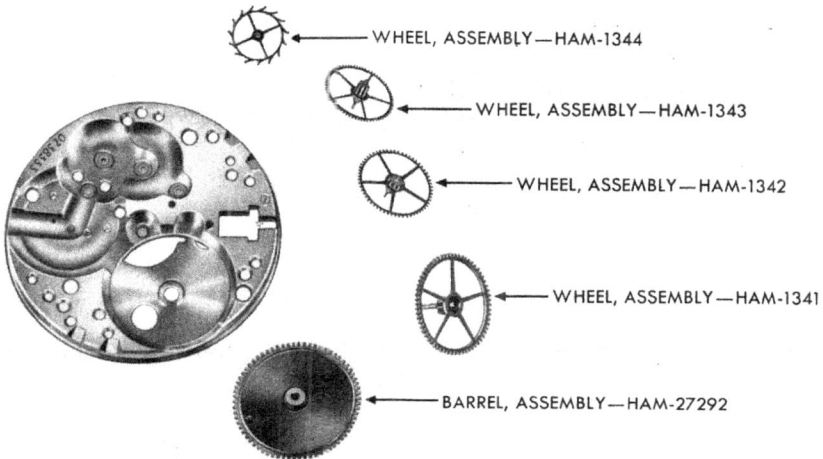

WHEEL, ASSEMBLY—HAM-1344

WHEEL, ASSEMBLY—HAM-1343

WHEEL, ASSEMBLY—HAM-1342

WHEEL, ASSEMBLY—HAM-1341

BARREL, ASSEMBLY—HAM-27292

RA PD 79065

Figure 124 — Hamilton Wrist Watch — Train Wheels and Barrel Assembly Removed

c. **Replace Train Wheels and Barrel Assembly** (fig. 124). Place mainspring barrel assembly on pillar plate. Replace train wheels in order: escape, fourth, third, and center wheels.

d. **Replace Bridges** (fig. 123). Replace the barrel bridge assembly, alining the pivots of the center and third wheels in their respective pivot holes. Secure in place with bridge screws. Replace train bridge assembly, alining the pivots of the fourth and escape wheels in their respective holes. Secure bridge with bridge screws.

e. **Replace Winding Wheels and Click** (fig. 122). Replace winding wheel and winding wheel hub and secure with winding wheel screw. Place click spring in recess in under side of click. Insert both ends of click spring into recess of click and push into position with a screwdriver. Replace click assembly on its stud and secure with click screw. Replace ratchet wheel, fitting it on square of mainspring barrel arbor, and secure with screw.

f. **Replace Setting Mechanism and End Stone Cap Assembly** (fig. 121). Replace lower end stone balance cap assembly and secure with cap screws. Replace winding pinion and winding and setting clutch in their respective places; then insert winding stem, allowing it to pass through the winding pinion and winding and setting clutch. Replace setting lever, placing the larger stud in the recess of the stem and the hole directly over the setting lever screw. Place the index finger of the left hand over the setting lever, holding it in place. Invert movement; turn setting lever screw clockwise, securing setting

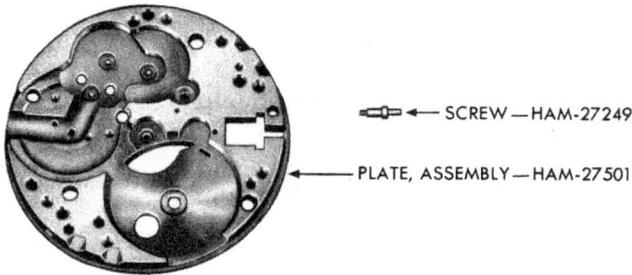

=◁□= ←— SCREW—HAM-27249

◄——————PLATE, ASSEMBLY—HAM-27501

RA PD 79015

*Figure 125 — Hamilton Wrist Watch — Setting Lever Screw Removed
From Pillar Plate*

lever and locking stem into the movement. Replace clutch lever on its stud, inserting end of lever in the recess of the clutch. Place clutch spring around its stud; hold clutch lever spring in position with one screwdriver and pull the long end of the spring back until it falls into place back of the clutch lever. Replace the cannon pinion. Place setting and minute wheels on their respective studs.

g. **Replace Setting Cap Spring** (fig. 120). Replace setting cap spring, positioning the spring end behind setting lever stud. Replace screws and secure. At this point, an examination must be made to check freedom of the train. This is done by turning the crown one full turn and allowing the train to rotate; if wheels of the train backlash on reaching the end of the winding, train has perfect freedom. If they slow down or stop abruptly, a bind exists and must be corrected.

h. **Replace Pallet and Pallet Bridge** (fig. 119). Replace pallet assembly. Replace pallet bridge assembly, carefully alining the pallet arbor pivot in its hole. Secure the pallet bridge with the two pallet bridge screws. Check freedom of pallet assembly; then check the action of pallet assembly and escape wheel.

i. **Replace Balance and Balance Cock** (fig. 118). Place upper end stone cap assembly on bench with polished surface down. Place balance cock inverted on end stone cap assembly. Aline screw holes, replace end stone cap assembly screws, and secure. NOTE: *Upper end stone cap assembly screws have highly polished ends.* Replace regulator assembly, allowing it to snap into place around the end stone cap assembly setting. Invert balance and loosen the hairspring stud screw. Grasp the balance wheel assembly with tweezers and insert hairspring stud in hole in balance cock, allowing the overcoil of the hairspring to be placed between the regulator pins simultaneously. Secure hairspring stud screw. Grasp balance cock assembly

ELGIN WRIST WATCH, 8/0 SIZE, 7- OR 15-JEWEL

with tweezers and invert carefully in order not to distort the hairspring. Place balance under center wheel and engage roller jewel pin in the slot of the pallet fork; then cautiously set balance cock in place. Replace balance cock screw and secure.

j. Replace Hour Wheel (fig. 117). Invert movement on movement block and replace hour wheel.

k. Replace the Dial (fig. 116). Back dial foot screws out three turns and replace dial. Secure by tightening foot screws.

l. Replace Hands (fig. 114). Replace seconds hand. Replace hour hand with the point at the twelfth hour. Replace minute hand in the same position.

m. Replace Movement in Lower Portion of Case (fig. 115). Carefully place movement in lower portion of case with stem over cut-out in case; cautiously push movement until it is seated in its proper position.

n. Replace Bezel (fig. 113). Place bezel on lower portion of case with cut-out over stem and snap into place. Check to make sure movement is centered and stem does not bind.

Section VI

ELGIN WRIST WATCH, 8/0 SIZE, 7- OR 15-JEWEL

58. IDENTIFICATION.

a. Three Elgin models have been issued, all 8/0 size, having 7, 15, and 16 jewels. The 7- and 15-jewel standard watches are the same in construction, the difference being in the number of jewels and the ordnance markings on the exterior back of the case. The 7-jewel watch has the prefix "OD" before the serial number, and the standard 15-jewel has the prefix "OC" before the serial number. The 16-jewel (Hack) type A 11, differs from the standard Elgin wrist watch in that it is equipped with a waterproof case, a sweep second hand, and a black dial. Although they are normally issued to the Air Corps as a navigation watch, some have been issued, however, to ground troops. The ordnance marking on the exterior back of the case has the prefix "OFA" before the serial number. The 7- and 15-jewel watches pictured in figure 126 in cup-type cases are now issued in a waterproof case. The hour dials are graduated in minutes and arabic numerals indicate the hours. The second dial orbits are graduated in seconds, with 10-second divisions indicated by numerals. The hour numerals and the hour, minute, and sweep second hands are coated with a radium luminous material for night use. The second hands are all of blued steel.

RA PD 86949

7 JEWEL

15 JEWEL

Figure 126 — Elgin Wrist Watches — 7- and 15-jewel, 8/0 Size — Front and Back

ELGIN WRIST WATCH, 8/0 SIZE, 7- OR 15-JEWEL

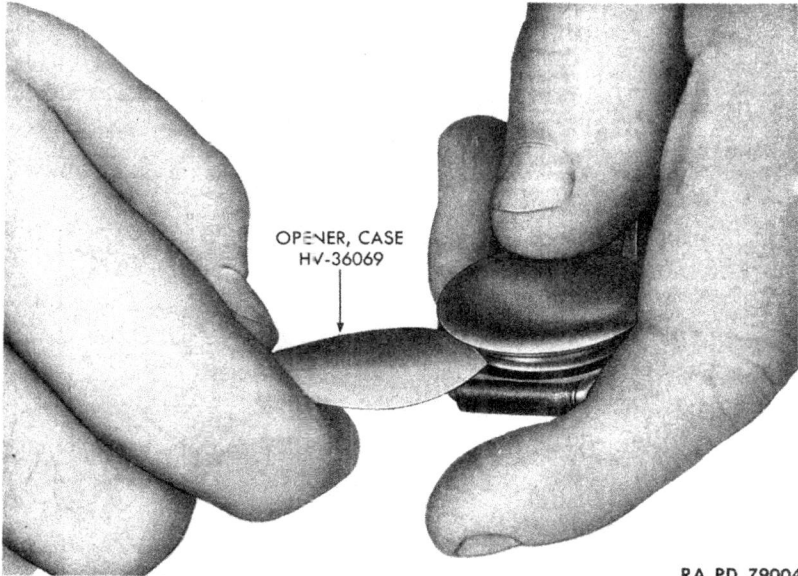

RA PD 79004

Figure 127 — Elgin Wrist Watch — Opening Case With Case Opener

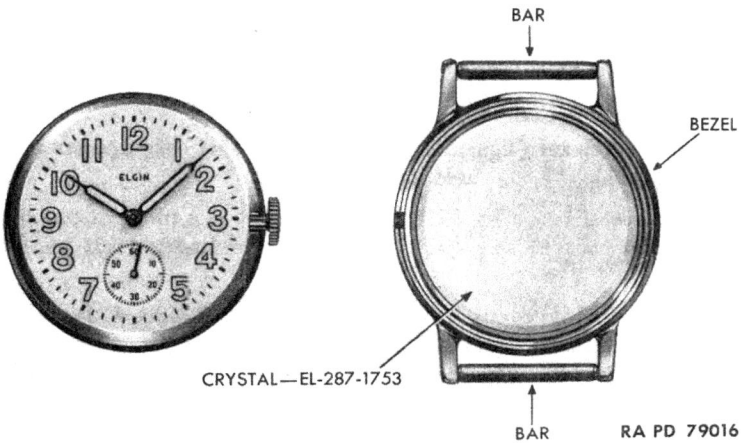

Figure 128 — Elgin Wrist Watch — Bezel Removed

143

HAND—EL-328-692-L

HAND
EL-328-519C

HAND—EL-328-693L

RA PD 79035

Figure 129 — Elgin Wrist Watch — Hands Removed

CASE—EL-1160-1753

RA PD 78907

Figure 130 — Elgin Wrist Watch — Movement Removed From Case

59. DISASSEMBLY OF ELGIN WRIST WATCH, 8/0 SIZE, 7- OR 15-JEWEL.

a. **Remove Bezel** (figs. 127 and 128). Insert case opener in slot in bottom portion of case and pry bezel off.

b. **Remove Hands** (fig. 129). Cut a V-slot in a piece of paper and slide it under hands to protect dial. Remove hands with hand remover.

c. **Remove Movement From Case** (figs. 130 and 131). Place edge of case opener under flange of movement and pry it loose at two sides. Remove movement, being careful not to hook balance wheel on case.

d. **Release Unused Power of Mainspring** (fig. 52). Release unused power of mainspring by holding crown with thumb and index finger. Disengage click with a small screwdriver and allow the crown

ELGIN WRIST WATCH, 8/0 SIZE, 7- OR 15-JEWEL

RA PD 78982

Figure 131 — Elgin Wrist Watch — Removing Movement From Case

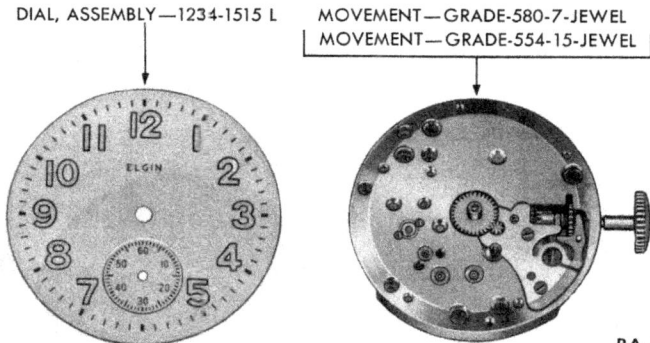

DIAL, ASSEMBLY—1234-1515 L

MOVEMENT—GRADE-580-7-JEWEL
MOVEMENT—GRADE-554-15-JEWEL

RA PD 79017

Figure 132 — Elgin Wrist Watch — Dial Removed

to turn slowly between the fingers, releasing power of mainspring.

e. **Remove Dial** (fig. 132). Back out dial foot screws two turns from contour of pillar plate and remove dial. Screw dial foot screws back into position.

ORDNANCE MAINTENANCE — WRIST WATCHES, POCKET WATCHES, STOP WATCHES, AND CLOCKS

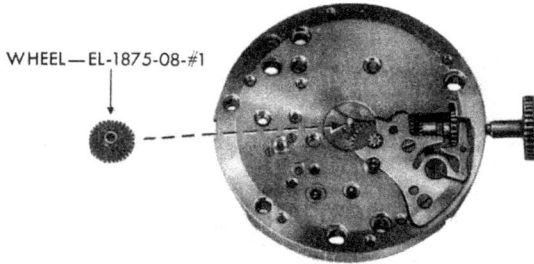

WHEEL — EL-1875-08-#1

RA PD 79051

Figure 133 — Elgin Wrist Watch — Hour Wheel Removed

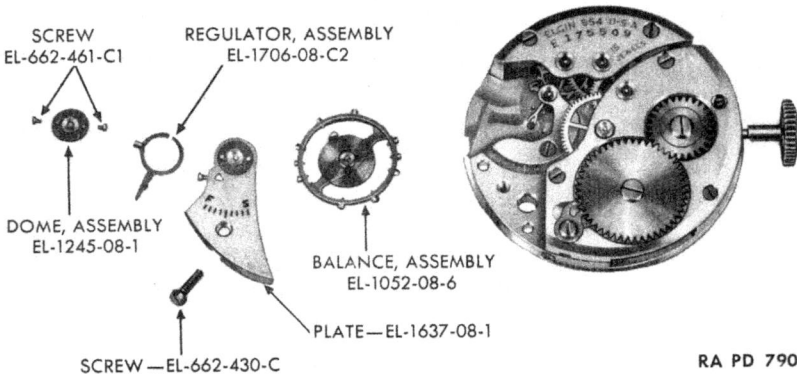

SCREW
EL-662-461-C1

REGULATOR, ASSEMBLY
EL-1706-08-C2

DOME, ASSEMBLY
EL-1245-08-1

BALANCE, ASSEMBLY
EL-1052-08-6

SCREW — EL-662-430-C

PLATE — EL-1637-08-1

RA PD 79036

*Figure 134 — Elgin Wrist Watch — Balance Cock and Balance
Assembly Removed*

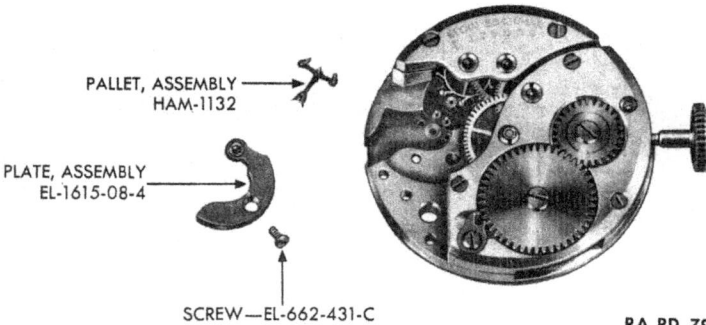

PALLET, ASSEMBLY
HAM-1132

PLATE, ASSEMBLY
EL-1615-08-4

SCREW — EL-662-431-C

RA PD 79018

*Figure 135 — Elgin Wrist Watch — Pallet Bridge and Pallet
Assembly Removed*

ELGIN WRIST WATCH, 8/0 SIZE, 7- OR 15-JEWEL

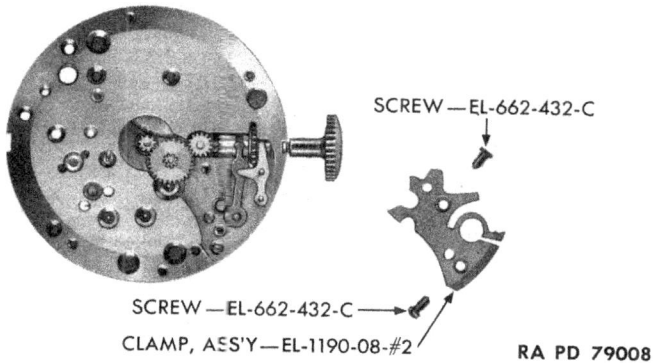

SCREW—EL-662-432-C

SCREW—EL-662-432-C

CLAMP, ASS'Y—EL-1190-08-#2

RA PD 79008

Figure 136 — Elgin Wrist Watch — Minute Wheel Clamp Assembly Removed

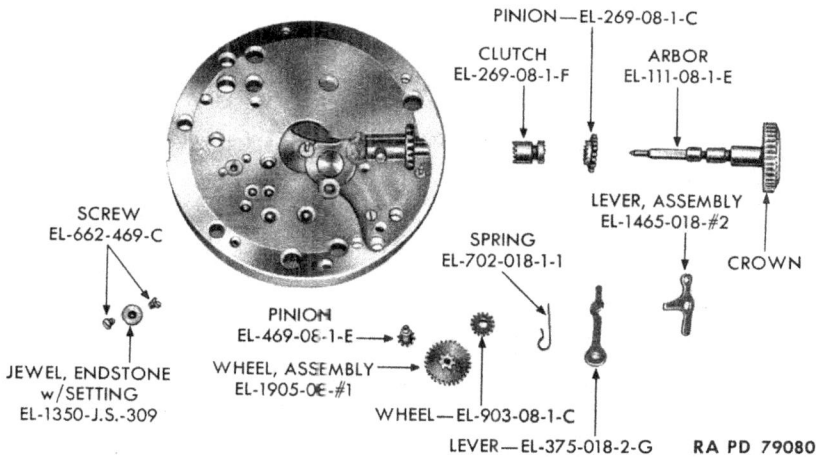

PINION—EL-269-08-1-C

CLUTCH
EL-269-08-1-F

ARBOR
EL-111-08-1-E

SCREW
EL-662-469-C

LEVER, ASSEMBLY
EL-1465-018-#2

SPRING
EL-702-018-1-1

CROWN

PINION
EL-469-08-1-E

JEWEL, ENDSTONE
w/SETTING
EL-1350-J.S.-309

WHEEL, ASSEMBLY
EL-1905-0E-#1

WHEEL—EL-903-08-1-C

LEVER—EL-375-018-2-G

RA PD 79080

Figure 137 — Elgin Wrist Watch — Setting Mechanism Removed

f.   **Remove Hour Wheel** (fig. 133).   Remove hour wheel with tweezers.

g.   **Remove Balance Cock and Balance Assembly and Disassemble** (fig. 134).   Invert movement on movement block, train side up. Loosen hairspring stud screw with a small screwdriver and free stud from balance cock.   Remove balance cock screw and balance cock. If balance cock is tight, insert a screwdriver in slot underneath cock and pry it loose.   Secure stud screw to prevent its being lost.   Re-

ORDNANCE MAINTENANCE — WRIST WATCHES, POCKET WATCHES, STOP WATCHES, AND CLOCKS

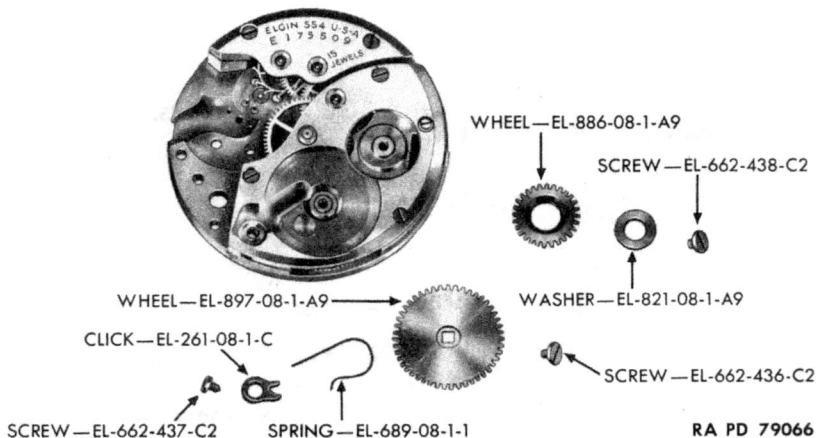

WHEEL—EL-886-08-1-A9

SCREW—EL-662-438-C2

WHEEL—EL-897-08-1-A9

WASHER—EL-821-08-1-A9

CLICK—EL-261-08-1-C

SCREW—EL-662-436-C2

SCREW—EL-662-437-C2   SPRING—EL-689-08-1-1

RA PD 79066

Figure 138 — Elgin Wrist Watch — Winding Wheels and Click Assembly Removed

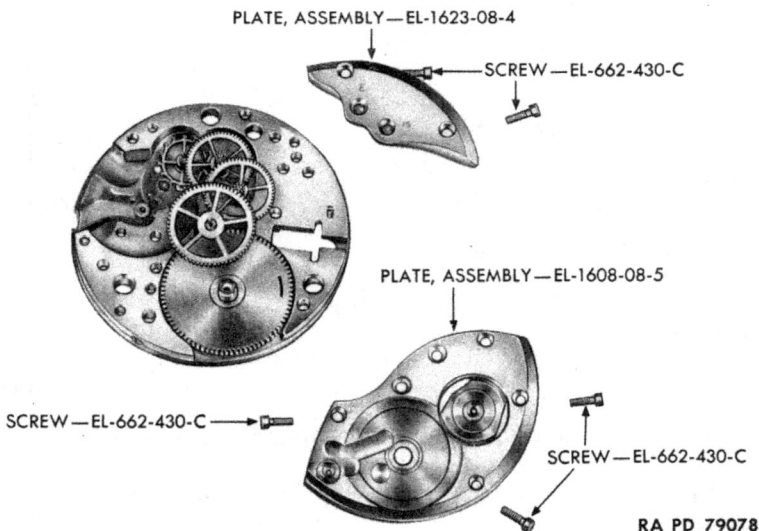

PLATE, ASSEMBLY—EL-1623-08-4

SCREW—EL-662-430-C

PLATE, ASSEMBLY—EL-1608-08-5

SCREW—EL-662-430-C

SCREW—EL-662-430-C

RA PD 79078

Figure 139 — Elgin Wrist Watch — Train and Barrel Plate Assemblies Removed

move balance assembly with tweezers. Invert balance cock on bench and remove upper balance end stone cap assembly screws; this permits removal of end stone cap assembly setting and regulator assembly.

ELGIN WRIST WATCH, 8/0 SIZE, 7- OR 15-JEWEL

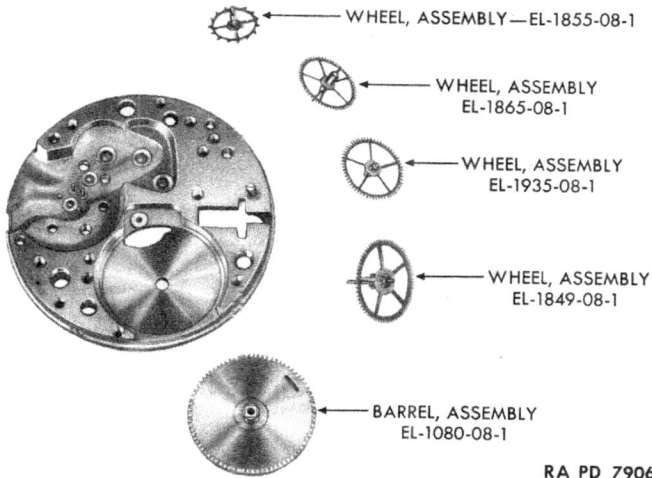

WHEEL, ASSEMBLY—EL-1855-08-1

WHEEL, ASSEMBLY
EL-1865-08-1

WHEEL, ASSEMBLY
EL-1935-08-1

WHEEL, ASSEMBLY
EL-1849-08-1

BARREL, ASSEMBLY
EL-1080-08-1

RA PD 79069

*Figure 140 — Elgin Wrist Watch — Train Wheels and Barrel
Assembly Removed*

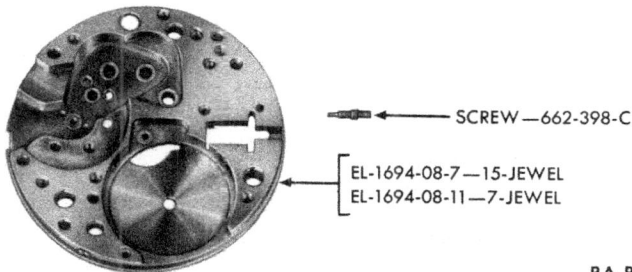

SCREW —662-398-C

EL-1694-08-7 — 15-JEWEL
EL-1694-08-11 — 7-JEWEL

RA PD 79031

*Figure 141 — Elgin Wrist Watch — Pillar Plate and Setting
Lever Screw Removed*

h. Remove Pallet Bridge and Pallet Assembly (fig. 135). Remove pallet bridge screws and pallet bridge. Remove pallet with tweezers.

i. Remove Minute Wheel Clamp (fig. 136). Remove minute wheel clamp screws and minute wheel clamp.

j. Remove Setting Mechanism and Lower End Stone Cap Assembly (fig. 137). Remove minute and setting wheels. Remove clutch lever spring by placing end of index finger over clutch spring

ORDNANCE MAINTENANCE — WRIST WATCHES, POCKET WATCHES, STOP WATCHES, AND CLOCKS

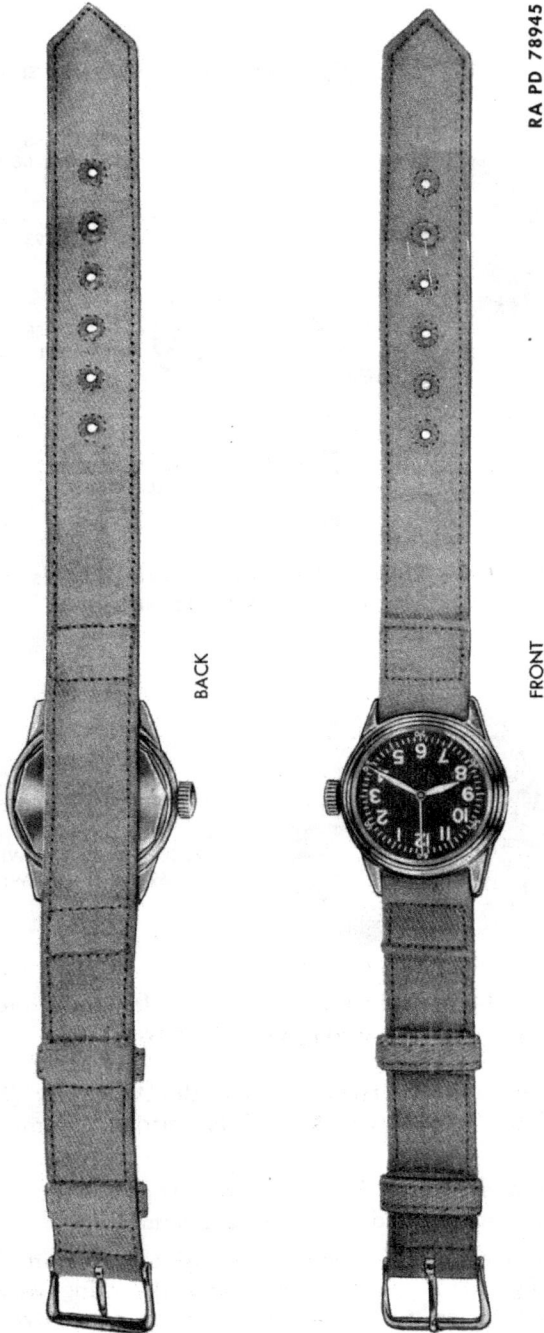

RA PD 78945

BACK

FRONT

Figure 142 — Elgin Wrist Watch — 16-jewel, 8/0 Size — Front and Back

ELGIN WRIST WATCH, 8/0 SIZE, 7- OR 15-JEWEL

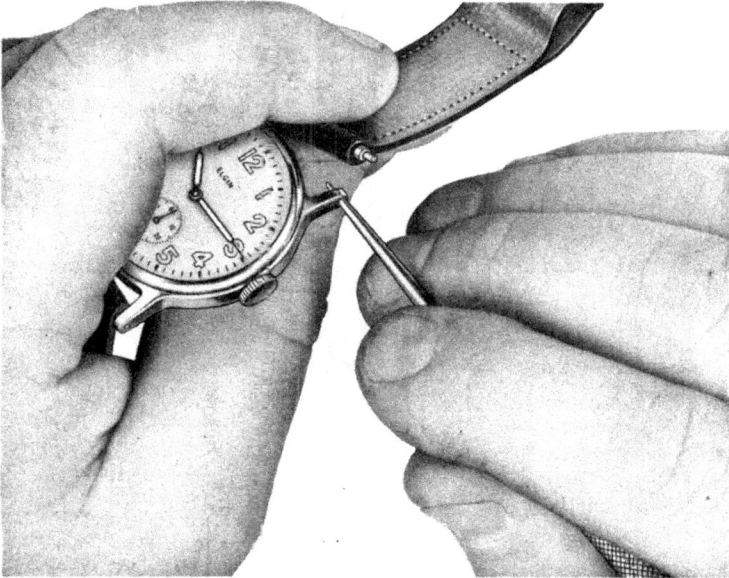

RA PD 78964

Figure 143 — Elgin Wrist Watch — Removing Wrist Band

and stud to prevent it from being lost; then remove clutch lever.

k.   Remove Winding Wheels and Click (fig. 138).   Remove crown wheel screw by turning it clockwise; remove crown wheel washer and crown wheel.   Remove ratchet wheel screw and ratchet wheel.   Remove click screw, click, and click spring.

l.   Remove Train and Barrel Bridges (fig. 139).   Remove train and barrel bridge screws and remove bridges.   If bridges are tight, insert screwdriver in slots provided in pillar plate and pry loose carefully.

m.   Remove Train Wheels and Barrel Assemblies (fig. 140).   Remove center, third, fourth, and escape wheels, and barrel assembly.

n.   Remove Setting Lever Screw (fig. 141).   Remove the setting lever screw and lift the setting lever off the pillar plate.   This completes the disassembly of the movement, stripping it down to the pillar plate and leaving only the hole jewel assembly settings in place.

o.   Remove Mainspring From Barrel (fig. 71).   Hold the mainspring barrel between the thumb and index finger while the barrel is supported on the anvil, place a screwdriver of the proper size within the slot provided in the cap, and pry off the cap.   Remove barrel

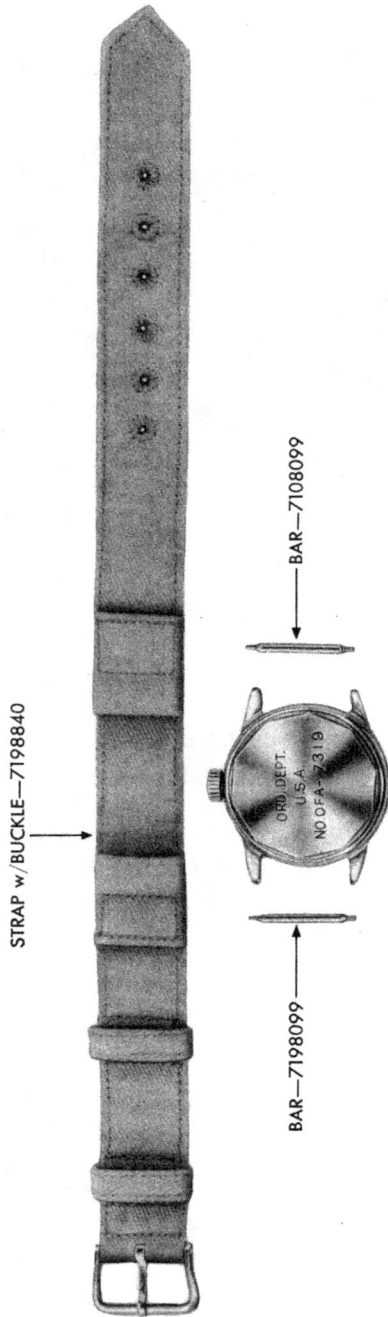

ORDNANCE MAINTENANCE — WRIST WATCHES, POCKET WATCHES, STOP WATCHES, AND CLOCKS

RA PD 78984

STRAP w/BUCKLE—7198840

BAR—7108099

ORD. DEPT.
U.S.A.
No OFA-7319

BAR—7198099

Figure 144 — Elgin Wrist Watch — Wrist Band Removed

ELGIN WRIST WATCH, 8/0 SIZE, 7- OR 15-JEWEL

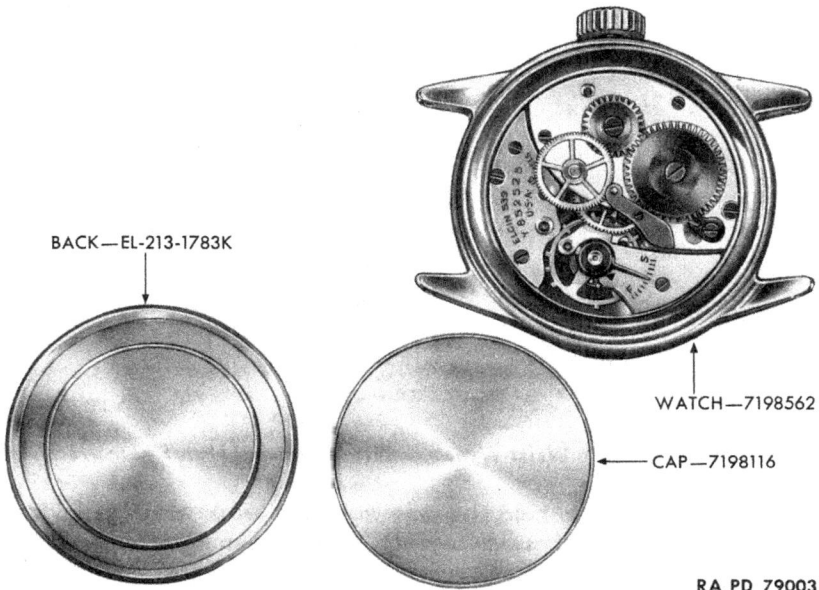

BACK—EL-213-1783K

WATCH—7198562

CAP—7198116

RA PD 79003

Figure 145 — Elgin Wrist Watch — Back and Dust Cover Removed

arbor, grasp the inside coil of the mainspring with tweezers, and pull it out of the barrel slowly, letting it uncoil as it comes out. Refrain from handling mainspring with bare fingers as much as possible.

60. DISASSEMBLE ELGIN WRIST WATCH, MODEL 1783, GRADE 539, WATERPROOF CASE.

a. General. The Elgin wrist watch, model 1783, grade 539, is equipped with a waterproof case with a screw-type back and a sweep second hand. The movement is 16-jewel. The addition of the sweep second hand requires a hollow center wheel pinion, a sweep second pinion bridge assembly, and an upper third wheel. The mainspring barrel bridge is drilled and tapped to permit attachment of the sweep second pinion bridge with a screw. The third wheel pinion is longer to permit attachment of the upper third wheel.

b. Remove Wrist Band (figs. 143 and 144). Press in on either end of the spring bar with a small screwdriver to release it from the case lug; then slide it from the lug, and pull it out of the opposite lug. The other spring bar is removed in the same manner.

c. Remove Back and Dust Cover (fig. 145). Unscrew the case back, using a case wrench. If the case back is screwed on very tight,

153

HAND—7198021

BLOCK, MOVEMENT

RA PD 78976

Figure 146 — Elgin Wrist Watch — Sweep Second Hand Removed

it may be necessary to hold the case in a case block while removing the back. Case wrenches are furnished by all manufacturers. Snap off the dust cover with a case opener.

d. Release Unused Power of Mainspring. Grasp the crown between thumb and index finger. Release the click with a small screwdriver and let crown turn slowly between the fingers, unwinding the unused power of the mainspring (fig. 52).

e. Remove Stem and Crown. Loosen the setting lever screw two turns to remove stem and crown from movement and case.

f. Remove Movement From Case. Lay the movement on the bench, tap lightly on the case, and lift the case off the movement. If the movement is very tight in the case, it may be necessary to loosen it with a small screwdriver by prying at various points around the bridge plates. The movement is not held in the case with screws.

g. Remove Sweep Seconds Hand (fig. 146). Protect the dial with paper and remove the sweep seconds hand, using the hand remover.

h. Remove Sweep Seconds Bridge (fig. 147). Invert the movement and remove the screw from the sweep seconds bridge. Lift off the bridge.

i. Remove Sweep Seconds Pinion (fig. 148). Grasp the sweep seconds pinion with tweezers and lift it out of the hollow center wheel staff.

j. Remove Movement Ring. Remove two movement ring screws and separate movement and ring.

ELGIN WRIST WATCH, 8/0 SIZE, 7- OR 15-JEWEL

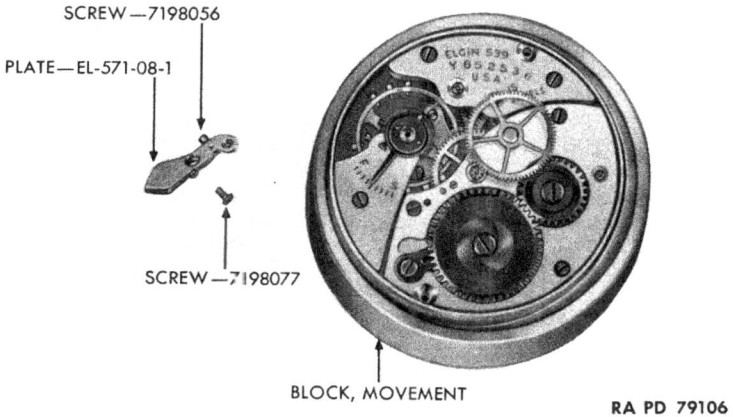

SCREW —7198056

PLATE—EL-571-08-1

SCREW —7198077

BLOCK, MOVEMENT

RA PD 79106

Figure 147 — Elgin Wrist Watch — Sweep Seconds Pinion Bridge Removed

k. **Disassemble Rest of Movement.** The rest of the movement is disassembled in the same sequence as the 7- or 15-jewel wrist watch outlined in paragraph 59 with the exception of the upper third wheel and the balance stop assembly.

l. **Remove Upper Third Wheel.** After the barrel bridge is lifted off the movement, enclose lower third wheel pinion in a pin vise. Holding the barrel bridge in the left hand with the index finger on the upper third wheel, pull and turn the pin vise carefully until the two wheels are separated.

m. **Remove Balance Stop Assembly.** Remove balance stop assembly screw and lift off balance stop assembly.

61. ASSEMBLY OF ELGIN WRIST WATCH, 8/0 SIZE, 7- OR 15-JEWEL.

a. **Wind in Mainspring** (figs. 68, 69, and 70). Select proper mainspring winder and wind mainspring into it slowly. Insert mainspring winder into barrel, hook end of mainspring on barrel hook, and press plunger which transfers mainspring into barrel. Insert barrel arbor and replace barrel cap, snapping it into its recess.

b. **Replace Setting Lever Screw** (fig. 141). Place pillar plate on proper size movement block and replace setting lever screw in its hole in pillar plate.

c. **Replace Train Wheels and Barrel** (fig. 140). Place mainspring barrel assembly on pillar plate. Replace train wheels in this order: escape, fourth, third, and center wheels.

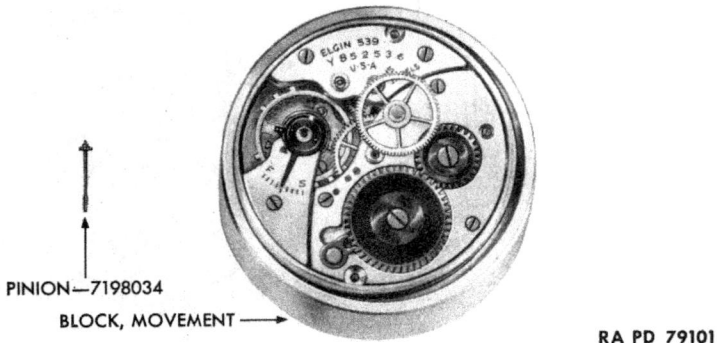

PINION—7198034

BLOCK, MOVEMENT ——→

RA PD 79101

Figure 148 — Elgin Wrist Watch — Sweep Seconds Pinion Removed

d. Replace Bridges (fig. 139). Replace the barrel bridge assembly alining the pivots of the center and third wheels in their respective pivot holes. Secure in place with bridge screws. Replace train bridge assembly, alining the pivots of fourth and escape wheels in their respective holes. Secure in place with bridge screws.

e. Replace Winding Wheels and Click (fig. 138). Replace crown wheel and washer; replace crown wheel screw and secure. Replace click spring in its recess in the barrel bridge. Replace click on its stud and secure in place with the click screw. Replace ratchet wheel, fitting it on the square of the mainspring arbor, and secure with ratchet wheel screw.

f. Replace Setting Mechanism and End Stone Cap Assembly (fig. 137). Replace the clutch and the bevel pinion. Place the minute wheel and setting wheels on their studs on the pillar plate. Replace the clutch lever, engaging it with the clutch and, with the tweezers, insert the clutch lever spring. Place the setting lever in position over the setting lever screw and tighten the setting lever screw to hold the setting lever in position. Insert the crown and arbor and tighten the setting lever screw. Insert the lower end stone cap and secure with two screws.

g. Replace Minute Wheel Clamp (fig. 136). Replace minute wheel clamp assembly, placing the spring end behind the setting lever stud. Replace minute wheel clamp screws and secure. Check freedom of train by rotating the crown one turn, allowing the train to revolve; if train wheels do not backlash on reaching the end of the winding, perfect freedom of the train does not exist and must be corrected.

ELGIN WRIST WATCH, 8/0 SIZE, 7- OR 15-JEWEL

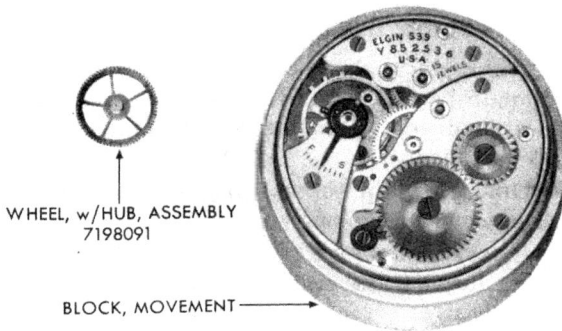

WHEEL, w/HUB, ASSEMBLY
7198091

BLOCK, MOVEMENT

RA PD 78985

Figure 149 — Elgin Wrist Watch — Upper Third Wheel Removed

h. Replace Pallet and Pallet Bridge Assembly (fig. 135). Replace pallet assembly. Replace pallet bridge, alining the pallet arbor pivot in its hole. Replace bridge screws and secure. Check freedom of the pallet assembly; then check action of the pallet and escape wheel.

i. Replace Balance and Balance Cock Assembly (fig. 134). Follow procedure outlined in paragraph 57.

j. Replace Hour Wheel (fig. 133). Invert movement on movement block and replace hour wheel.

k. Replace Dial (fig. 132). Back dial foot screws out two turns and replace dial. Secure by tightening dial foot screws.

l. Replace Hands (fig. 129). Replace seconds hand; replace hour hand with the point at the twelfth hour and replace minute hand in the same position. Check hands for clearance at the dial and make sure they do not hook on each other when turned through a complete revolution.

m. Replace Movement in Lower Portion of Case (fig. 130). Carefully place movement in lower portion of case with stem out over cut-out in case. Push movement in until it is seated in its proper position.

n. Replace Bezel (fig. 128). Place bezel on lower portion of case with cut-out over stem and snap it into place. Check to make sure movement is centered and stem does not bind. NOTE: *For assembly of Elgin wrist watch, model 1783, grade 539, refer to paragraph 62.*

62. ASSEMBLY OF ELGIN WRIST WATCH, MODEL 1783, GRADE 539, WATERPROOF CASE.

a. General. After replacing balance stop assembly, duplicate the assembly of the 7- or 15-jewel Elgin wrist watch, as outlined in paragraph 55; eight additional steps are necessary to complete the assembly of model 1783 as follows:

(1) REPLACE UPPER THIRD WHEEL (fig. 149). Replace upper third wheel over center wheel pinion.

(2) REPLACE SWEEP SECONDS PINION (fig. 148). Replace the sweep seconds pinion through the center wheel, being careful not to bend pinion.

(3) REPLACE SWEEP SECONDS PINION BRIDGE (fig. 147). Replace the sweep seconds pinion bridge; secure with bridge screw.

(4) REPLACE SWEEP SECONDS HAND (fig. 146). Invert the movement and install the sweep seconds hand on the sweep seconds pinion, alining the point at the twelfth hour. Check the sweep seconds hand for clearance.

(5) REPLACE MOVEMENT RING. Remove the stem and crown and replace the movement ring, alining the hole in the ring with the stem position on the movement. Secure with two ring screws.

(6) REPLACE CRYSTAL. If the crystal has to be replaced, obtain the correct size disk and cone and install them in the crystal pliers, and cup the crystal and snap it into the bezel ring.

(7) REPLACE MOVEMENT IN CASE. Replace movement in case and install stem and crown. Turn the stem to center movement in case and tighten the setting lever screw. Check the hands for clearance at the crystal by turning them one complete revolution. Replace the dust cover and screw the back into place securely with the case wrench.

(8) REPLACE WRIST BAND (figs. 143 and 144). Place the spring bars in the wrist band loops and insert one end of the spring bar in a case lug; compress the opposite end and slide it between its lug, snapping it into place. Install the other end of band in the same manner.

Section VII

WALTHAM WRIST WATCH, 6/0 SIZE, 9-JEWEL, MODEL 10609 AND 6/0 SIZE, 17-JEWEL, MODEL 10617

63. IDENTIFICATION.

a. There are two Waltham wrist watches used as service timepieces; the 6/0 size, 9-jewel and the 6/0 size, 17-jewel. The manufacturer's name is printed on the dial. The ordnance serial number

**WALTHAM WRIST WATCH, 6/0 SIZE, 9-JEWEL, MODEL 10609
AND 6/0 SIZE, 17-JEWEL, MODEL 10617**

RA PD 78961

INCHES

BACK

FRONT

Figure 150 — Waltham Wrist Watch, 9-jewel, 6/0 Size — Front and Back

159

ORDNANCE MAINTENANCE — WRIST WATCHES, POCKET WATCHES, STOP WATCHES, AND CLOCKS

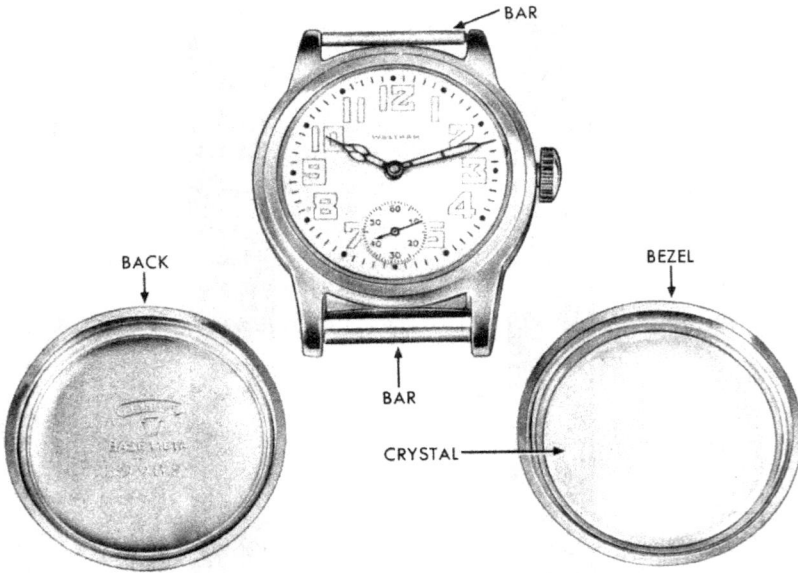

RA PD 78882

Figure 151 — Waltham Wrist Watch — Case Back and Bezel Removed

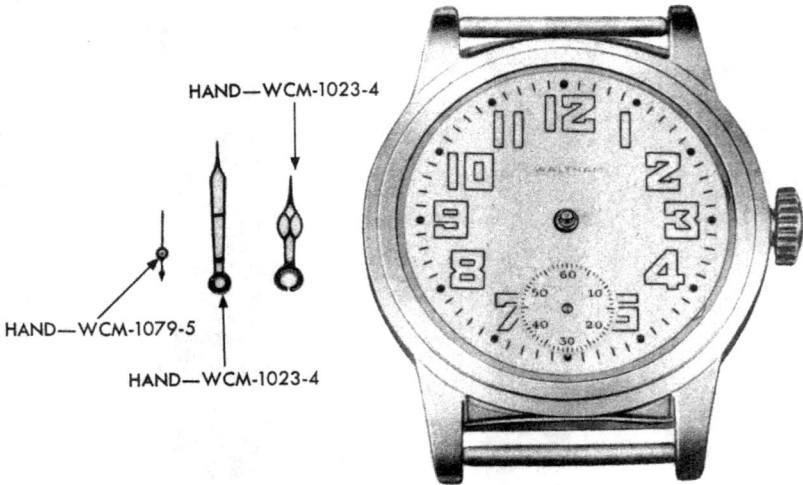

RA PD 79041

Figure 152 — Waltham Wrist Watch — Hands Removed

WALTHAM WRIST WATCH, 6/0 SIZE, 9-JEWEL, MODEL 10609
AND 6/0 SIZE, 17-JEWEL, MODEL 10617

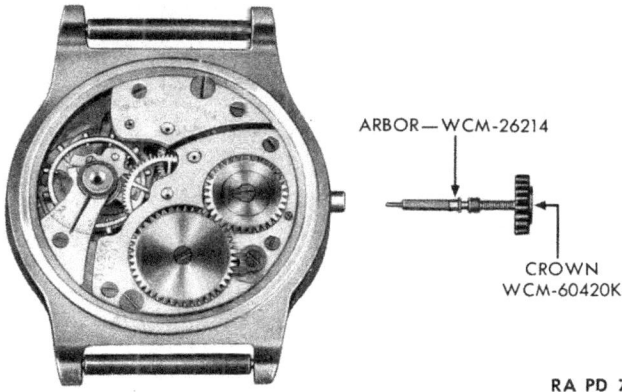

ARBOR—WCM-26214

CROWN
WCM-60420K

RA PD 78895

Figure 153 — Waltham Wrist Watch — Arbor and Crown Removed

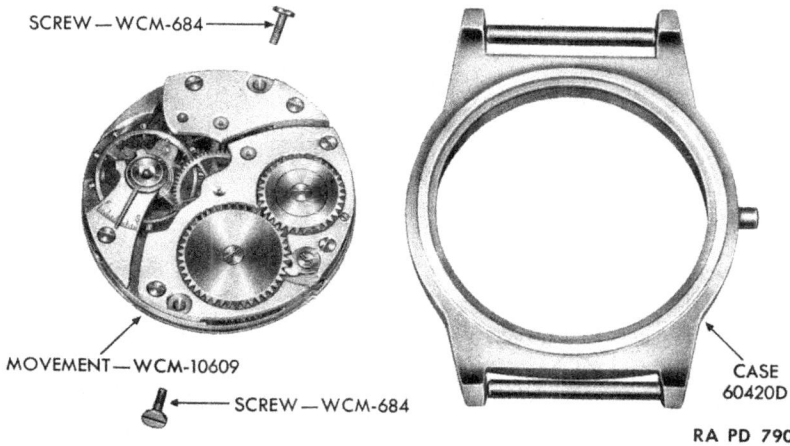

SCREW—WCM-684

MOVEMENT—WCM-10609

SCREW—WCM-684

CASE
60420D

RA PD 79062

Figure 154 — Waltham Wrist Watch — Movement Removed From Case

and grade is marked on the exterior back of the case. The prefix "OC" before the serial number will identify the 9-jewel, and the 17-jewel models are indicated by the prefix "OD" before the serial number. NOTE: *The 6/0 size, 17-jewel is normally issued and maintained by the Air Corps. Both of these watches are now issued in waterproof-type cases, but the illustrations in this section deal only with the cup-type case.*

MOVEMENT—WCM-10609   DIAL—WCM-61-L   RA PD 79019

Figure 155 — Waltham Wrist Watch — Dial Removed

WHEEL—WCM-26032

RA PD 79052

Figure 156 — Waltham Wrist Watch — Hour Wheel Removed

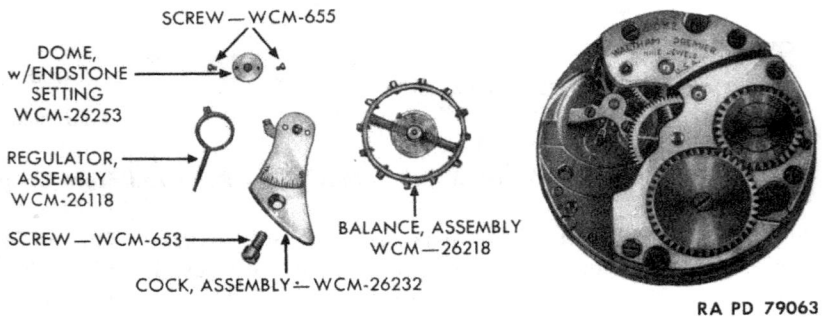

SCREW — WCM-655

DOME,
w/ENDSTONE
SETTING
WCM-26253

REGULATOR,
ASSEMBLY
WCM-26118

SCREW — WCM-653

COCK, ASSEMBLY — WCM-26232

BALANCE, ASSEMBLY
WCM—26218

RA PD 79063

Figure 157 — Waltham Wrist Watch — Balance Cock and Balance Assembly Removed

WALTHAM WRIST WATCH, 6/0 SIZE, 9-JEWEL, MODEL 10609
AND 6/0 SIZE, 17-JEWEL, MODEL 10617

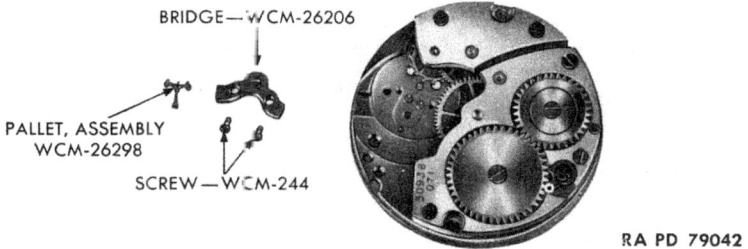

*Figure 158 — Waltham Wrist Watch — Pallet Bridge and Pallet
Assembly Removed*

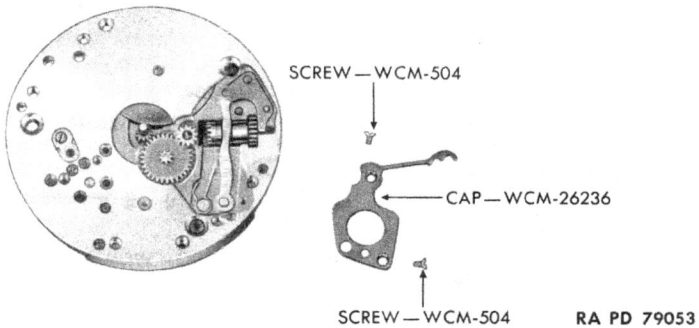

Figure 159 — Waltham Wrist Watch — Shipper Cap Assembly Removed

64. DISASSEMBLY.

a. **Remove Case Back and Bezel** (fig. 151). Insert a case opener in slot in back and pry it off. Remove bezel in the same manner. A few 6/0's have been issued in screw-type cases. Check for this carefully before attempting to pry off back and bezel.

b. **Remove Hands** (fig. 152). Cut a V-slot in a piece of paper and slide it under the hands to protect dial. Remove hands with hand remover.

c. **Release Unused Power of Mainspring** (fig. 52). Release unused power of mainspring by holding crown with thumb and index finger; then disengage click with a small screwdriver and allow crown to turn slowly between fingers.

ORDNANCE MAINTENANCE — WRIST WATCHES, POCKET WATCHES, STOP WATCHES, AND CLOCKS

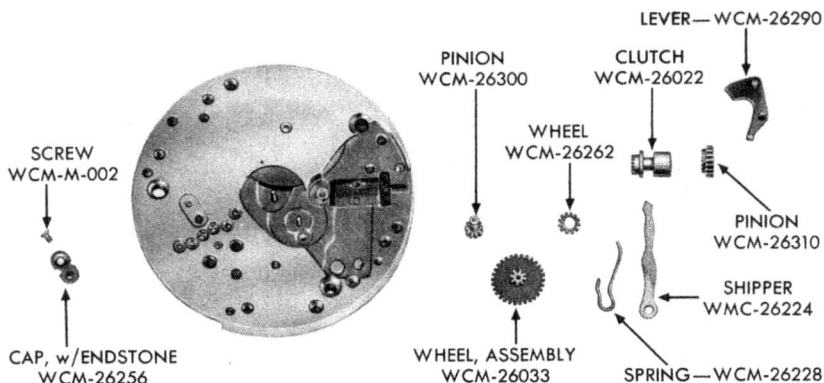

RA PD 79070

Figure 160 — Waltham Wrist Watch — Setting Mechanism Removed

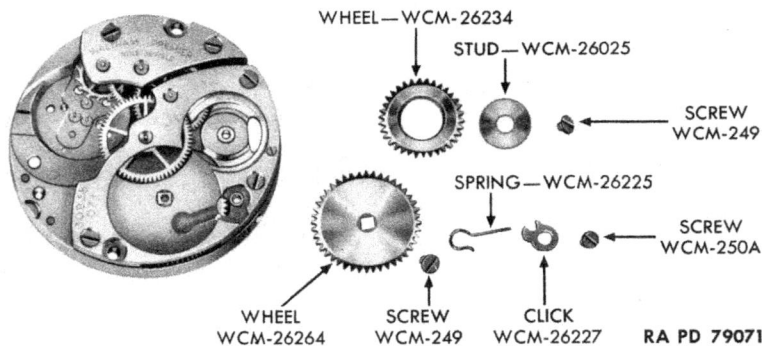

Figure 161 — Waltham Wrist Watch — Winding Wheel and Click Assembly Removed

d. **Remove Arbor and Crown** (fig. 153). Place movement on movement block of proper size, train side up. Loosen setting lever screw until arbor can be pulled out of movement.

e. **Remove Movement From Case Band** (fig. 154). Remove two case screws. Hold movement in place on movement block and lift off case band.

f. **Remove Dial** (fig. 155). Back out dial foot screws two turns from contour of pillar plate and remove dial. Screw dial foot screws back into place to avoid losing them.

WALTHAM WRIST WATCH, 6/0 SIZE, 9-JEWEL, MODEL 10609
AND 6/0 SIZE, 17-JEWEL, MODEL 10617

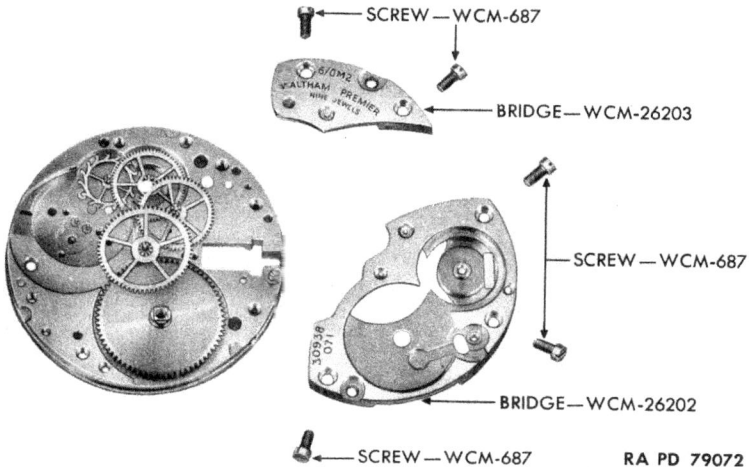

*Figure 162 — Waltham Wrist Watch — Train and Barrel Bridge
Assemblies Removed*

g. **Remove Hour Wheel** (fig. 156). Remove hour wheel by lifting it off with tweezers.

h. **Remove Balance Cock and Balance Assembly** (fig. 157). Invert movement on movement block, train side up; loosen hairspring stud screw with a small screwdriver and free stud from balance cock. Remove balance cock screw and balance cock. If balance cock is tight, insert a screwdriver in slot underneath cock and pry it loose. Remove balance assembly with tweezers. Secure stud screw to avoid losing it. Invert balance cock on bench and remove upper balance end stone cap assembly screws, thus permitting removal of end stone cap assembly setting and regulator assembly.

i. **Remove Pallet Bridge and Pallet Assembly** (fig. 158). Remove pallet bridge screws and pallet bridge. Remove pallet with tweezers.

j. **Remove Shipper Cap** (fig. 159). Invert movement on movement block and remove shipper cap screws and shipper cap.

k. **Remove Setting Mechanism and Lower End Stone Cap Assembly** (fig. 160). Remove minute wheel and setting wheel. Remove cannon pinion. Remove minute and setting wheels. To remove shipper lever spring, place end of index finger over shipper lever spring and stud to avoid losing it, and remove shipper lever spring with tweezers. Remove shipper lever. Place index finger on setting lever

WHEEL, ASSEMBLY — WCM-26254

WHEEL, ASSEMBLY — WCM-26276

WHEEL, ASSEMBLY — WCM-26270

WHEEL, ASSEMBLY — WCM-26247

BARREL, ASSEMBLY

RA PD 79086

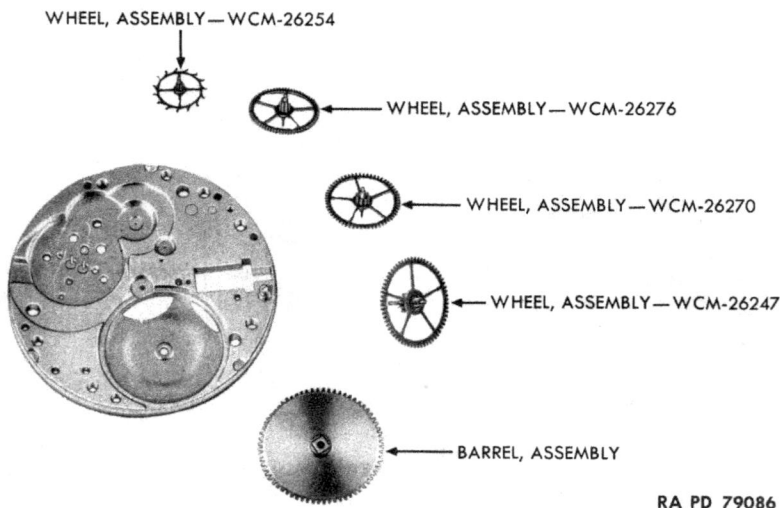

Figure 163 — Waltham Wrist Watch — Train Wheels and Barrel Assemblies Removed

and invert movement; then unscrew setting lever screw until setting lever is released. Reinvert movement and remove setting lever. Pull out stem and crown; remove winding pinion and winding and setting clutch. Remove lower end stone balance assembly cap screw and lower end stone cap assembly.

l. **Remove Winding Wheels and Click Assembly** (fig. 161). Remove crown wheel screw. Remove crown wheel stud and crown wheel. Remove winding wheel screw and winding wheel. Remove click screw, click, and click spring.

m. **Remove Bridges** (fig. 162). Remove barrel and train bridge assembly screws and bridge assemblies. If the bridges are tight, insert a screwdriver in slots provided in pillar plate and pry loose carefully.

n. **Remove Train Wheels and Barrel Assemblies** (fig. 163). Remove center, third, fourth, and escape wheels, and barrel assembly.

o. **Remove Setting Lever Screw** (fig. 164). Lift the setting lever screw off the pillar plate. This completes the disassembly of the movement, stripping it down to the pillar plate and leaving only the hole jewel assembly settings in place.

p. **Remove Mainspring From Barrel** (fig. 71). To disassemble the mainspring barrel assembly, remove the arbor; turn the main

WALTHAM WRIST WATCH, 6/0 SIZE, 9-JEWEL, MODEL 10609
AND 6/0 SIZE, 17-JEWEL, MODEL 10617

PLATE—WCM-26200 ➤   ➤◀—SCREW—WCM-604A

RA PD 79057

*Figure 164 — Waltham Wrist Watch — Pillar Plate With Setting
Lever Screw Removed*

wheel clockwise to release the hub from the mainspring and lift off
the main wheel. Grasp the inside coil of the mainspring with
tweezers and pull it out of the barrel slowly, letting it uncoil as it
comes out. Refrain from handling mainspring with bare fingers as
much as possible.

**65. ASSEMBLY OF WALTHAM WRIST WATCH, 6/0 SIZE,
9-JEWEL, MODEL 10609, AND THE 17-JEWEL, 8¾
LIGNE, MODEL 870.**

   a. Wind in Mainspring (figs. 68, 69, and 70). Select proper
mainspring winder and wind mainspring into it slowly. Insert mainspring winder into barrel, hook end of mainspring on barrel hook,
and press plunger which transfers mainspring into barrel. Insert
main wheel, hook inner end of mainspring on main wheel hub, replace arbor, and snap into square of barrel.

   b. Replace Setting Lever Screw (fig. 164). Place pillar plate on
proper size movement block and replace setting lever screw in its
hole.

   c. Replace Train Wheels and Barrel (fig. 163). Place mainspring barrel assembly on pillar plate. Replace train wheels in the
following order: escape, fourth, third, and center wheels.

   d. Replace Bridges (fig. 162). Replace the barrel bridge assembly, alining the pivots of the center and third wheel in their respective pivot holes. Secure in place with bridge screws. Replace train
bridge assembly, alining the pivots of the fourth and escape wheels
in their respective holes. Secure in place with bridge screws.

   e. Replacing Winding Wheels and Click (fig. 161). Replace
click spring and click, and secure in place with click screw. Replace

winding wheel, fitting it on the square of the mainspring barrel arbor, and secure in place with winding wheel. Replace crown wheel and crown wheel stud, and secure in place with crown wheel screw.

f. Replace Setting Mechanism and End Stone Cap Assembly (fig. 160). Replace lower end stone cap assembly and secure with cap screw. Replace setting lever, with bent end in toward train side of pillar plate, and with hole above setting lever screw. Place the index finger over the setting lever and invert movement; then turn setting lever screw enough to hold lever in place. Replace winding pinion and clutch in cut-out in pillar plate. Replace shipper on its stud, with end of shipper resting in recess in clutch. Place shipper spring around its stud, hold in position with one screwdriver, and pull long end of spring until it falls into place behind shipper. Replace cannon pinion. Replace minute and setting wheels on their respective studs.

g. Replace Shipper Cap Assembly (fig. 159). Replace shipper cap, placing spring end behind setting lever stud. Replace cap screws and secure. At this point an examination must be made to check freedom of the train by inserting the stem and crown temporarily and rotating crown one turn, allowing train to revolve. If wheels of the train backlash on reaching the end of the winding, train has perfect freedom. If they slow down or stop abruptly, a bind exists and must be corrected.

h. Replace Pallet and Pallet Bridge Assembly (fig. 158). Replace pallet assembly. Replace pallet bridge assembly, carefully alining the pallet arbor pivot in its hole. Check freedom of pallet assembly and then check the action of the pallet assembly and escape wheel. Rotate crown two turns and check action of pallet assembly and escape wheels. Remove stem and crown.

i. Replace Balance and Balance Cock Assembly (fig. 157). This procedure is identical with that described in paragraph 57 i.

j. Replace Hour Wheel (fig. 156). Invert movement on movement block and replace hour wheel.

k. Replace Dial (fig. 155). Back dial foot screws out two turns and replace dial. Secure by tightening dial foot screws.

l. Replace Movement in Case (fig. 154). Invert movement on movement block. Place case band over movement and aline winding arbor hole with winding pinion and clutch hole. Replace two case screws and secure.

m. Replace Winding Arbor and Crown (fig. 153). Insert winding arbor into its hole in case band, slightly revolving crown in order to properly set arbor in center of clutch. Tighten setting lever until

BULOVA WRIST WATCH, MODEL 10 AK, 10½ LIGNE SIZE, 15-JEWEL,
WATERPROOF CASE

arbor is locked in movement. Center movement to prevent binding in winding arbor.

n. **Replace Hands** (fig. 152). Replace seconds hand. Replace hour hand with point at twelfth hour; replace minute hand in same position. Check hands for clearance at dial, making sure they do not hook on each other when turned through a complete revolution.

o. **Replace Back and Bezel** (fig. 151). Replace back and bezel on case band and snap into position.

Section VIII

BULOVA WRIST WATCH, MODEL 10 AK, 10½ LIGNE SIZE, 15-JEWEL, WATERPROOF CASE

66. IDENTIFICATION.

a. The Bulova wrist watch, model 10 AK, 10½ ligne size, 15-jewel movement, may be identified by a black dial with the manufacturer's name on it. It is a waterproof case, stem wound and stem set. The case is of the screw-back type, sealed with a rubber washer and dust cover. The bezel is formed as an integral part of the case ring and is equipped with an unbreakable crystal. The movement is secured with a case ring and is not held in the case with screws.

67. DISASSEMBLY.

a. **Remove Wrist Band.** Press in on either end of the spring bar with a small screwdriver and release it from the lug; slide it from the lug and pull it out of the opposite lug. Remove the other spring bar in the same manner.

b. **Remove Back, Gasket, and Dust Cover** (fig. 166). Unscrew the back, using a case wrench. Remove the rubber gasket and snap out the dust cover with a case opener.

c. **Release Unused Power of Mainspring** (fig. 52). Grasp crown between thumb and index finger, release click with a small screwdriver, and let the crown turn slowly between the fingers to unwind the unused power of the mainspring.

d. **Remove Stem and Crown** (fig. 167). Loosen the setting lever screw two turns and remove stem and crown from the movement and case.

e. **Remove Movement From Case** (fig. 168). Lay the movement on the bench, tap lightly on the case, and lift case off the movement.

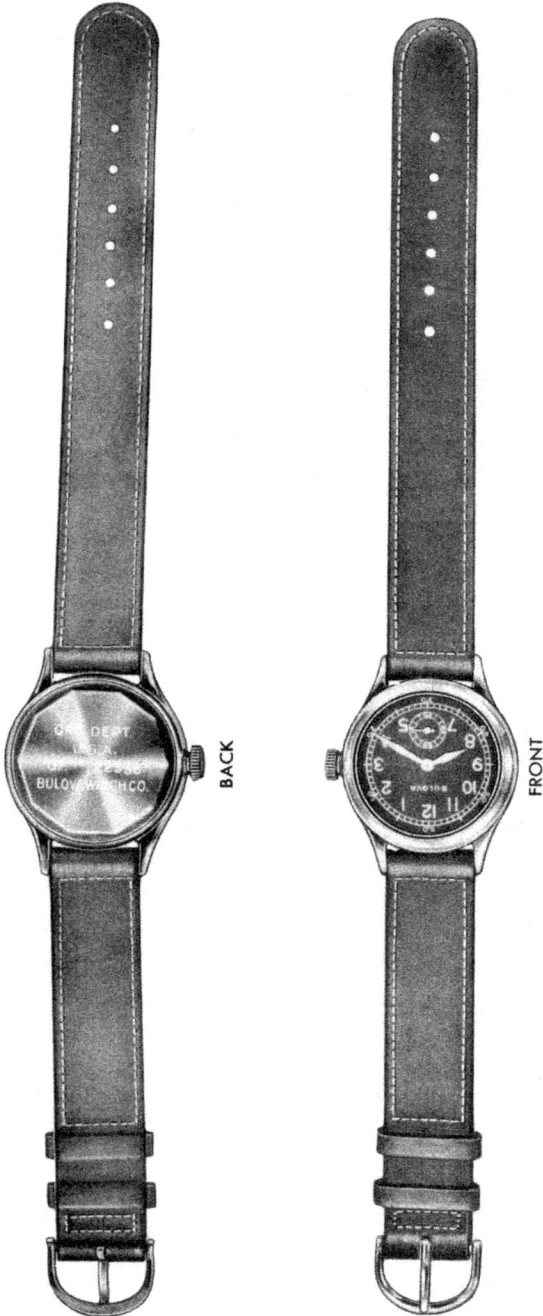

RA PD 78979

BACK

FRONT

Figure 165 — Bulova Wrist Watch — 15-jewel, 10½ Ligne Size — Front and Back

BULOVA WRIST WATCH, MODEL 10 AK, 10½ LIGNE SIZE, 15-JEWEL,
WATERPROOF CASE

RA PD 78975

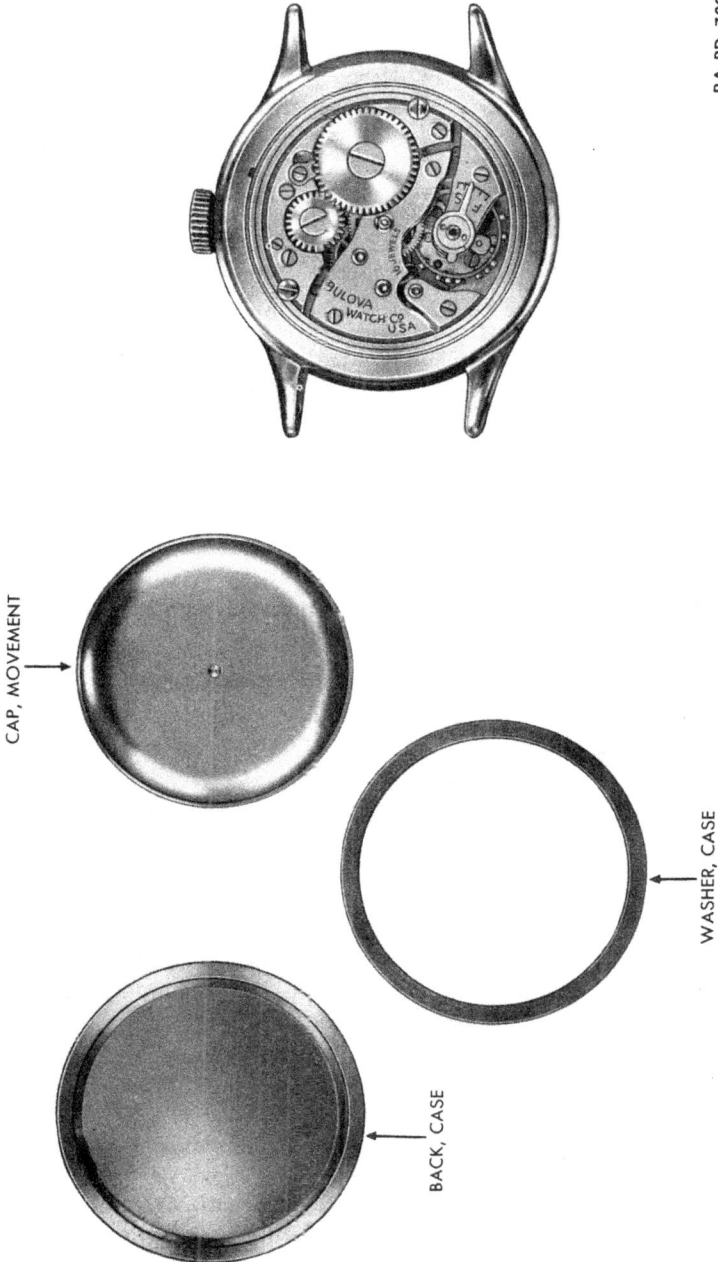

CAP, MOVEMENT

WASHER, CASE

BACK, CASE

Figure 166 — Bulova Wrist Watch — Back Removed

ORDNANCE MAINTENANCE—WRIST WATCHES, POCKET WATCHES, STOP WATCHES, AND CLOCKS

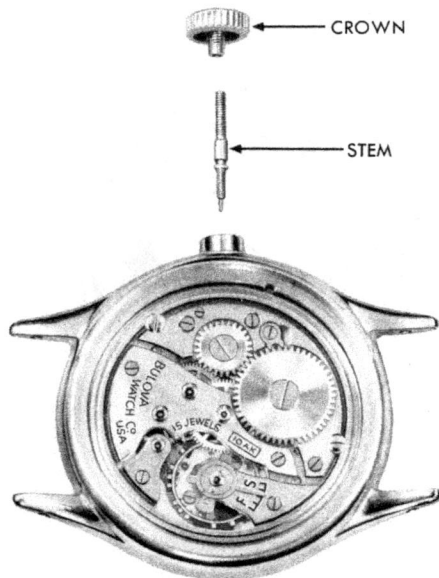

RA PD 79076

Figure 167 — Bulova Wrist Watch — Stem and Crown Removed

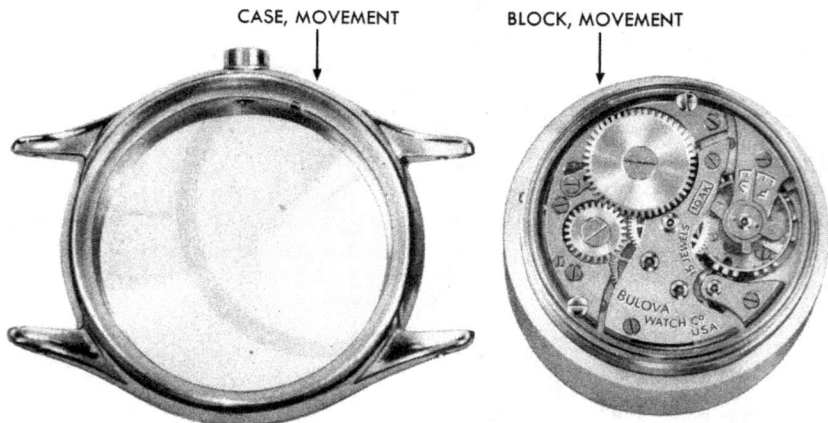

RA PD 79059

Figure 168 — Bulova Wrist Watch — Movement Removed From Case

If the movement is tight in the case, loosen it with a small screwdriver by prying at various points around the bridge plates. The movement is not held in the case with screws.

BULOVA WRIST WATCH, MODEL 10 AK, 10½ LIGNE SIZE, 15-JEWEL, WATERPROOF CASE

RA PD 78974

Figure 169 — Bulova Wrist Watch — Hands Removed

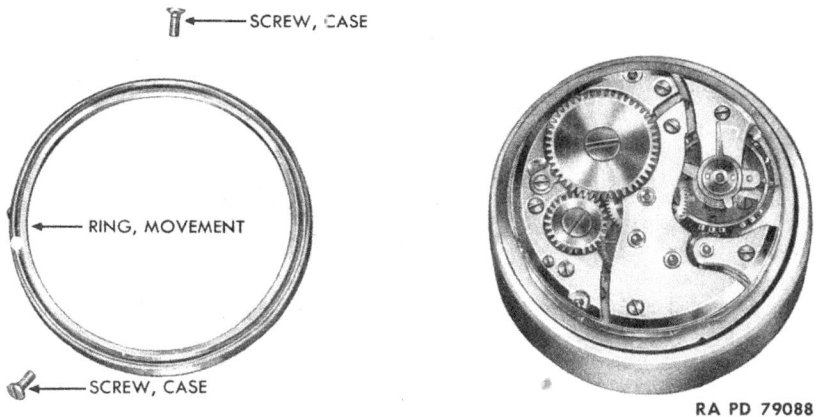

RA PD 79088

Figure 170 — Bulova Wrist Watch — Movement Ring Removed

f. Remove Hands (fig. 169). Protect the dial with paper and remove the hands, using a hand remover.

g. Remove Movement Ring (fig. 170). Remove two movement ring screws, and separate movement and movement ring.

h. Remove Dial (fig. 171). Loosen two dial foot screws two turns and lift off dial; then tighten dial foot screws to avoid losing them.

i. Remove Hour Wheel (fig. 172). Grasp the hour wheel with tweezers, lift it off cannon pinion, and remove brass dial washer.

j. Remove Cannon Pinion (fig. 174). Grasp cannon pinion with pin vise and lift it up and off.

k. Remove Setting Bridge (fig. 175). Remove two setting bridge screws and lift off the setting bridge.

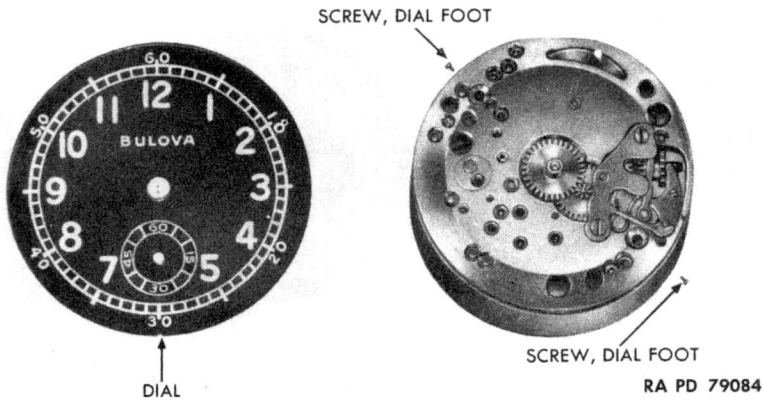

Figure 171 — Bulova Wrist Watch — Dial Removed

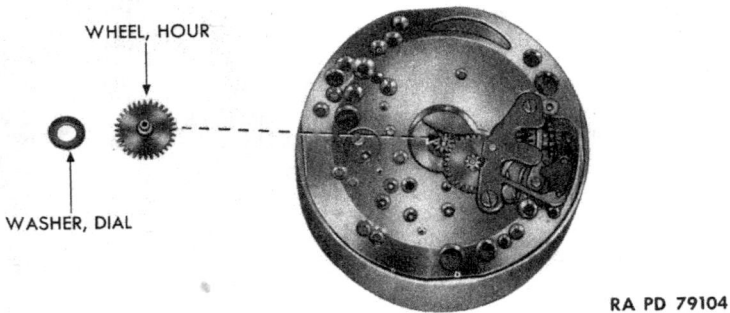

Figure 172 — Bulova Wrist Watch — Hour Wheel Removed

l. **Remove Minute and Setting Wheels** (fig. 176). Lift minute and setting wheels off of their respective posts.

m. **Remove Winding and Setting Assembly** (fig. 177). Hold clutch lever spring in place and lift off clutch lever and clutch lever spring. Remove clutch and winding pinion. Invert movement on the movement block and unscrew the setting lever screw. Lift off the setting lever.

n. **Remove Balance Cock and Balance Assembly** (fig. 178). Loosen the hairspring stud screw and free stud from balance cock. Remove the balance cock screw and the balance cock. If balance cock is tight, insert screwdriver between balance cock and plate and

BULOVA WRIST WATCH, MODEL 10 AK, 10½ LIGNE SIZE, 15-JEWEL, WATERPROOF CASE

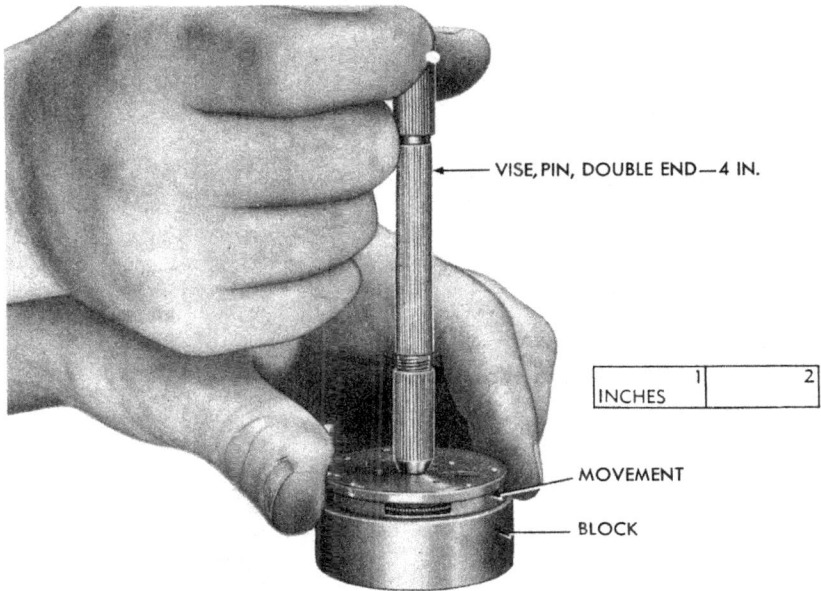

VISE, PIN, DOUBLE END—4 IN.

INCHES | 1 | 2

MOVEMENT

BLOCK

RA PD 78997

Figure 173 — Removing Cannon Pinion With Pin Vise

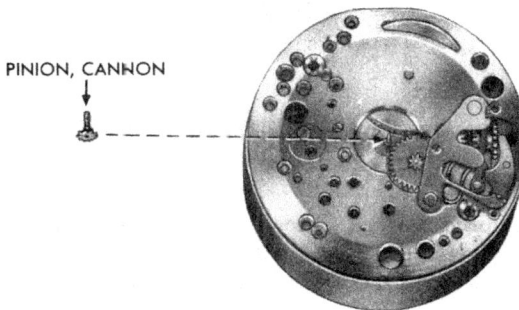

PINION, CANNON

RA PD 79089

Figure 174 — Bulova Wrist Watch — Cannon Pinion Removed

pry it loose. Invert balance and remove two dome screws. Lift dome and regulator off the balance cock.

o. **Remove Pallet Bridge and Pallet Assembly** (fig. 179). Remove two pallet bridge screws and lift off pallet bridge. Remove pallet assembly.

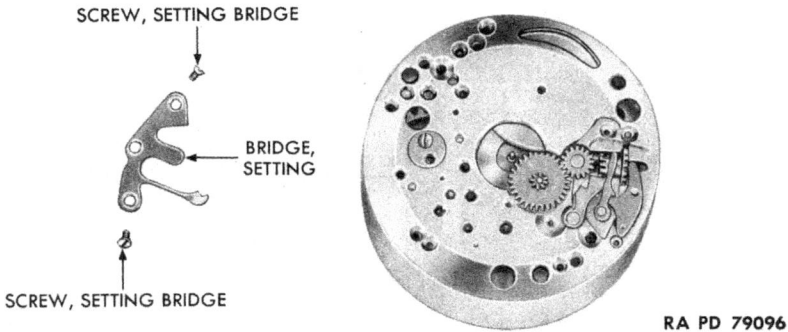

SCREW, SETTING BRIDGE

BRIDGE,
SETTING

SCREW, SETTING BRIDGE

RA PD 79096

Figure 175 — Bulova Wrist Watch — Setting Bridge Removed

WHEEL, SETTING

WHEEL, MINUTE

RA PD 79090

*Figure 176 — Bulova Wrist Watch — Minute and Setting Wheels
Removed*

p. **Remove Ratchet Wheel, Crown Wheel, and Click** (fig. 180). Remove ratchet wheel screw and ratchet wheel. Remove crown wheel screw by turning it clockwise. Lift off the crown wheel. Remove click screw and click. Remove click spring.

q. **Remove Barrel Bridge** (fig. 181). Remove the barrel bridge screws and lift off the barrel bridge. Remove setting lever screw.

r. **Remove Train Bridge** (fig. 182). Remove train wheel bridge screws and lift off bridge.

s. **Remove Train Wheels and Mainspring Barrel Assembly** (fig. 183). Remove center wheel, third wheel, fourth wheel, escape wheel, and mainspring barrel assembly.

BULOVA WRIST WATCH, MODEL 10 AK, 10½ LIGNE SIZE, 15-JEWEL, WATERPROOF CASE

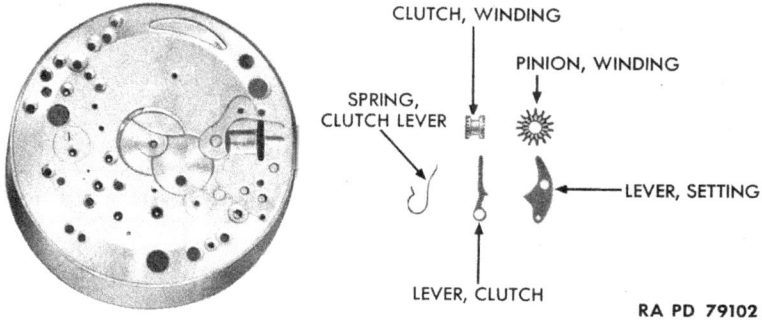

Figure 177 — Bulova Wrist Watch — Winding and Setting Assembly Removed

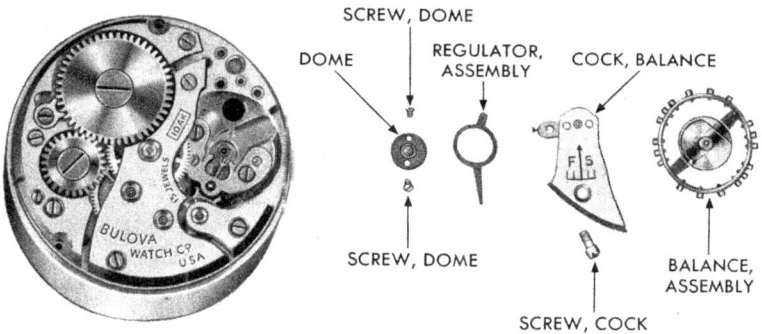

Figure 178 — Bulova Wrist Watch — Balance Cock and Balance Assembly Removed

t. **Remove End Stone Cap Assembly** (fig. 183). Invert movement on movement block, remove end stone cap screws, and lift off end stone cap assembly.

u. **Remove Mainspring** (fig. 185). Hold the mainspring barrel between the thumb and index finger, while the barrel is supported on the anvil, and place a screwdriver of the proper size within the slot provided in the cap and pry off the cap. Turn arbor counterclockwise until it disengages from mainspring; then lift out arbor. Grasp inner coil of mainspring with tweezers and slowly uncoil it out of mainspring barrel.

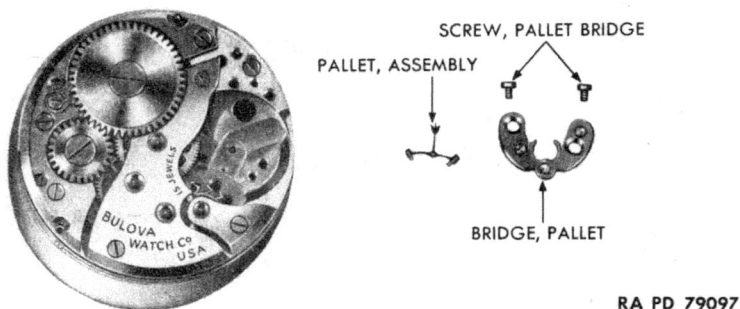

RA PD 79097

Figure 179 — Bulova Wrist Watch — Pallet Bridge and Pallet Assembly Removed

RA PD 79098

Figure 180 — Bulova Wrist Watch — Ratchet Wheel, Crown Wheel, and Click Removed

v. Remove Crystal. Install the proper size disk and cone in the crystal pliers; cup crystal and remove it from bezel ring only if replacement is necessary.

68. ASSEMBLY OF BULOVA WRIST WATCH, MODEL 10 AK, 10½ LIGNE SIZE, 15-JEWEL.

a. Replace Lower End Stone Cap Jewel. Place the lower end stone cap jewel in its place on pillar plate and secure it with end stone cap jewel screws (fig. 184).

b. Replace Upper Cap Jewel and Regulator (fig. 178). Place regulator on cap jewel. Invert the balance cock on the bench and place balance cock on the cap jewel and regulator; secure in place with two screws.

BULOVA WRIST WATCH, MODEL 10 AK, 10½ LIGNE SIZE, 15-JEWEL, WATERPROOF CASE

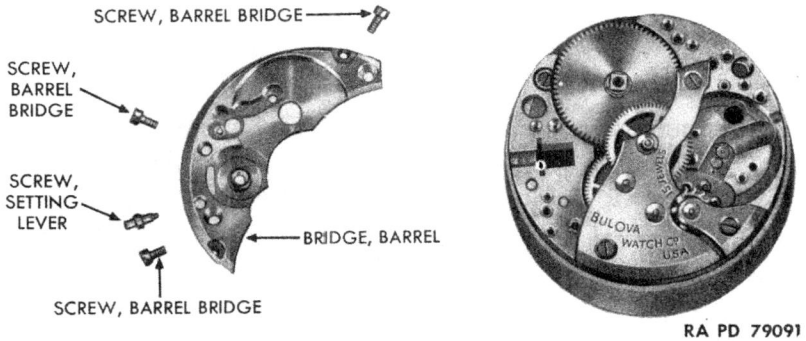

Figure 181 — Bulova Wrist Watch — Mainspring Barrel Bridge Removed

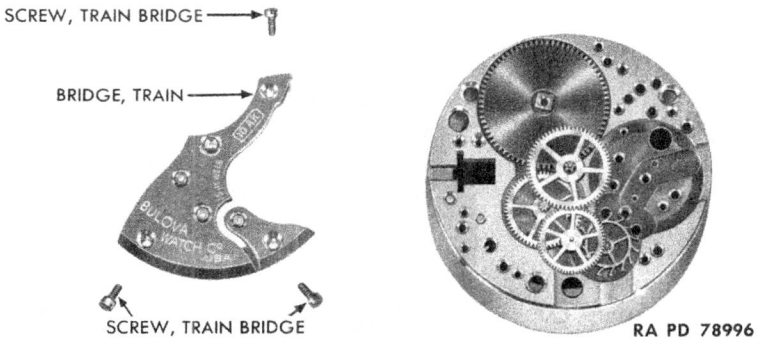

Figure 182 — Bulova Wrist Watch — Train Wheel Bridge Removed

c. **Wind in Mainspring** (figs. 68, 69, and 70). Obtain the correct size mainspring winder and carefully wind the mainspring into it. Place winder in mainspring barrel and hook end of mainspring on the barrel hook. Press plunger and transfer the mainspring into barrel. Insert arbor and turn it clockwise until the hook on the arbor engages the mainspring. Place mainspring barrel cap on the barrel and snap it into its groove.

d. **Replace Train Wheels and Mainspring Barrel** (fig. 183). Place the movement on a movement block, dial side down. Place the mainspring barrel assembly on the plate in its position. Place the escape wheel, fourth wheel, third wheel, and center wheel in their respective positions on the plate and replace the setting lever screw in its hole in the pillar plate.

179

ORDNANCE MAINTENANCE — WRIST WATCHES, POCKET WATCHES, STOP WATCHES, AND CLOCKS

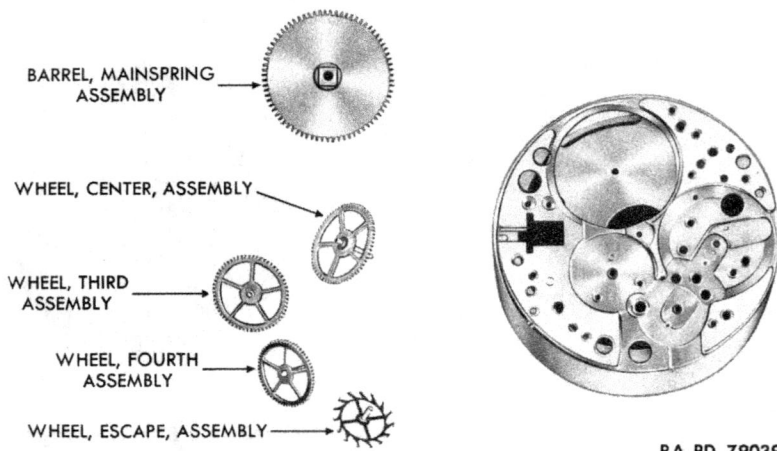

BARREL, MAINSPRING
ASSEMBLY

WHEEL, CENTER, ASSEMBLY

WHEEL, THIRD
ASSEMBLY

WHEEL, FOURTH
ASSEMBLY

WHEEL, ESCAPE, ASSEMBLY

RA PD 79039

Figure 183 — Bulova Wrist Watch — Train Wheel and Barrel Assembly Removed

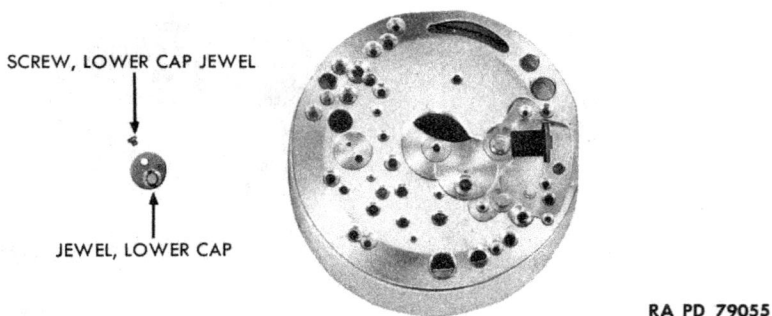

SCREW, LOWER CAP JEWEL

JEWEL, LOWER CAP

RA PD 79055

Figure 184 — Bulova Wrist Watch — Lower Cap Jewel Removed

e. **Replace Train Wheel Bridge** (fig. 182). Replace the train wheel bridge, alining the pivots of the escape, fourth, third, and center wheels to their respective bearings; secure the bridge in place with three bridge screws.

f. **Replace Mainspring Barrel Bridge** (fig. 181). Replace the mainspring barrel bridge, alining the mainspring barrel arbor with its bearing in the bridge. Secure the bridge in place with three bridge screws.

g. **Replace Click Spring and Click** (fig. 180). Insert the click spring in its recess in the barrel bridge. Place click on its post on the bridge and secure it with screw.

BULOVA WRIST WATCH, MODEL 10 AK, 10½ LIGNE SIZE, 15-JEWEL,
WATERPROOF CASE

RA PD 79092

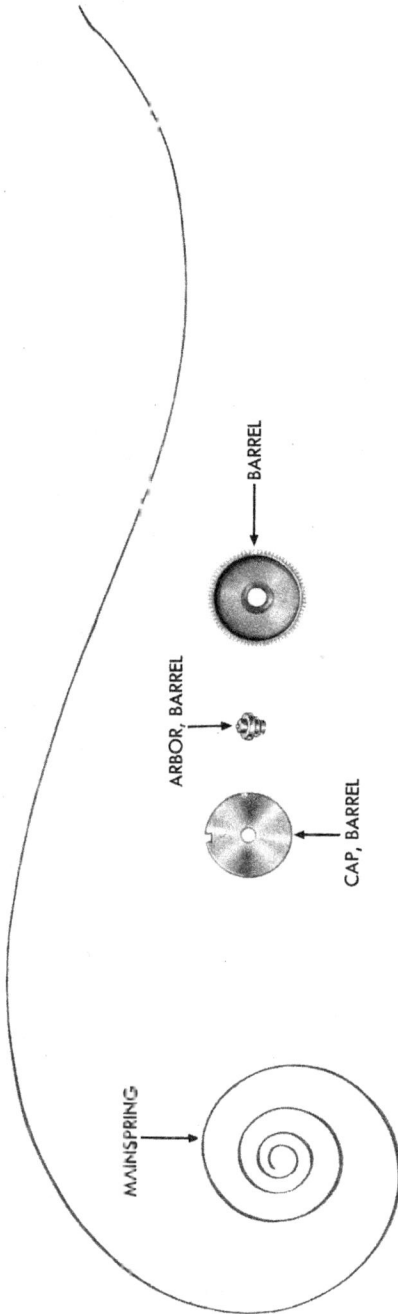

BARREL

ARBOR, BARREL

CAP, BARREL

MAINSPRING

Figure 185 — Bulova Wrist Watch — Mainspring Barrel Assembly Disassembled

h. Replace Ratchet Wheel and Crown Wheel (fig. 180). Replace the ratchet wheel and secure it with screw. Replace the crown wheel and secure it with its screw by turning counterclockwise.

i. Replace Cannon Pinion (fig. 174). Invert the movement on movement block and support the upper center wheel pivot while pressing the cannon pinion on its seat.

j. Replace Winding and Setting Assembly (fig. 177). Place the setting lever on its screw and cover the end of the index finger with watchmakers' paper. Hold the setting lever in place, turn the movement up on its edge, and secure the setting lever screw. Replace the winding pinion; replace the clutch matching the teeth with those of the pinion. Replace the clutch lever spring and clutch lever.

k. Replace Minute and Setting Wheel (fig. 176). Replace the minute wheel. Replace setting wheel with the beveled side down.

l. Replace Setting Bridge (fig. 175). Replace the setting bridge and secure it with its screws. At this point, check the freedom of the train, and winding and setting assembly. Assemble the stem and crown to the movement, rotate the crown two turns, and observe the movement of the train. If the gears backlash at the end of the winding, perfect freedom of the train is present. If they slow down or come to an abrupt stop, a bind exists and must be corrected.

m. Replace Pallet Assembly and Pallet Bridge (fig. 179). Place the pallet assembly in its place in the movement and replace the pallet bridge, alining the upper pivot of the pallet to its bearing in the bridge. Check the pallet for freedom, being careful that the pallet stones do not hit the escape wheel teeth. Secure the pallet bridge in place with bridge screws.

n. Replace Balance Cock and Balance Assembly (fig. 178). Invert balance cock and place balance assembly on balance cock. Insert hairspring stud in its position in balance cock, alining the overcoil of the hairspring simultaneously between regulator pins. Tighten the hairspring stud screw and invert balance and balance cock assembly. Place assembly in its position in the movement, alining the roller jewel with slot in pallet. Aline the balance pivots to their respective jewels and press bridge into place. Secure the bridge with its screw and check freedom of balance, making sure that the hairspring is level and centered. Wind the watch and observe action of escapement.

o. Replace Hour Wheel and Dial Washer (fig. 172). Replace the hour wheel and dial washer.

p. Replace Dial (fig. 171). Loosen dial foot screws, install, and aline the dial, and secure dial foot screws.

BULOVA WRIST WATCH, MODEL 10 AK, 10½ LIGNE SIZE, 15-JEWEL, WATERPROOF CASE

q. **Replace Hands** (fig. 169). Replace the hands, alining the tips of the hour and minute hands at the twelfth hour. Check the hands for clearance by turning them a complete revolution.

r. **Replace Movement Ring** (fig. 170). Remove the stem and crown and replace the movement ring, alining the hole in the ring to the stem position in the movement. Secure the ring in place with its screws.

s. **Replace the Crystal.** If replacement is necessary, obtain the correct size crystal, install the correct size cup and cone, cup the crystal, and snap it into the bezel ring which is part of the case ring.

t. **Replace Movement in Case.** Replace the movement in the case and insert the stem and crown. Turn the crown to aline the movement and secure the setting lever screw. Check hands for clearance at the crystal.

u. **Replace Dust Cover, Gasket, and Back** (fig. 166). Replace the dust cover and rubber gasket, and screw the case back into place, securing it with the case wrench.

v. **Replace Wrist Band.** Place the spring bars in the band loops and then insert one end of the spring bar in the hole in a lug; compress the other end of the spring bar and slide it along the inner surface of the opposite lug until it snaps into place in the hole. Install the other end of the band and spring bar in the same way.

CHAPTER 3

ELGIN STOP WATCHES

Section I

CHARACTERISTICS OF ELGIN STOP WATCHES

69. CHARACTERISTICS.

a. General. Several types of time-interval records and stop watches have been issued. All models except the Elgin stop watch are obsolete (fig. 186). It is used to indicate minutes, seconds, and fractions of a second.

70. THE ELGIN STOP WATCH, TYPE B, CLASS 15 (LONG AND SHORT PENDANT).

a. The Elgin stop watch, type B, has a 7-jewel movement and is identical to the standard Elgin 16 size (fig. 186). It has an additional stop works mechanism located under the dial. The major movement is a continuous running movement. When the stem plunger is pressed the first time, it allows the connecting pinion to

ELGIN, 16-SIZE, LONG PENDANT   ELGIN, 16-SIZE, SHORT PENDANT

RA PD 77454

Figure 186 — Stop Watches

TROUBLE SHOOTING, ADJUSTMENT, AND REPAIR OF STOP WATCH

mesh with the seconds wheel, which starts the seconds hand in motion. Pressing the plunger the second time disengages the connecting pinion, and the seconds hand immediately comes to a stop. Pressing the plunger the third time allows the hand to return to zero.

b. The Elgin stop watch, in addition to a main dial graduated in fifths of a second, has a minute recording orbit divided into 30 one-minute graduations. In recording longer intervals than 1 minute, the seconds hand, after revolving one complete turn, sets the intermittent wheel in motion which, in turn, pushes the minute recording wheel one space. The minute recording wheel in moving one space will register 1 minute on the minute recording orbit.

c. There have been several changes in the design of parts of the stop works mechanism. ORD 8 SNL F-36 (addendum) lists changes made.

Section II

TROUBLE SHOOTING, ADJUSTMENT, AND REPAIR OF STOP WATCH

71. STOP WORKS MECHANISM — ELGIN TIMER.

a. **Watch Stops When Mechanism Is Engaged.**

(1) This may be caused by rust on the second wheel pivots, pinion, or arbor; stop mechanism dirty or gummy; second wheel staff bent or broken; intermediate minute wheel assembly binding; connecting lever binding on connecting pinion; friction spring improperly adusted; hands catching on each other or sweep hand rubbing on dial or crystal; or burs on seconds wheel teeth. To determine the cause, press plunger and observe operation of hands. Remove the bezel and hands. Remove dial and determine which of the above malfunctions exist.

(2) To correct the condition, replace any rusted, bent, or broken pivots, pinions, or arbors. If the intermediate minute wheel assembly binds, adjust it for clearance and depthing. If the connecting lever is binding on the connecting pinion, adjust it. If the friction spring is improperly tensioned, adjust for proper tension. If the minute hand or sweep second hand rub on the dial or catch on each other, position them for clearance. If the stop mechanism is dirty or gummy, the watch will have to be cleaned and oiled.

b. **Depressing Crown Does Not Start Hands.**

(1) This may be caused by a broken stud on the large or small end of the actuating lever; cam hook screw loose, broken, or missing; connecting lever rusted to stud; broken or worn cam hook; broken actuating lever spring; actuating cam screw loose or broken; broken

ORDNANCE MAINTENANCE — WRIST WATCHES, POCKET WATCHES, STOP WATCHES, AND CLOCKS

pivot on seconds wheel pinion; worn pivot holes for connecting pinion; or actuating cam pawl, pawl spring, or intermediate lever screw worn, broken, or missing. To determine the cause, remove the bezel, hands, and dial and inspect for cause.

(2) To correct the condition, replace actuating lever if either of the studs are worn or broken. Replace cam hook screw if threads are stripped, or stud is bent or broken. Replace connecting lever if rusted to stud. Replace broken or worn cam hook. Replace connecting lever spring if worn or broken. Replace actuating cam screw if loose, stripped, or broken. Replace seconds wheel if pivots are broken or bent. Replace connecting lever if the pivot holes are worn.

c. **Second Hand Will Rotate but Minute Hand Will Not.**

(1) This may be caused by the intermediate minute wheel spring being loose, broken, or weak; seconds wheel driver loose, worn, bent, or broken; intermediate wheel assembly out of adjustment or rusted to stud; or burs on the portion of the actuating cam which engages the intermediate wheel assembly. To determine the cause, remove the bezel, hands, and dial, and press the crown in to engage the mechanism. Observe the action to locate the cause of trouble.

(2) If the intermediate minute wheel spring is loose, broken, or weak, replace it. If the seconds wheel driver is loose, worn, bent, or broken, replace it. If the intermediate wheel assembly is out of adjustment, adjust it; if the connecting lever is rusted to stud, replace the assembly. If the actuating cam is burred at point of contact, replace actuating cam.

d. **Minute Recording Hand Will Not Rotate Properly.**

(1) This may be caused by a loose hand; bent, loose, or broken minute recording pawl spring; broken, worn, or missing minute recording wheel pawl spacer; worn or bent seconds wheel driver; bent, broken, or worn tooth on intermediate wheel or minute wheel; or a bent minute wheel pivot. To determine the cause, remove the bezel, hands, and dial and depress the crown, thus engaging the mechanism, and observe the action.

(2) If the minute recording pawl spring or spacer is loose, bent, or broken, replace them. Replace worn, bent, or broken seconds wheel driver. Replace intermediate wheel or minute wheel if a tooth is worn, bent, or broken. Replace minute wheel if pivots are bent or broken.

e. **Minute or Second Hand Will Rotate but Will Not Fly Back.**

(1) This may be caused by a loose, bent, or broken fly-back lever spring; heart cam loose on staff; broken or bent fly-back lever; fly-back lever rusted to stud or flyback lever screw; burs on heart cams; or second and minute hands loose on staffs. To determine

TROUBLE SHOOTING, ADJUSTMENT, AND REPAIR OF STOP WATCH

the cause, remove bezel, hands, and dial and depress crown and observe the cause.

(2)   If the fly-back lever spring is bent or broken, replace it. If the fly-back lever is bent, broken, or rusted to stud or screw, replace it. If the heart cams are burred, replace them. If hands are loose on staffs, refit them.

f.   Second and Minute Hands Will Not Fly Back to Zero.

(1)   This may be caused by loose or weak fly-back lever spring; burs on the contacting point of fly-back lever; burs on heart cams; or minute recording wheel pawl spring not properly tensioned. To determine cause, remove bezel, hands, and dial and depress plunger and observe the action.

(2)   If the fly-back lever spring is loose or weak, replace it. If the contacting points of the fly-back lever are burred, remove burs and polish or replace. If heart cams are burred, replace them. If the minute recording wheel pawl spring is not tensioned properly, readjust it.

g.   Minute and Second Hand Will Rotate but Not Stop.

(1)   This may be caused by the connecting lever being rusted, or burs on the contacting portion of the connecting lever which engages with actuating cam. To determine the cause, remove bezel, hands, and dial and depress the crown to engage the mechanism and observe the action.

(2)   If the connecting lever is rusted, it must be replaced. If the connecting lever is burred, stone off the burs and polish, or replace.

h.   Watch Stops at Same Time Every Minute With Stop Works Engaged.

(1)   This may be caused by dirt or burs on seconds wheel teeth. To determine the cause, remove bezel, hands, and dial and depress the crown to engage the mechanism and observe the cause.

(2)   If the trouble is caused by dirt, clean the watch. If the seconds wheel teeth are burred, replace the seconds wheel assembly.

i.   Watch Stops Several Times Each Minute With Stop Works Mechanism Engaged.

(1)   This may be caused by dirt, burs, rust, or a missing leaf on connecting pinion. To determine cause, remove bezel, hands, and dial and depress the crown to engage the mechanism and observe the action.

(2)   Clean the watch if the trouble is caused by dirt. If it is due to a burred, a rusted, or a missing leaf, the connecting pinion must be replaced.

Section III

ELGIN STOP WATCHES, TYPE B, CLASS 15

72. IDENTIFICATION.

a. **Elgin Stop Watches** (figs. 186 and 187). There are two types of Elgin stop watches authorized to all branches of the service. They are open-faced, of the plain timer type. The movements are 16 size and have 7 jewels. They are of American manufacture and may be distinguished by the long and short pendant, and the manufacturer's name on the dial.

73. DISASSEMBLY OF ELGIN STOP WATCH, TYPE B, CLASS 15.

a. **Remove Bezel** (fig. 188). Remove bezel by prying open with case opener.

b. **Remove Hands** (fig. 189). Cut a V-slot in a piece of paper and slide it under the hands to protect the dial. Remove hands with hand remover (fig. 50).

c. **Remove Movement From Case** (fig. 190). Loosen the case pendant screw and remove crown and stem assembly. Open case backs, using case opener. Remove two case screws and remove movement from case from dial side, using methods and precautions as for pocket watches (par. 47 g).

d. **Remove Dial** (fig. 192). Loosen dial foot screws, which are located in pillars above pillar plate. Lift off dial. Tighten screws to avoid losing them.

e. **Remove Actuating Lever Spring and Actuating Lever** (fig. 193). Remove actuating lever spring screw and spring. Remove actuating lever screw and actuating lever. Remove hook cam screw and hook cam.

f. **Remove Connecting Lever Assembly and Connecting Pinion** (fig. 194). Remove connecting lever spring screw and remove spring. Remove connecting lever screw and lever. Remove connecting pinion by grasping it with tweezers, but do not grasp pinion by the teeth, which are easily damaged. Use care when lifting pinion out of movement in order to protect it from hooking the third wheel.

g. **Remove Fly-back Lever and Spring** (fig. 195). Remove fly-back lever spring screw and spring. Remove fly-back lever screw and lift fly-back lever off its stud.

h. **Remove Minute Register Wheel and Seconds Wheel Bridge** (fig. 196). Remove minute register wheel pawl and spacer screw,

ELGIN STOP WATCHES, TYPE B, CLASS 15

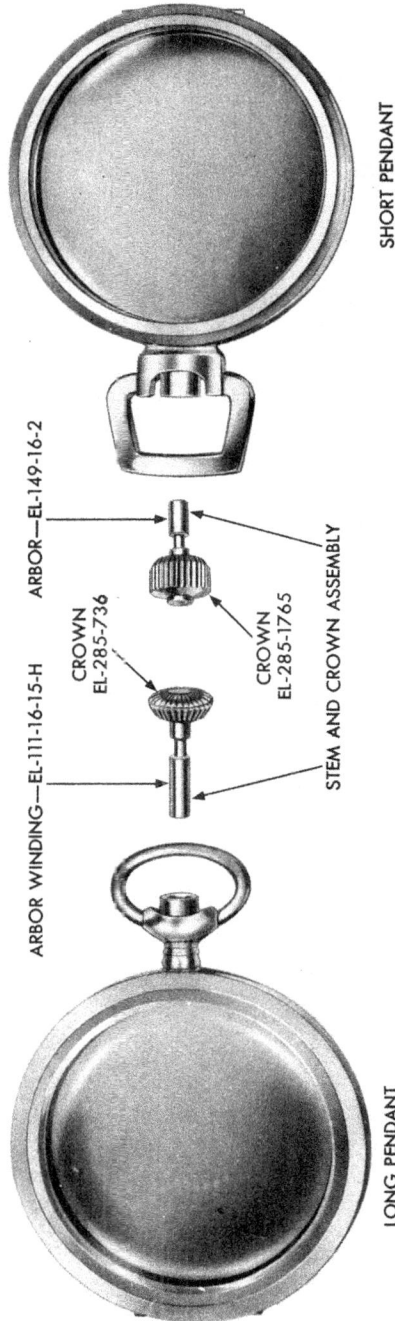

RA PD 79099

SHORT PENDANT

ARBOR—EL-149-16-2

STEM AND CROWN ASSEMBLY

CROWN
EL-285-1765

CROWN
EL-285-736

ARBOR WINDING—EL-111-16-15-H

LONG PENDANT

Figure 187 — Elgin Stop Watches — Showing Long and Short Pendants

BEZEL

CRYSTAL

RA PD 78875

Figure 188 — Elgin Stop Watch — Bezel Removed

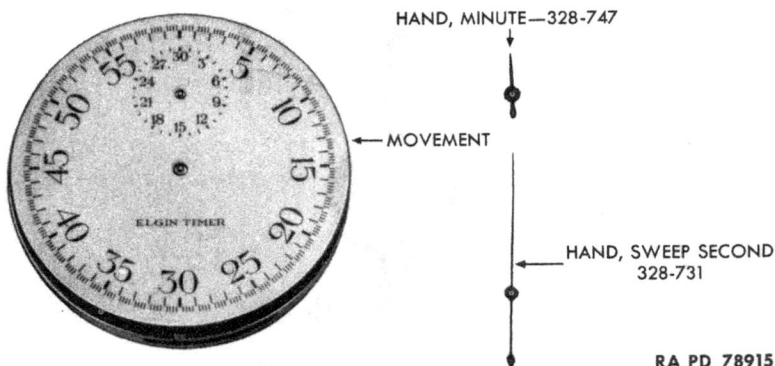

HAND, MINUTE—328-747

← MOVEMENT

HAND, SWEEP SECOND
328-731

RA PD 78915

Figure 189 — Elgin Stop Watch — Hands Removed

and remove pawl and spacer. Remove seconds wheel bridge screw and seconds wheel bridge.

i. **Remove Wheel Assemblies and Friction Spring** (fig. 197). Remove seconds and minute register wheels by grasping wheel spokes with tweezers and carefully lift out of movement. Remove friction spring screw and friction spring.

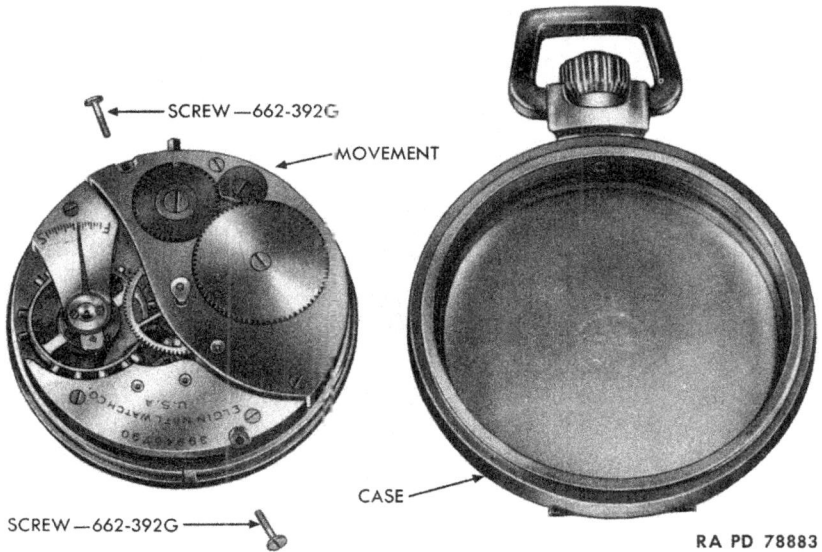

Figure 190 — Elgin Stop Watch — Movement Removed From Case

j. **Remove Intermittent Lever and Wheel** (fig. 198). Remove the intermittent lever spring screw and remove spring. Remove intermittent lever screw and remove intermittent lever and wheel assembly. To disassemble intermittent lever in order to free intermittent wheel, invert lever on bench. Remove three screws and the lever will split, allowing removal of wheel from its stud.

k. **Remove Cam Pawl and Cam** (fig. 199). Remove cam pawl spring screw and remove cam pawl spring. Remove cam screw and cam.

l. This completes the disassembly of the stop works mechanism. Disassemble rest of movement by following the procedure for the Elgin pocket watch, size 16, outlined in paragraph 50.

74. ASSEMBLY OF ELGIN STOP WATCH, TYPE B, CLASS 15.

a. **Assemble Major Unit of Movement.** Follow procedure outlined in paragraph 51.

b. **Replace Actuating Cam Assembly.** Replace cam and cam screw. Replace cam pawl spring and secure with cam pawl screw (fig. 199).

c. **Replace Intermittent Lever and Wheel Assembly.** Replace intermittent wheel on its stud on lever. Place top half of the lever

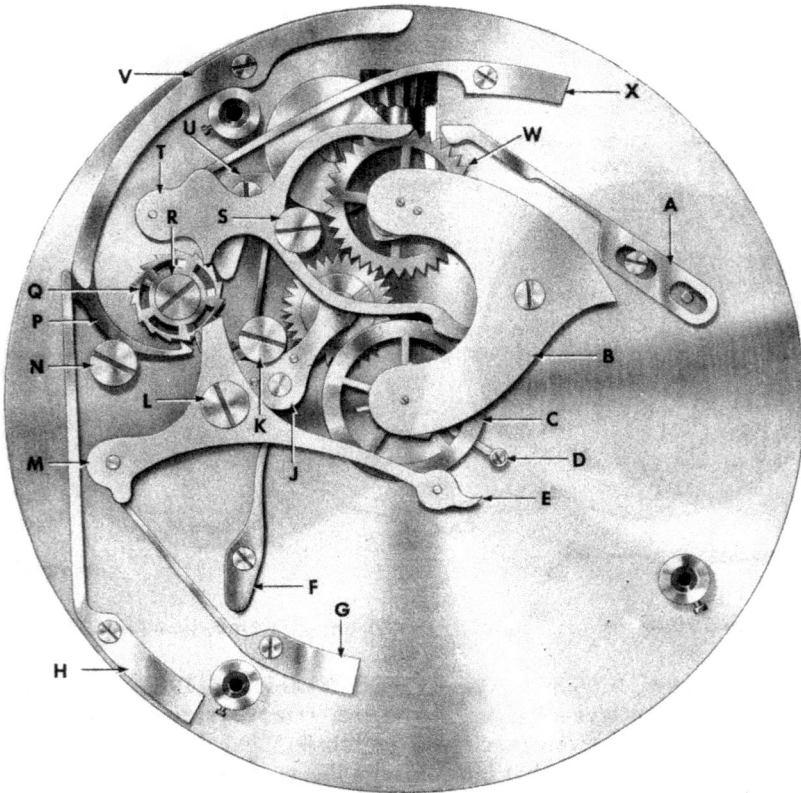

A—MINUTE REGISTER PAWL
AND SPACER

B—SECONDS WHEEL AND MINUTE
REGISTER WHEEL BRIDGE

C—SECONDS WHEEL

D—SECONDS WHEEL FRICTION
SPRING

E—CONNECTING LEVER PINION

F—INTERMITTENT LEVER SPRING

G—CONNECTING LEVER SPRING

H—ACTUATING LEVER SPRING

J—INTERMITTENT LEVER AND
WHEEL ASSEMBLY

K—INTERMITTENT LEVER SCREW

L—CONNECTING LEVER SCREW

M—CONNECTING LEVER

N—CAM HOOK SCREW

P—CAM HOOK

Q—ACTUATING CAM

R—ACTUATING CAM SCREW

S—FLYBACK LEVER SCREW

T—FLYBACK LEVER

U—CAM, PAWL AND SCREW

V—ACTUATING LEVER

W—MINUTE REGISTER WHEEL

X—FLYBACK LEVER SPRING

RA PD 86935

*Figure 191 — Elgin Stop Watch, Type B, Showing Relative Position of
Parts*

ELGIN STOP WATCHES, TYPE B, CLASS 15

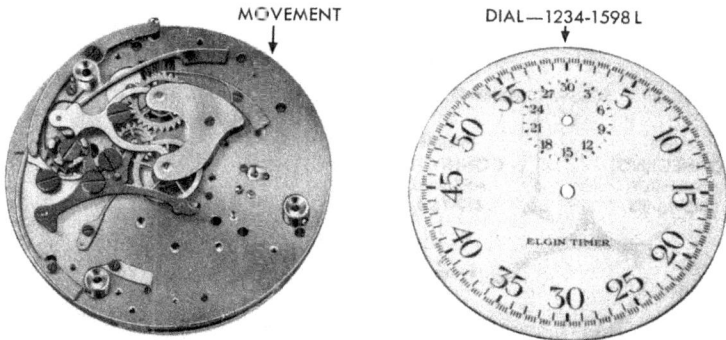

MOVEMENT   DIAL—1234-1598 L

RA PD 78920

Figure 192 — Elgin Stop Watch — Dial Removed

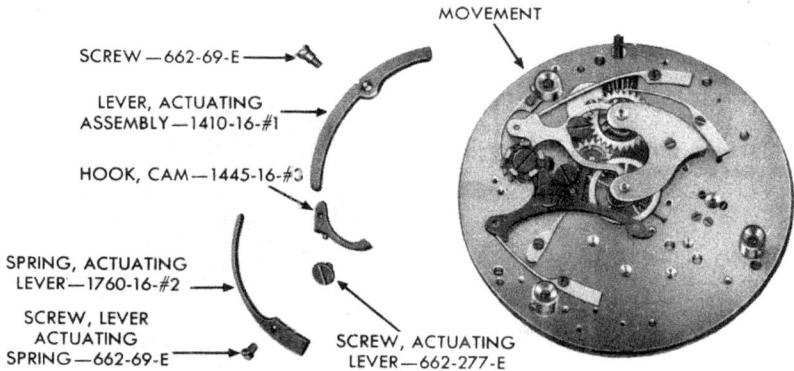

MOVEMENT

SCREW —662-69-E

LEVER, ACTUATING
ASSEMBLY—1410-16-#1

HOOK, CAM—1445-16-#3

SPRING, ACTUATING
LEVER—1760-16-#2

SCREW, LEVER
ACTUATING
SPRING—662-69-E

SCREW, ACTUATING
LEVER—662-277-E

RA PD 78994

Figure 193 — Elgin Stop Watch — Actuating Lever Assembly Removed

in place and secure with three screws. Replace intermittent lever and wheel assembly on its stud on the pillar plate and secure with intermittent lever screw (fig. 198).

d. Replace Seconds and Minute Register Wheels and Friction Spring. Replace friction spring and friction spring screw. Replace seconds and minute register wheels by grasping a spoke of the wheels with tweezers and carefully inserting their pivots in their respective bearings (fig. 197).

e. Replacing Fly-back Lever Assembly. Replace fly-back lever on its stud on the pillar plate. Replace lever spring and secure with screw. Replace fly-back lever screw (fig. 195).

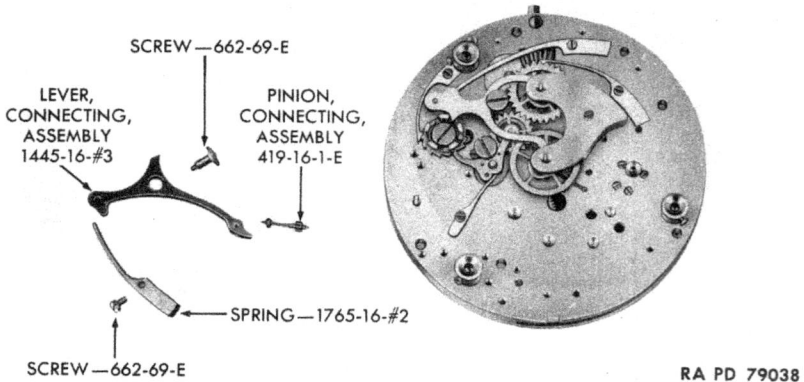

Figure 194 — Elgin Stop Watch — Connecting Lever Assembly Removed

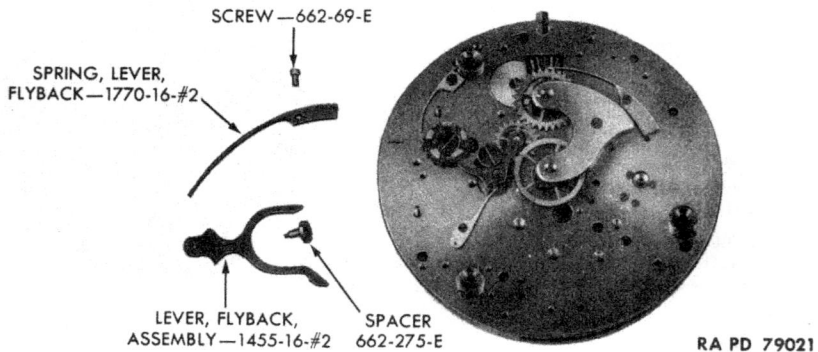

Figure 195 — Elgin Stop Watch — Fly-back Lever Assembly Removed

f. Replace Seconds and Minute Register Wheel Bridge. Replace bridge, alining pivots of wheels in their respective bearings. Replace bridge screw and secure. Replace friction spring and secure with screw. Replace minute register wheel pawl and spacer, and secure in proper position with screw (fig. 196).

g. Replace Connecting Pinion and Connecting Lever Assembly. Replace connecting pinion, carefully alining pivot in its bearing. Replace connecting lever carefully, placing pinion arbor pivot in its hole in lever, and secure with connecting lever screw. Replace connecting lever spring and secure with screw (fig. 194).

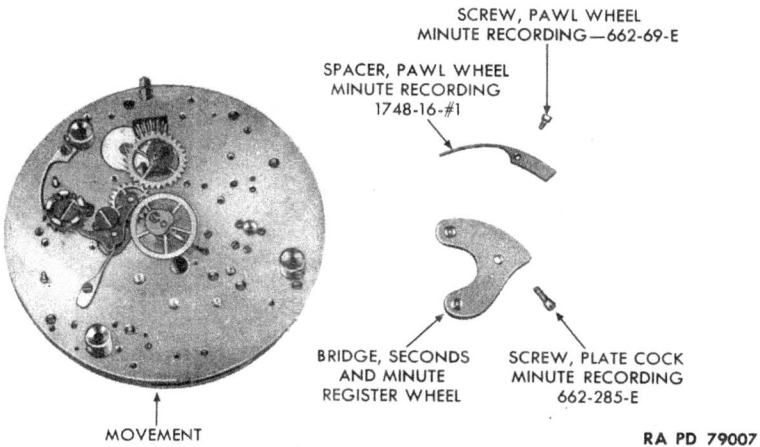

SCREW, PAWL WHEEL
MINUTE RECORDING—662-69-E

SPACER, PAWL WHEEL
MINUTE RECORDING
1748-16-#1

BRIDGE, SECONDS
AND MINUTE
REGISTER WHEEL

SCREW, PLATE COCK
MINUTE RECORDING
662-285-E

MOVEMENT

RA PD 79007

Figure 196 — Elgin Stop Watch — Seconds and Minute Wheel Bridge Assembly Removed

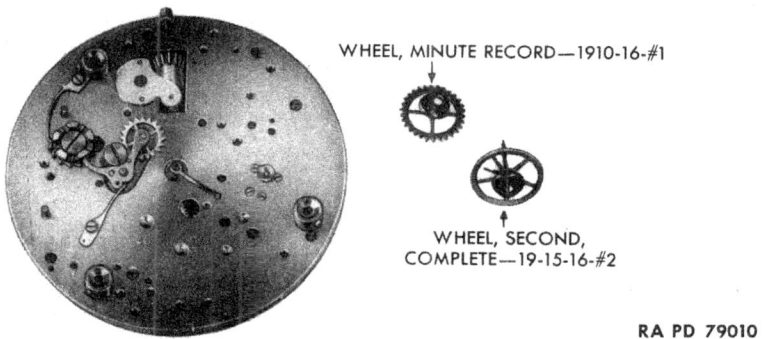

WHEEL, MINUTE RECORD—1910-16-#1

WHEEL, SECOND,
COMPLETE—19-15-16-#2

RA PD 79010

Figure 197 — Elgin Stop Watch — Seconds and Minute Wheel Assembly Removed

h. Replace Actuating Lever Assembly. Replace cam hook and screw. Replace actuating lever, placing stud on end of lever in hole of cam hook. Replace actuating lever screw and secure. Replace actuating lever spring and secure in place with screw (fig. 193).

i. Replace Dial. Loosen dial foot screws and replace dial. Lock dial in position by tightening dial foot screws (fig. 192).

ORDNANCE MAINTENANCE—WRIST WATCHES, POCKET WATCHES, STOP WATCHES, AND CLOCKS

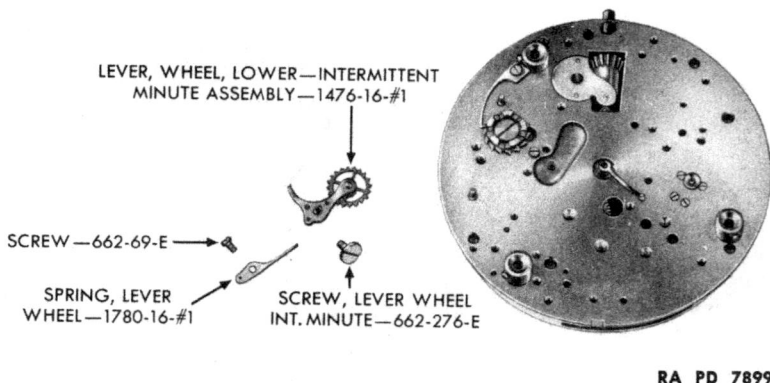

LEVER, WHEEL, LOWER—INTERMITTENT
MINUTE ASSEMBLY—1476-16-#1

SCREW—662-69-E

SPRING, LEVER
WHEEL—1780-16-#1

SCREW, LEVER WHEEL
INT. MINUTE—662-276-E

RA PD 78995

*Figure 198 — Elgin Stop Watch — Intermittent Lever and Wheel
Assembly Removed*

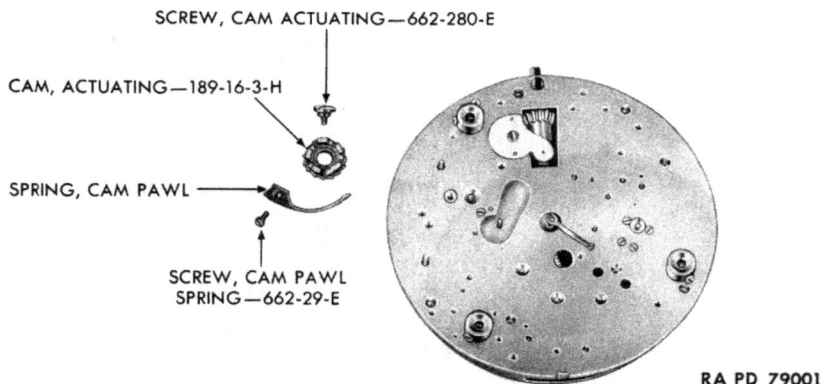

SCREW, CAM ACTUATING—662-280-E

CAM, ACTUATING—189-16-3-H

SPRING, CAM PAWL

SCREW, CAM PAWL
SPRING—662-29-E

RA PD 79001

Figure 199 — Elgin Stop Watch — Cam Assembly Removed

j. Replace Movement in Case. Replace movement in case and center movement; replace case screws and secure (fig. 190).

k. Replace Hands. Replace minute register hand with its point at zero. Replace sweep seconds hand with its point at zero (fig. 189).

l. Replace Bezel and Close Backs. Replace bezel by snapping it into place. Close dust cover and outer cover, and snap them shut (fig. 188).

m. There are two type B, class 15 Elgin stop watches issued for service, namely: the long pendant and the short pendant. The only difference in the two watches is in the length of the pendants (fig. 187.)

CHAPTER 4

MESSAGE CENTER CLOCK M1

75. IDENTIFICATION.

a. The message center clock is mounted in a hardwood carrying case. The clock movement is of the 8-day type, fitted with an 11-jewel watch movement. The dial has a black background, with the name, "CLOCK, MESSAGE CENTER, M1" outlined in white. Clocks of later manufacture have arabic numerals running from 13 to 00 and a double hour hand so that it may be used with the 24-hour system of keeping time used by the armed forces.

76. DISASSEMBLY OF MESSAGE CENTER CLOCK M1.

a. **Remove Clock From Carrying Case.** Remove the three screws which attach clock to mounting panel in wooden case and remove the clock (fig. 202).

b. **Remove Bezel.** Remove bezel by unscrewing it counterclockwise (fig. 203).

c. **Remove Hands.** Protect dial with paper and remove hands, using the hand remover (fig. 204).

d. **Remove Reflector.** Remove the three screws which attach reflector to dial and lift off reflector (fig. 205).

e. **Remove Movement From Case.** Remove setting knob screw and knob. Hold hand over dial, invert case, and slide movement out of case (fig. 206).

f. **Remove Dial and Dial Ring.** Remove three screws which attach dial to plate and lift off dial. Remove three grasshoppers from the dial ring feet under dial plate and lift off dial ring (fig. 207).

g. **Remove Setting Mechanism** (fig. 208). Remove hour wheel. Remove minute wheel screw and minute wheel. Remove setting pinion screw and setting pinion assembly. Remove cannon pinion. Remove setting pinion screw and gear; remove setting stem screw and pull out the stem which permits removal of compression spring from setting bridge.

h. **Release Unused Power of Mainspring.** Release the unused power of the mainspring, exercising caution because the mainspring is very strong.

i. **Remove Back Plate.** Remove the four back plate screws and back plate. Do not lay movement on the bench dial side down, unless the center pinion is protected with a movement block (fig. 209).

RA PD 78861

Figure 200 — Message Center Clock M1

j. Remove Fourth Bridge Plate. Remove the three fourth bridge pillar screws and fourth bridge plate (fig. 210).

k. Remove Regulator Staff, Train Bridge, Fourth and Third Wheels, and Escape Wheel Bridge and Wheel. Loosen regulator staff screw and lift out regulator staff assembly. Remove the three train plate screws and train plate. Remove two escape wheel bridge screws and remove bridge. Lift off fourth, third, and escape wheel assemblies (fig. 211).

l. Remove Mainspring Barrel and Train Wheels. Remove

MESSAGE CENTER CLOCK M1

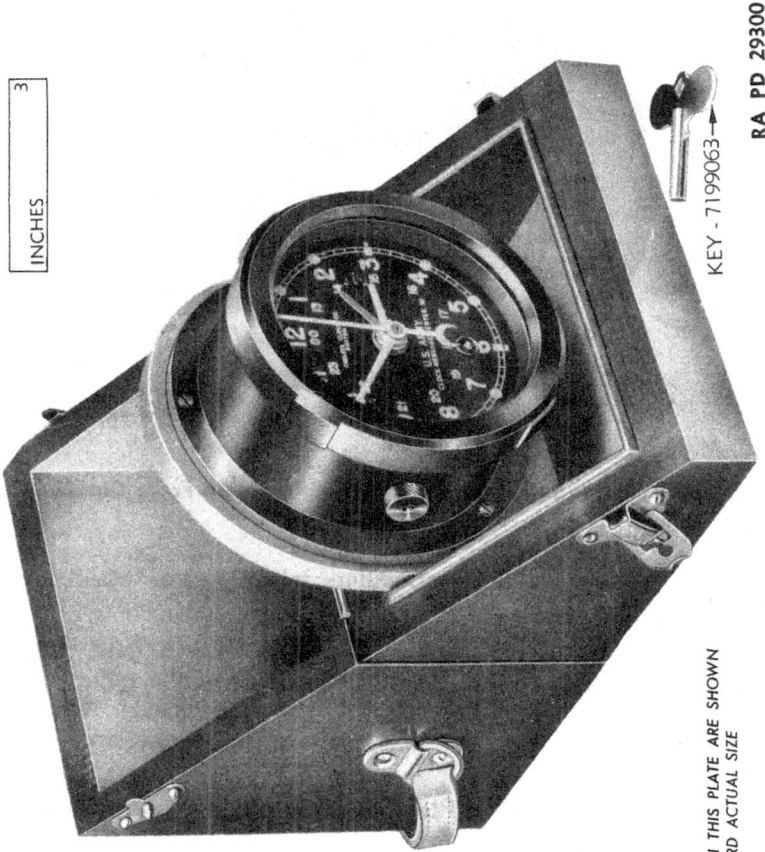

RA PD 29300

KEY - 7199063 →

INCHES

3

Figure 201 — Message Center Clock M1 (Later Manufacture)

PARTS IN THIS PLATE ARE SHOWN
ONE-THIRD ACTUAL SIZE

ORDNANCE MAINTENANCE — WRIST WATCHES, POCKET WATCHES, STOP WATCHES, AND CLOCKS

SCREW, CASE →

SCREW, CASE

SCREW, CASE

RA PD 79011

Figure 202 — Message Center Clock M1 — Removed From Carrying Case

mainspring barrel assembly, intermediate wheel, center wheel, and ratchet wheel (fig. 212).

m. **Remove Regulator Worm Assembly, Click, and Click Spring.** Remove two screws from the train side of the pillar plate and lift off the worm assembly. Remove ratchet wheel. Remove the click screw and click. Remove click spring screw and click spring (fig. 213).

n. **Remove Center Wheel Plate, Escapement Plate, and Assembly.** Remove two screws from underneath the intermediate and center wheel plate, releasing the balance and escapement assembly plate. Lift off the assembly (fig. 214).

o. **Remove Balance and Escapement Assembly From Train Plate.** Push the regulator to the extreme fast position, loosen the hairspring stud screw, and free the hairspring stud with a pin pusher from the balance cock. Remove the balance cock screw and balance cock. If the balance cock fits tightly, insert screwdriver in slot underneath balance cock and pry it loose. Remove balance cock assembly with tweezers and secure the hairspring stud screw to

MESSAGE CENTER CLOCK M1

GLASS—CLC-51031

BEZEL—CLC-12100

Figure 203 — Message Center Clock M1 — Bezel Removed

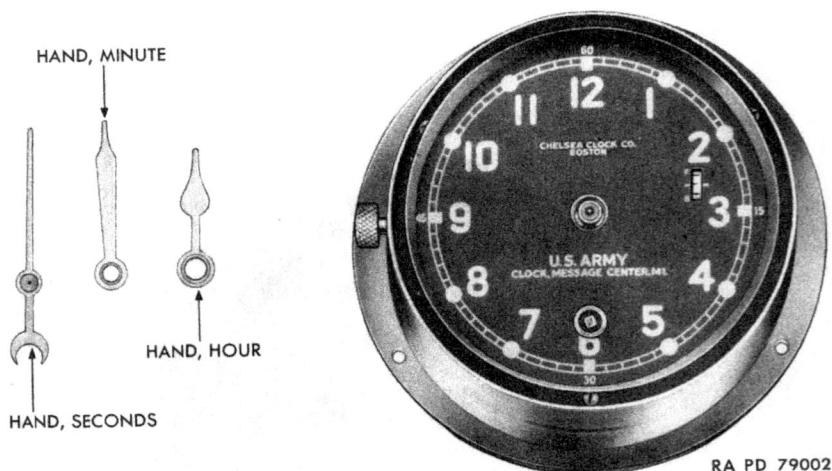

Figure 204 — Message Center Clock M1 — Hands Removed

prevent losing it. Remove two upper dome screws from balance cock, and remove balance cock cap jewel and regulator. Remove two lower cap jewel screws, grasp the lower cap jewel with tweezers, and lift it out of plate (fig. 214).

p. Remove Pallet Bridge and Pallet Assembly. Remove two pallet bridge screws and lift off pallet bridge assembly. Remove pallet assembly (fig. 216).

q. Remove Mainspring Assembly. Tap the mainspring barrel arbor with a brass mallet and snap the barrel cap out its groove. Remove barrel cap. Remove barrel arbor by turning it clockwise to release it from mainspring. Remove mainspring from the barrel by grasping it by the inside coil with pliers and slowly unwinding it from the barrel. Do not remove the mainspring from the barrel unless it is necessary to do so for replacement (fig. 218).

77. ASSEMBLY OF MESSAGE CENTER CLOCK M1.

a. Winding in Mainspring. Select the proper size mainspring winder and wind the mainspring into it slowly. Insert the mainspring winder into the barrel, hook the end of mainspring on barrel hook, and press plunger which transfers mainspring into the barrel. Insert the barrel arbor, turning it counterclockwise till the mainspring engages the arbor hook. Snap barrel cap into its recess in barrel (figs. 68, 69, and 70).

MESSAGE CENTER CLOCK M1

RA PD 78928

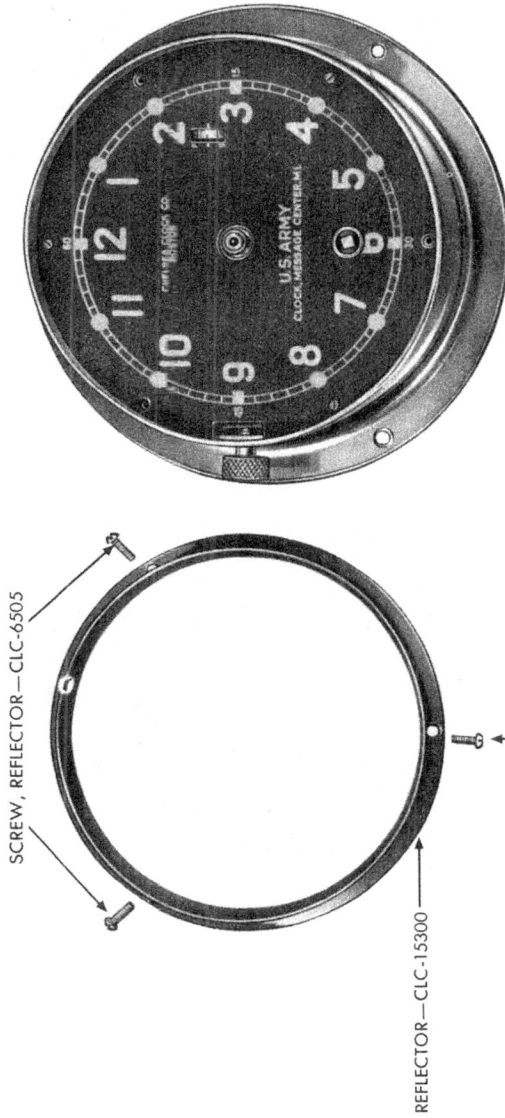

Figure 205 — Message Center Clock M1 — Reflector Removed

SCREW, REFLECTOR—CLC-6505

SCREW, REFLECTOR—CLC-6505

REFLECTOR—CLC-15300

ORDNANCE MAINTENANCE — WRIST WATCHES, POCKET WATCHES, STOP WATCHES, AND CLOCKS

RA PD 78929

CASE—CLC-13098

MOVEMENT

SCREW—CLC-51679

KNOB—CLC-8248

U.S. ARMY
CLOCK, MESSAGE CENTER M1

Figure 206 — Message Center Clock M1 — Movement Removed From Case

MESSAGE CENTER CLOCK M1

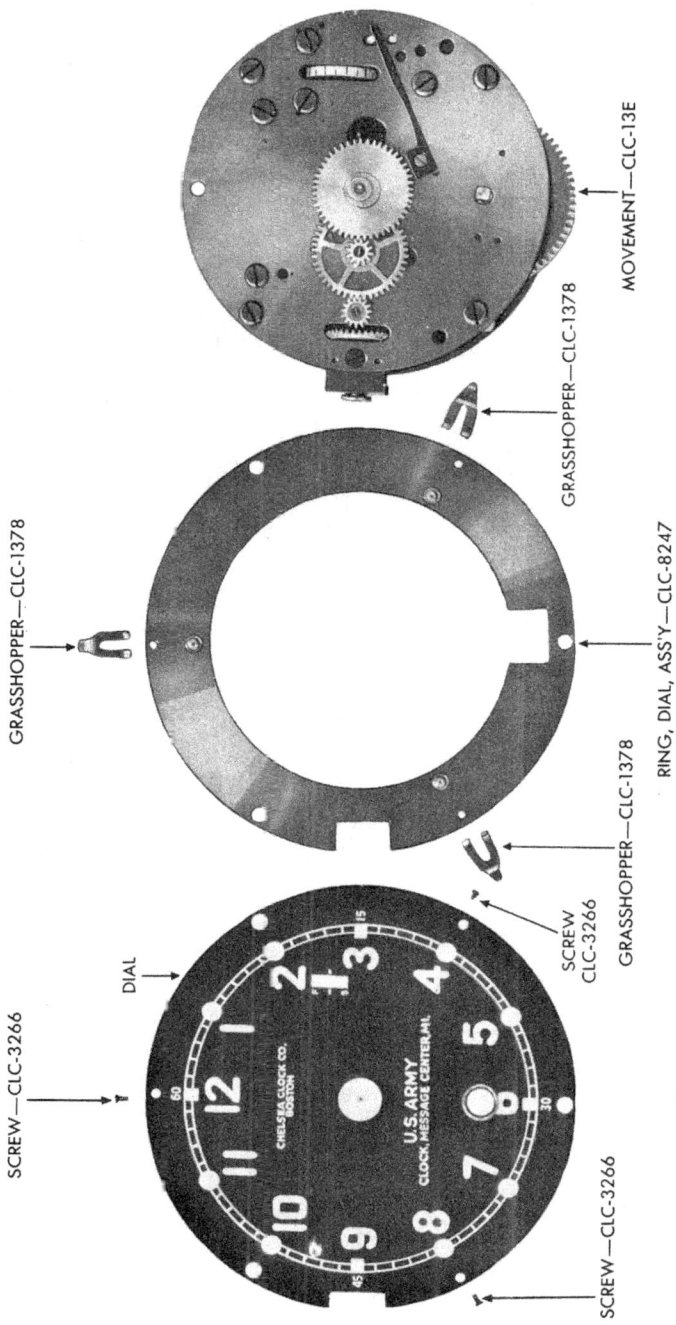

RA PD 79046

MOVEMENT—CLC-13E

GRASSHOPPER—CLC-1378

GRASSHOPPER—CLC-1378

RING, DIAL, ASS'Y—CLC-8247

GRASSHOPPER—CLC-1378

SCREW CLC-3266

DIAL

SCREW—CLC-3266

SCREW—CLC-3266

CHELSEA CLOCK CO. BOSTON

U.S. ARMY CLOCK, MESSAGE CENTER.M1

Figure 207 — Message Center Clock M1 — Dial and Dial Ring Removed

ORDNANCE MAINTENANCE — WRIST WATCHES, POCKET WATCHES, STOP WATCHES, AND CLOCKS

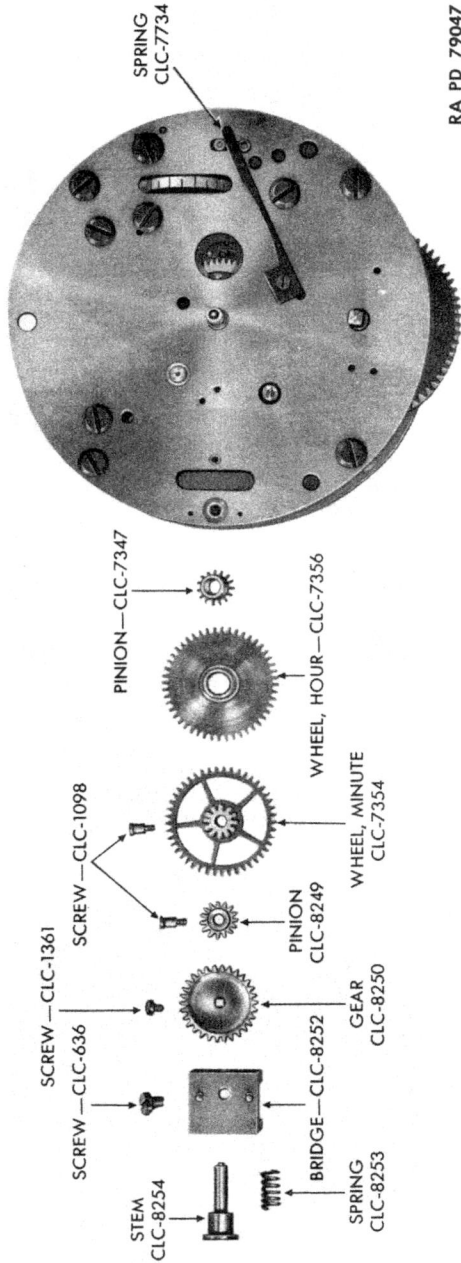

RA PD 79047

SPRING
CLC-7734

PINION—CLC-7347

WHEEL, HOUR—CLC-7356

SCREW—CLC-1098

SCREW—CLC-1361

WHEEL, MINUTE
CLC-7354

PINION
CLC-8249

GEAR
CLC-8250

SCREW—CLC-636

BRIDGE—CLC-8252

SCREW—CLC-636

STEM
CLC-8254

SPRING
CLC-8253

Figure 208 — Message Center Clock M1 — Setting Mechanism Removed

MESSAGE CENTER CLOCK M1

RA PD 78954

SCREW—CLC-633

SCREW—CLC-633

PLATE
CLC-8472

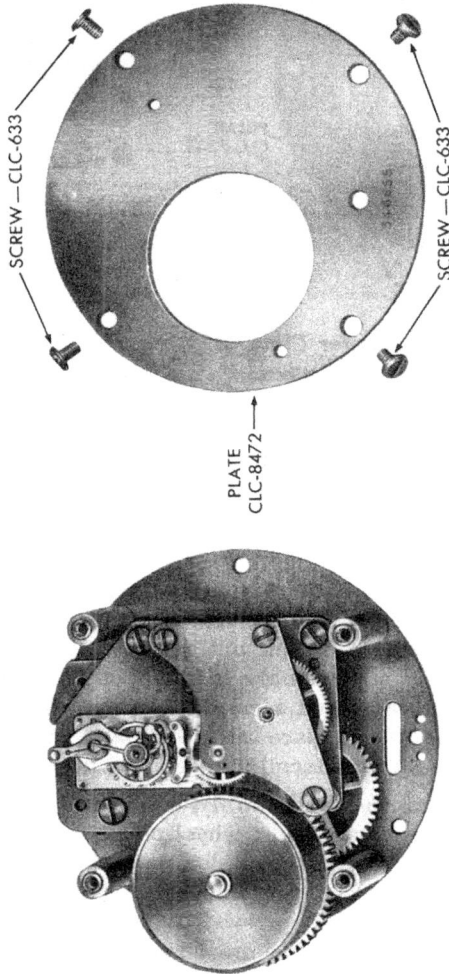

Figure 209 — Message Center Clock M1 — Back Plate Removed

ORDNANCE MAINTENANCE — WRIST WATCHES, POCKET WATCHES, STOP WATCHES, AND CLOCKS

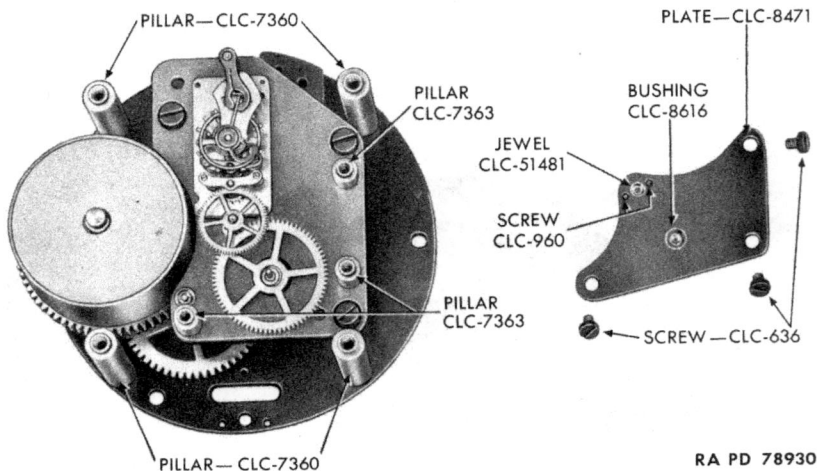

*Figure 210 — Message Center Clock M1 — Fourth Bridge Plate
Removed*

   b.   **Replace Cap Jewels.** Grasp the balance end stone cap with tweezers, place it on the escape plate, and secure with balance end stone cap screws. Replace the dome and regulator and secure in place with upper cap jewel screws. Carefully protect the regulator pins when replacing regulator.

   c.   **Replace the Setting Pinion Assembly** (fig. 208). Place the compression spring on stem and insert the assembly through large hole in bridge, compressing the spring until the stem extends through small hole in bridge. Hold assembly in this position, install gear with teeth away from bridge, and secure it in place with its screw. Install the setting assembly in place on lower plate, placing gear in center of slot in plate. Secure assembly in place with screws.

   d.   **Replace Regulator Index Assembly, Click, and Click Spring** (fig. 213). Place the regulator index wheel assembly on train side of lower plate, aline wheel to center of slot, and secure with screws. Place regulator gear so slot in gear alines with pin in lower plate. Replace click and secure with its screws; then replace click spring and secure with screw. NOTE: *The movement should be supported on a movement block during the balance of assembly.*

   e.   **Replace Train Wheels and Mainspring Barrel** (fig. 212). Place center wheel in position on train side of plate. Place intermediate wheel assembly in position on plate. Place ratchet wheel in position on the mainspring barrel arbor with the teeth facing

MESSAGE CENTER CLOCK M1

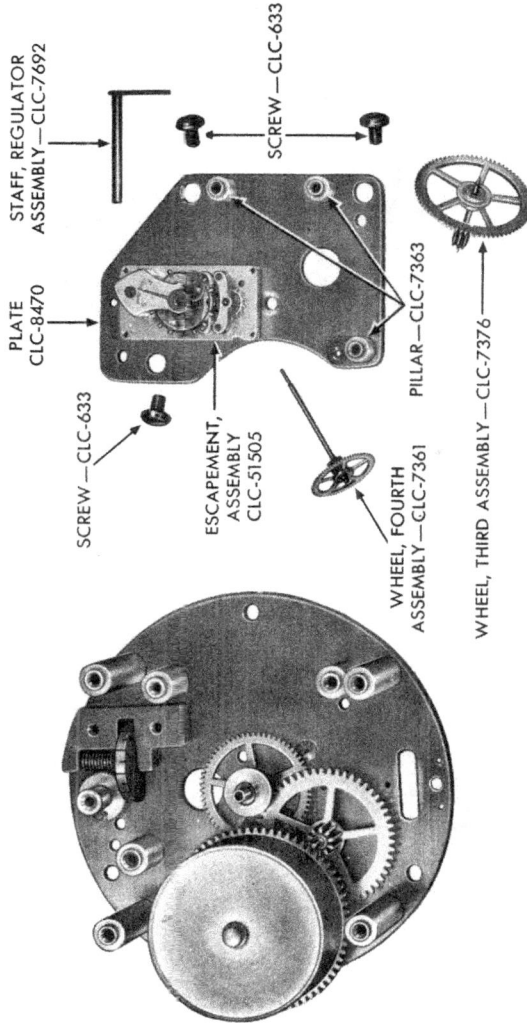

STAFF, REGULATOR ASSEMBLY—CLC-7692

SCREW—CLC-633

SCREW—CLC-633

PLATE CLC-8470

PILLAR—CLC-7363

SCREW—CLC-633

ESCAPEMENT, ASSEMBLY CLC-51505

WHEEL, FOURTH ASSEMBLY—CLC-7361

WHEEL, THIRD ASSEMBLY—CLC-7376

RA PD 79068

Figure 211 — Message Center Clock M1 — Regulator Staff, Train Bridge Assembly, and Fourth and Third Wheels Removed

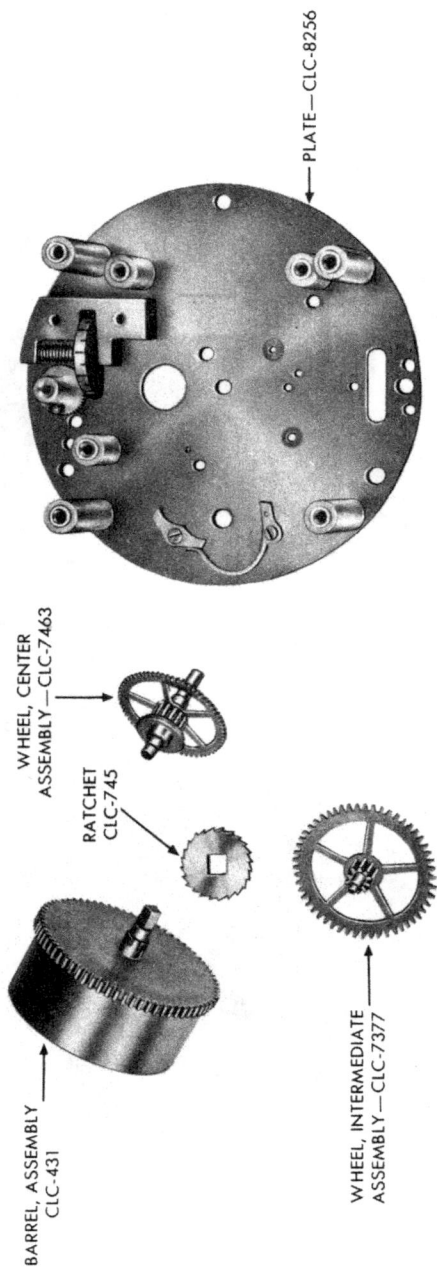

ORDNANCE MAINTENANCE—WRIST WATCHES, POCKET WATCHES, STOP WATCHES, AND CLOCKS

RA PD 79048

PLATE—CLC-8256

WHEEL, CENTER
ASSEMBLY—CLC-7463

RATCHET
CLC-745

WHEEL, INTERMEDIATE
ASSEMBLY—CLC-7377

BARREL, ASSEMBLY
CLC-431

Figure 212 — Message Center Clock M1 — Center Wheel, Intermediate Wheel, Mainspring Barrel, and Ratchet Wheel Removed

MESSAGE CENTER CLOCK M1

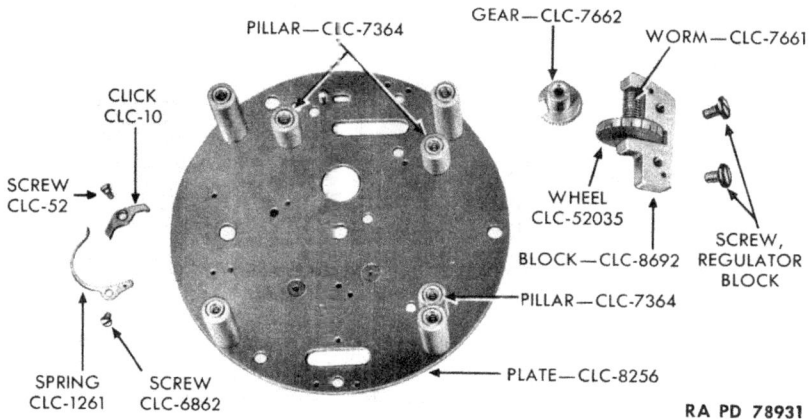

Figure 213 — Message Center Clock M1 — Regulator Index Wheel Assembly, Ratchet Wheel Click, and Click Spring Removed

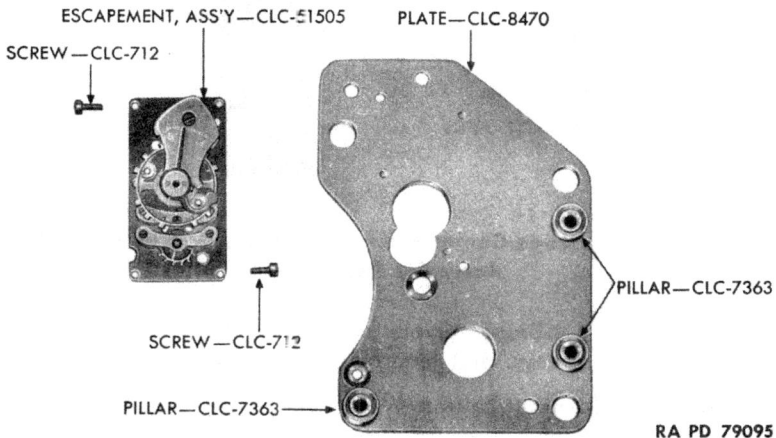

Figure 214 — Message Center Clock M1 — Escapement and Balance Assembly Removed From Train Plate

counterclockwise. Place mainspring barrel assembly in position on plate.

f. **Replace Escape Plate** (fig. 214). Place escape plate in position on the intermediate and fourth wheel plate and secure with escape plate screws. Place intermediate and fourth wheel plate in

211

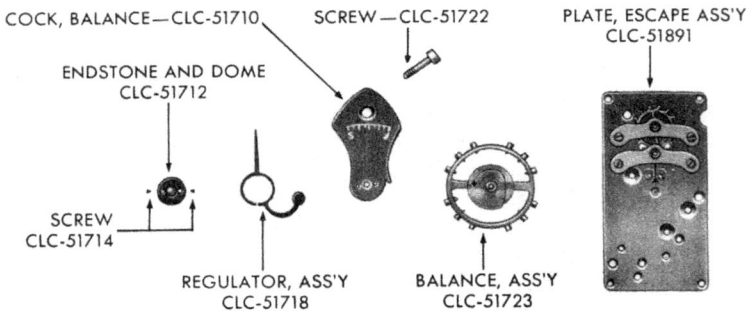

COCK, BALANCE—CLC-51710

SCREW—CLC-51722

PLATE, ESCAPE ASS'Y
CLC-51891

ENDSTONE AND DOME
CLC-51712

SCREW
CLC-51714

REGULATOR, ASS'Y
CLC-51718

BALANCE, ASS'Y
CLC-51723

RA PD 79049

Figure 215 — Message Center Clock M1 — Balance Cock and Balance Assembly Removed

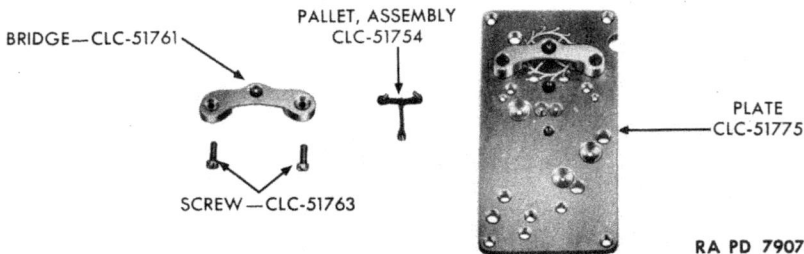

BRIDGE—CLC-51761

PALLET, ASSEMBLY
CLC-51754

PLATE
CLC-51775

SCREW—CLC-51763

RA PD 79075

Figure 216 — Message Center Clock M1 — Pallet Bridge and Pallet Assembly Removed

position, carefully alining pivots of the intermediate and center wheels in their bearings, and secure plate with screws.

g. Replace Cannon Pinion. Support center wheel arbor and bushing, and center and intermediate wheel plate; press cannon pinion into place on center wheel arbor from the dial side.

h. Replace Third Wheel Assembly (fig. 211). Place the third wheel assembly in position, seating the lower pivot in its bearing in lower plate.

i. Replace Escape Wheel and Pinion Assembly. Place escape wheel and pinion in position on escape plate (fig. 217).

j. Replace Fourth Wheel Assembly (fig. 211). Insert fourth wheel pinion through center wheel arbor into its seat.

MESSAGE CENTER CLOCK M1

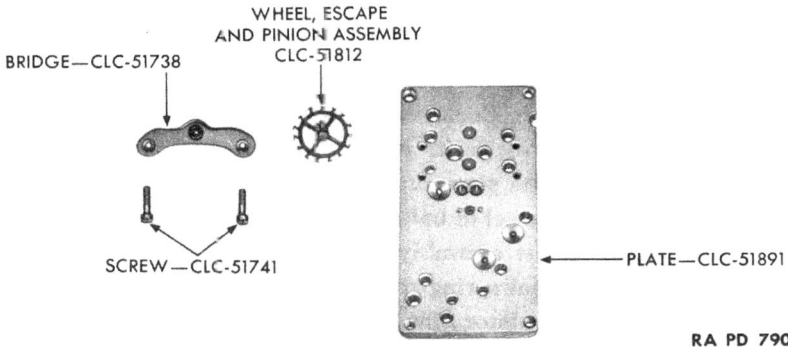

Figure 217 — Message Center Clock M1 — Escape Wheel Bridge and Escapement Removed

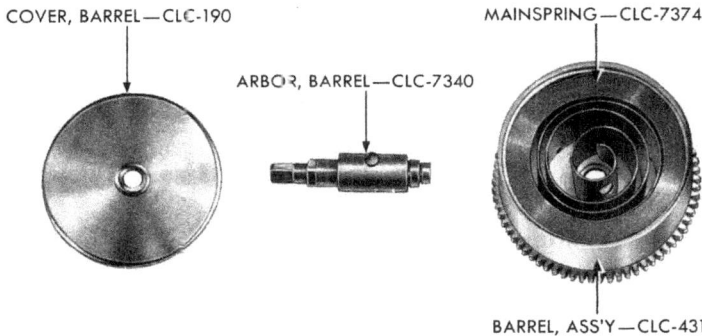

Figure 218 — Message Center Clock M1 — Mainspring Barrel Assembly Cap and Arbor Removed

k. Replace Third and Fourth Wheel Plate (fig. 210). Place the third and fourth wheel plate in position, alining the pivots of the third and fourth wheels in their bearings. Secure with bridge plate screws. NOTE: *Care should be exercised not to damage the fourth wheel jewel.*

l. Replace Escape Wheel Bridge Assembly (fig. 217). Replace the escape wheel bridge, alining the pivot of the escape wheel to its jewel, and secure with bridge screws. This completes the assembly of the train. At this point check freedom of the intermediate wheel to the escape wheel.

ORDNANCE MAINTENANCE—WRIST WATCHES, POCKET WATCHES, STOP WATCHES, AND CLOCKS

m. **Replace Pallet and Pallet Bridge Assembly** (fig. 216). Replace pallet assembly. Place pallet bridge over the pallet assembly, alining pivot of the pallet to its jewel. Secure bridge in place with screws. Check the action of the pallet.

n. **Replace Balance Cock and Balance Assembly** (fig. 215). Place lower balance pivot in its jewel on the escape plate assembly. Place balance cock in its place on the escape assembly plate, alining the upper pivot to its jewel in balance cock. Aline the roller jewel to its position in the pallet assembly and secure balance cock in place with its screw. Place hairspring stud in cock and aline the overcoil of hairspring between regulator pins simultaneously. Secure hairspring stud screw. NOTE: *The hairspring must be level when stud screw is secured.*

o. **Replace Regulator Staff Assembly** (fig. 211). Aline regulator gear with holes in plate. Insert staff through hole in plate into gear and through lower plate. Place tension spring against staff so that gear and worm will be held in mesh. Place pollywog over regulator. Aline retaining screw hole in gear and staff and install screw.

p. **Replace Back Plate** (fig. 209). Aline back plate on pillars and secure with screws.

q. **Replace Minute Wheel Assembly** (fig. 208). Invert the movement on movement block and place minute wheel in its position between cannon pinion and setting pinion. Secure in place with minute wheel screw.

r. **Replace Dial Ring Assembly** (fig. 207). Place the dial ring feet through the holes in dial plate. Place a grasshopper spring on each of them on train side of dial plate, securing dial ring in place.

s. **Replace Hour Wheel.** Replace hour wheel on cannon pinion. Replace dial and secure with three dial screws.

t. **Replace Hands** (fig. 204). Place hour hand on the post of hour wheel with point at the twelfth hour. Place minute hand on cannon pinion seat with point at the twelfth hour. Place sweep seconds hand on the fourth wheel pinion with point at the twelfth hour. Turn hands through a complete revolution around dial, checking them for position at the twelfth hour. If hands do not line up properly at the twelfth hour, remove sweep seconds and minute hands and realine them.

MESSAGE CENTER CLOCK M1

u. Replace Movement in Case (fig. 205). Carefully protect the hands and place movement in case. Aline holes in dial with holes in case. Replace the reflector, alining retaining screw holes with holes in dial and case. Secure with screws. Replace setting knob and secure retaining screw.

v. Replace Bezel (fig. 203). Screw the bezel into place clockwise, making sure the glass does not touch sweep seconds hand or fourth wheel pinion.

w. Replace Clock in Mounting Case (fig. 202). Place the clock against the mounting panel of the case, aline the screw holes, and secure with three mounting screws.

CHAPTER 5

REFERENCES

78. PUBLICATIONS INDEXES.

The following publications indexes should be consulted frequently for latest changes or revisions of references given in this chapter and for new publications relating to materiel covered in this manual:

a. Ordnance supply catalog index (index to SNL's) ..ASF Cat. ORD 2

b. Ordnance major items and combinations, and pertinent publications ....SB 9-1

c. List of publications for training (listing CCBP's, FM's, FT's, MTP's, TB's, TM's, TR's, TC's, and LO's) ....FM 21-6

d. List of training films, film strips, and film bulletins FM 21-7

e. Military training aids (listing graphic training aids, models, devices, and displays)................FM 21-8

f. List and index of administrative and supply publications (listing new AR's, Cir's, GO's, WDB's, T/O & E's, T/O's, T/E's, T/A's, T/BA's, MR's, RR's, WDP's, SB's, MWO's and forms)...........WD Pam 12-6

79. STANDARD NOMENCLATURE LISTS.

a. Clock, message center, M1 ....SNL F-194
b. Watches, pocket, wrist and stop ....SNL F-36

80. EXPLANATORY PUBLICATIONS.

a. Auxiliary fire control instruments ....TM 9-575

INDEX

INDEX

INDEX

NOTES

NOTES

www.ingramcontent.com/pod-product-compliance
Lightning Source LLC
Chambersburg PA
CBHW071421090426
42737CB00011B/1531